The Revolution
in Real Estate
Finance

ANTHONY DOWNS

The Revolution in Real Estate Finance

THE BROOKINGS INSTITUTION
Washington, D.C.

ce,

Copyright © 1985 by

THE BROOKINGS INSTITUTION

1775 Massachusetts Avenue, N.W., Washington, D.C. 20036

Library of Congress Cataloging in Publication data:

Downs, Anthony.
　The revolution in real estate finance.

　Includes bibliographies and index.
　1. Mortgages—United States.　2. Real estate
investment—United States.　3. Housing—United States—
Finance.　I. Brookings Institution.　II. Title.
HG5095.D68　1985　　332.7'22'0973　　85-14941
ISBN 0-8157-1918-3
ISBN 0-8157-1917-5 (pbk.)

9　8　7　6　5　4　3　2　1

THE BROOKINGS INSTITUTION is an independent organization devoted to nonpartisan research, education, and publication in economics, government, foreign policy, and the social sciences generally. Its principal purposes are to aid in the development of sound public policies and to promote public understanding of issues of national importance.

The Institution was founded on December 8, 1927, to merge the activities of the Institute for Government Research, founded in 1916, the Institute of Economics, founded in 1922, and the Robert Brookings Graduate School of Economics and Government, founded in 1924.

The Board of Trustees is responsible for the general administration of the Institution, while the immediate direction of the policies, program, and staff is vested in the President, assisted by an advisory committee of the officers and staff. The by-laws of the Institution state: "It is the function of the Trustees to make possible the conduct of scientific research, and publication, under the most favorable conditions, and to safeguard the independence of the research staff in the pursuit of their studies and in the publication of the results of such studies. It is not a part of their function to determine, control, or influence the conduct of particular investigations or the conclusions reached."

The President bears final responsibility for the decision to publish a manuscript as a Brookings book. In reaching his judgment on the competence, accuracy, and objectivity of each study, the President is advised by the director of the appropriate research program and weighs the views of a panel of expert outside readers who report to him in confidence on the quality of the work. Publication of a work signifies that it is deemed a competent treatment worthy of public consideration but does not imply endorsement of conclusions or recommendations.

The Institution maintains its position of neutrality on issues of public policy in order to safeguard the intellectual freedom of the staff. Hence interpretations or conclusions in Brookings publications should be understood to be solely those of the authors and should not be attributed to the Institution, to its trustees, officers, or other staff members, or to the organizations that support its research.

Foreword

Since the mid-1970s revolutionary changes have occurred in both the methods of financing real estate investments in the United States and the institutions that do such financing. These changes accelerated in the 1980s and will probably continue into the 1990s. Shifts in the expectations of lenders and equity investors concerning future inflation, partial deregulation of financial institutions, dramatic changes in U.S. fiscal and monetary policies, and technical advances in electronic funds transfer and telecommunications all contributed to the new environment.

In this book Anthony Downs explores the profound implications of this revolution for many aspects of U.S. real estate markets. Because real estate constitutes by far the largest component of wealth in the United States, and is also the most widely held, the revolution will directly affect millions of Americans, and in surprisingly diverse ways. These include the reduction of new office space allotted to each worker, renovation of older downtown neighborhoods, a shift of new office development to the suburbs, and the development of sophisticated financial instruments for channeling household savings into mortgage markets.

This revolution has especially affected the financing of residential property—first-time buyers now find it very difficult to purchase a home. Downs describes the dimensions of this "housing affordability problem" and its possible implications for public policy.

Anthony Downs is a senior fellow in the Brookings Economic Studies program. He is grateful to his Brookings colleagues Henry J. Aaron, Barry P. Bosworth, Gary Burtless, Edward F. Denison, Robert E. Litan, Joseph A. Pechman, and Alice M. Rivlin for their valuable comments on early drafts of this volume. He is also grateful to Kevin Villani of the Federal Home Loan Mortgage Corporation, Tim Howard, Gary Kopff, and David Maxwell of the Federal National Mortgage Association, Raymond J. Struyk of the Urban Institute, and Katharine L. Bradbury of the Federal Reserve Bank of Boston for commenting on the manuscript; to James McEuen for editing it; to Janet L. Chakarian for checking its factual content and for research assistance; to Patricia Regan and Judy Kleinman for research assistance; to Jacquelyn G. Sanks for secretarial services; and to Florence Robinson for preparing the index. Financial assistance for the project was provided by the American Council of Life Insurance, the Ford Foundation, and the Federal National Mortgage Association.

The views expressed in this book are solely those of the author, and should not be ascribed to the persons or organizations whose assistance is acknowledged above, or to the trustees, officers, or other staff members of the Brookings Institution.

BRUCE K. MACLAURY
President

July 1985
Washington, D.C.

Contents

Tables

Figures

The Revolution in Real Estate Finance

1

Introduction and Overview

DURING the late 1970s and early 1980s, a revolution occurred in U.S. real estate finance and the institutions that provide it. This revolution was caused by sweeping changes in investors' perceptions, economic conditions, public policies, and communication technology. It already has profoundly influenced real estate markets, and it will continue to shape them throughout the 1980s and beyond. Real estate is the quantitatively largest and most widely held form of wealth in the United States. Because real estate is the principal asset of millions of households, the revolution in real estate affects the welfare of the entire nation.

Many real estate practitioners are aware of some of the causes of this revolution, but few have grasped their comprehensive effects. This book describes the revolution and traces its principal present and future effects. This initial chapter presents an overview of the book's analysis and findings.

Causes of the Revolution

Five radical changes have occurred since the mid-1970s in factors affecting real estate finance.

—Shifts in the expectations of capital suppliers—that is, of lenders and equity investors—about future inflation. Around 1980 capital suppliers changed from believing that inflation rates would remain low to believing that those rates would be relatively high. They have recently begun to think that inflation might again be low in the rest of the 1980s, but they are much less certain than they were in the 1970s.

1

—*Loss of housing's formerly favored position in credit markets.* This loss was the result of a combination of financial deregulation (discussed below) and tax-law changes that increased benefits from investing in industrial plant and equipment and in many kinds of real property other than owner-occupied housing. These changes reduced the relative tax benefits of homeownership.

—*A dual change in federal fiscal and monetary policies.* After 1979 the nation adopted stimulative fiscal policies involving large deficits, plus relatively restrictive monetary policies intended to restrain inflation. These shifts raised both nominal and real interest rates—especially the latter—above their average levels in 1950–79.

—*Partial deregulation of financial markets.* Many restraints on the activities that each financial institution could undertake were removed; legal ceilings on bank and thrift interest rates were ended, and use of many new types of mortgages and other financial instruments was permitted. Yet partial deregulation still left certain institutions—such as those covered by federal deposit insurance—with important fund-raising advantages.

—*Technical improvements in electronic funds transfer.* Advances in electronic technology cut the cost of raising funds for many financial institutions, speeded up the reaction times of investors around the world to unfolding events, and more closely linked the sale of property with obtaining financing for it.

These five changes are further described in chapter 2.

Neither partial deregulation of financial markets nor technical improvements in electronic communications can be reversed; their effects will be permanent. Housing probably cannot recover much of its once-sheltered position in credit markets, so effects of that loss will also last a long time. But both monetary and fiscal policy on the one hand, and the expectations of capital suppliers concerning inflation on the other, can be changed in the future. Monetary policy has already shifted back toward a more traditional form.

Yet the United States seems committed for the remainder of the 1980s to an economic strategy involving large federal deficits and relatively high nominal interest rates. That strategy will probably keep capital suppliers' expectations of inflation relatively high, even if inflation rates themselves stay low. Thus all five causes are likely to remain operative during most of the 1980s.

Two Main Effects of the Revolution

Together these revolutionary factors, plus other economic forces, have produced two main effects in real estate capital markets. The first is *a higher level of both real and nominal interest rates* than prevailed in the 1950s, 1960s, and 1970s. Real rates in the 1980s are especially far above those in the 1970s. In this analysis real interest rates are computed by subtracting each year's percentage increase in the consumer price index from that year's average nominal interest rate for each type of financial instrument (short-term, intermediate-term, or long-term). This can be done both before and after taking account of income taxes. After-tax real rates, however, have greater effects on behavior in real estate markets. Average real rates calculated in this way for recent periods are shown in table 1-1. Although the table uses home mortgage rates, real rates for commercial and industrial mortgages were quite similar during 1950–83. This dramatic rise in real interest rates—both before and after taxes—has been abetted by all five of the revolutionary causes described above.

The second main effect has been *institutional integration of housing capital markets with other formerly separate components of the general capital market.* This integration results mainly from partial deregulation of financial markets, which contributed to the loss of the sheltered credit position housing formerly enjoyed. Easier electronic transfer of funds also accelerated integration of world capital markets.

These two effects are both results and causes of greater uncertainty in capital markets about future movements in interest rates. Both effects are discussed further in chapter 3.

The Fundamental Structure of Real Estate Financial Markets

Financial markets in real estate involve annual flows of both real capital—labor, land, and materials—and financial capital—money, other forms of debt, and certificates of ownership—in transactions concerning real property. Financial capital flows are much larger

Table 1-1. *Average Annual Home Mortgage Interest Rates, 1951–84*
Percent

Period	Before income tax Nominal (1)	Change in CPI (2)	Real (col. 1 − col. 2) (3)	After income tax (30 percent tax bracket) Nominal (4)	Real (col. 1 − col. 2) (5)
1951–59	5.25	1.45	3.80	3.68	2.23
1960–69	6.29	2.39	3.90	4.40	2.01
1970–79	8.64	7.20	1.44	6.05	−1.15
1980–83	13.48	6.53	6.95	9.44	2.91
1983	12.35	3.21	9.14	8.65	5.44
1984	12.38	4.00	8.38	8.67	4.67

Sources: *Federal Home Loan Bank Board Journal*, various issues; U.S. Bureau of the Census, *Statistical Abstract of the United States* (Government Printing Office, various years); and Council of Economic Advisers, *Economic Indicators*, December 1984, March 1985.

than real capital flows each year because many existing properties change hands or are refinanced in transactions that do not involve changes in physical resources. Both kinds of capital are discussed in this book, but the emphasis is on financial capital flows.

Personal savings by households are the source for most of the added capital used in real estate transactions each year, just as they are the basis for many other financial transactions. Households also borrow additional amounts as large as their savings. During 1971–81, households combined such borrowings and savings to finance the total of about 13 percent of personal income they used to acquire financial assets of all kinds.

The fundamental paths of capital flows from saving households to final real estate capital users are shown in figure 1-1. The key actors in real estate financial markets are household savers, the depository institutions in which households place most of their savings, mortgage originators (sometimes the same as those depository institutions), transformers of mortgages into other types of financial instruments in secondary mortgage markets, equity syndicators, and final real estate capital users. The last group includes those who develop, buy, renovate, or refinance real properties.

Savings and loan associations have been the largest single institutional source of real estate capital in the past, in both originating and holding mortgages. Commercial banks ranked second in both activities. Mortgage companies were third in originations, but individuals and minor institutions together ranked third in holding mortgages. Mortgages of all kinds account for about one-third of all debt in the United States and are about four times larger than the next largest form of private debt, other bank loans.

Chapter 4 and appendix A describe in detail key actors in U.S. real estate financial markets and how they have behaved in the past. The description in chapter 4 sets the stage for subsequent chapters analyzing the effects of the revolution in real estate finance.

Further Effects of the Revolution

The two main effects cited above—higher interest rates and greater integration of capital markets—have produced the following further effects on real estate markets.

—Developers and users of *all* types of real property are under pressure to use the space built with new capital more intensively than in the past (chapter 5).

—Capital suppliers now place increased emphasis on equity participation in the non-owner-occupied housing projects they finance, rather than continuing to rely on "pure" debt financing such as mortgages (chapter 5).

—There is a built-in bias in capital markets that favors certain institutions that invest mainly in real estate. Whether these institutions finance owner-occupied housing or income properties depends on the level of nominal interest rates. When those rates are relatively high, as they have been recently, institutions will continue to put money into income properties even when the markets for such properties are overbuilt (chapter 5).

—The relative social priority of owner-occupied housing is lower than it was in the three preceding decades. This fall has created a problem of "housing affordability" (chapters 7, 8, and 9).

—Because deregulation of financial institutions has been only partial, it has created serious imbalances between the rewards, of risk taking and its costs and possible penalties. These imbalances exist both within specific types of institutions (especially banks and thrift institutions) and among different types of institutions. They have already imposed large costs of excessive risk taking on the public sector because of federal deposit insurance. Even more of such costs could similarly shift in the future (chapter 10).

Figure 1-1. *Structure of Real Estate Financial Markets*[a]

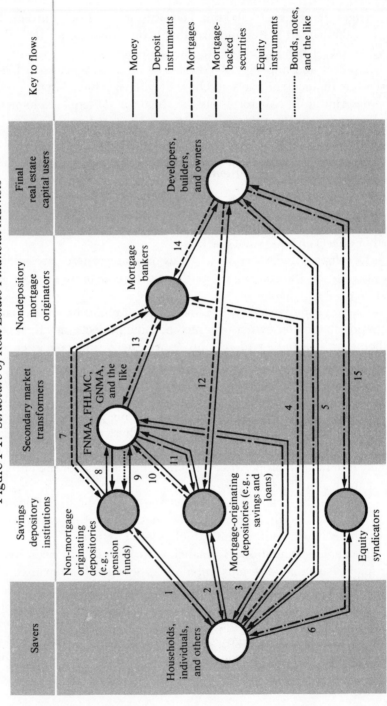

a. Flows are numbered for convenient reference in the text. See pages 64–67 for a full discussion of this diagram.

—Financial institutions that have traditionally supplied most real estate capital have experienced tremendous turmoil, for many including threats to their long-run viability (chapter 11). The thrift industry in particular (savings and loan associations and mutual savings banks) is in precarious condition, with its solvency maintained partly through semifictitious accounting practices approved by regulators. If interest-rate volatility continues, the industry might require a congressional rescue very costly to taxpayers.

—Secondary mortgage markets have become increasingly important channels for steering capital into real estate, especially to finance owner-occupied housing (chapters 12 and 13).

—The economic strategy of big federal deficits combined with high nominal interest rates that has prevailed in the United States during the early and mid-1980s is especially detrimental to housing finance. It should be changed if such finance is to be given relatively high social priority in the future (chapter 14).

Each effect is discussed at length in the chapters that follow. This discussion is summarized below.

Pressure to Use New Capital More Intensively

Higher real interest rates mean that money—a key ingredient in almost all real property transactions—costs more in relation to other resources than in the past. Therefore, real property developers and users are under pressure to use the space built with this more expensive money more intensively than before. The influences of this pressure will last as long as real interest rates remain well above their historic levels. These influences are analyzed in chapter 5.

Greater real capital costs pressure occupants to economize on space use. This cutting back means smaller areas per person for new homes, hotel rooms, industrial spaces, and offices (although office machines are taking up more space, largely offsetting this effect). Rising real incomes, however, usually lead to consumption of more space per person. Hence actually observed use of space will be a net result of these two opposite forces if both consumer and business real incomes keep increasing. Among space users with slowly rising real incomes, the pressure of higher real rates should dominate, and their use of space should observably contract.

In addition, both within and among firms, more activities that require expensive space will be separated from those that do not. The latter will move where rents are cheaper, and the two will be linked electronically. An example is keeping executives downtown for face-to-face contacts but locating lower-level employees in less costly suburban or rural space, or even abroad. Thus downtown areas are likely to capture a smaller share of future growth in office space.

Because real capital now costs more, developers also have greater incentive to renovate older structures built with cheaper capital than to build new ones. The relative value of older structures consequently will rise and cause more revitalization of older areas.

Higher real capital costs also dramatically affect housing markets. Because fewer newly formed households can qualify for mortgage loans, a higher fraction than in earlier post–World War II decades will rent rather than buy homes. The demand for rental housing will therefore increase, putting upward pressure on rents. But all types of housing cost more in real terms than in the 1970s, so fewer separate households will be formed out of any given population increase than formerly. Thus total new housing starts will be lower in the 1980s than in the 1970s, and the share of housing in total capital flows will be smaller.

Increased Equity Participation by Suppliers of Real Estate Capital

From 1945 through the mid-1970s, the major suppliers of real estate capital provided it in the form of long-term mortgage loans at fixed interest rates to developers, investors, builders, and home-buyers. These borrowers put up equity capital, usually from 0 percent to 25 percent of the total capital invested. The viability of this arrangement, however, was upset in the 1970s by inflation that was not anticipated by most capital suppliers. Because they had made long-term, fixed-rate loans at relatively low rates compared with actual inflation rates, they received low real returns on their capital.

To avoid suffering such low yields again in the climate of high inflation that they expected would occur in the 1980s, most capital suppliers shifted their behavior in two ways. They raised the initial nominal interest rates they demanded, as noted above. They also deemphasized provision of "pure" debt and emphasized provision of either equity or debt with some form of equity participation. This shift has dramatically changed the likely future distribution of rewards from profitable real estate investments between those parties who had traditionally put up equity and those institutions that had traditionally supplied debt capital.

It is true that nominal yields on *total capital invested* in income-producing real estate projects have probably risen in the 1980s compared with most earlier periods (except the late 1970s) because of higher interest rates generally. But the average yield on the *equity portion* of such capital has certainly fallen compared with its past levels, especially those in the 1970s. Capital suppliers are now capturing a higher share of the total yield from each property, and developers or other traditional transaction initiators a lower share. Moreover, a greater percentage of the total capital supplied now takes the form of equity, or some type of "quasi equity," and a smaller share is pure debt.

As a result, the multiplier effect on yields to equity of high leveraging with debt has been greatly reduced. Moreover, the average inflation rate in the 1980s appears likely to be lower than that in the 1970s, further reducing the benefits of leveraging for equity investors. Consequently, average yields to equity capital are lower than in the 1970s, whether measured in nominal or real terms or before or after taxes. Nevertheless, creating real estate projects may still be quite profitable—sufficiently so to generate a large supply of persons willing to try it.

Because the yield going to those who normally initiate new projects has fallen, market values of income property will probably appreciate less rapidly than they would have before this change. Such a slowdown in property appreciation appeared dramatically in 1982. Values of many income properties declined under pressure from immense overbuilding in most nonresidential markets. This drop was larger than the decline that typically occurs in similar recessions.

This negative change was partly offset in 1983 and 1984, however, by a huge inflow of money into real estate markets from thrift institutions and real estate syndicators. Thrifts were inundated with new deposits in early 1983 after financial deregulation lifted ceilings on savings interest rates. They promptly funneled this money into real estate. Syndicators experienced a large rise in demand for equities that was caused by favorable 1981 tax-shelter changes plus a fall in bond rates during 1982.

The result was intense competition among buyers of equity properties that drove prices up and yields down during 1983 and early 1984. But these effects are likely to be less permanent than the influences of other major elements in the revolution. Thrifts will not receive another big savings inflow because no further beneficial rule changes are in view. Syndication is likely to suffer somewhat from adverse tax-law changes enacted in 1984 and possibly to be enacted in 1985. Even if chronic oversupplies of money are available for investment in income properties (as discussed in the next section), the resultant overbuilding would keep rents from rising rapidly, thus inhibiting increases in property values in the long run.

The Real Estate Bias of Capital Markets

The nation's major financial institutions compete to raise capital from households, pension funds, and other investors of personal savings flows. They earn both fees and interest rate spreads from investing such capital in various uses. Partial deregulation of these institutions has created an overall bias among them that favors investment in real estate. Such preference arises because federal benefits to investors make two methods of raising capital less costly to financial institutions than all others. Both methods tend to direct the long-term capital they raise into real estate. One method is offering federally insured savings deposits; the other is selling equity ownership shares in real estate syndications. In both cases the federal government provides the ultimate investors with a significant benefit for which the financial institutions themselves do not have to pay the full cost.

In the case of banks and thrift institutions, this benefit is federal deposit insurance. The premiums these institutions pay for such insurance are much smaller than the full cost of similar private deposit insurance; hence savers who use these accounts receive a "surplus benefit." This benefit confers on such accounts a huge competitive advantage in attracting funds in comparison with uninsured accounts. Before deregulation, banks and thrifts could not capitalize on this advantage because the interest rates they could pay savers were limited by law. But deregulation removed these limits, allowing banks and thrifts to match the formerly higher rates offered by more competitive savings institutions such as money market funds. The competitive advantage shifted to banks and thrifts because of deposit insurance.

In the case of real estate syndication, the benefit is shelter from federal income taxes. Investors who buy syndication shares receive this benefit at no cost to the syndicators. Hence they get higher returns per dollar of cost to the syndicators than in other investments. Tax-law changes in 1981, plus dramatic developments in stock and bond markets in 1982, greatly increased the allure of syndication shares for investors in 1983 and 1984.

Only banks and thrift institutions can offer federally insured savings accounts. Banks invest most of the money they raise through such accounts in short-term uses, but thrifts invest most of theirs in long-term uses, mainly in real estate mortgages and equities. Thrifts have recently been empowered to make more non–real estate investments than in the past, but they still get huge tax benefits from focusing mainly on real estate. Real estate syndicators by definition *must* put their funds into buying real estate. So the major financial institutions using these two lowest-cost fund-raising methods are biased toward putting long-term money thus raised into real estate. Whenever these institutions raise a lot of capital, they are under tremendous pressure to invest it in real estate to cover the cost of the capital.

Because of this bias, the institutions concerned are likely to continue investing funds in real estate beyond the point at which the "pure" marginal returns from such investment—that is, nongovernmentally subsidized returns—approximate those from alternative investments. The resultant *surplus of funds invested in real estate* could cause overbuilding in real estate markets when large amounts of capital can be raised through these two methods.

Such overbuilding is not likely to become extensive in markets for owner-occupied housing for three reasons. One is the relation between nominal interest rates and the ability of potential buyers to qualify for loans. Another is the relatively short lead time required to build new homes. Whenever nominal interest rates are relatively high, as they have been in the early and mid-1980s, fewer households can qualify, so the demand for new homes falls. Homebuilders quickly perceive this and stop constructing new units before any big inventory of unsold homes is created. In practice, many homebuilders only build new units that are already sold. If nominal rates declined, more households could qualify, so the demand for new homes would rise substantially, absorbing likely increases in new construction.

The third reason is the inability of capital suppliers to become equity partners in financing owner-occupied housing. The ultimate occupants of such properties are home-owning households that do not want to share ownership with their funding sources. Capital suppliers cannot hedge against inflation by taking long-run equity positions as partners of the owners of such housing, as they can with the owners of income properties. Adjustable rate mortgages (ARMs) provide capital suppliers with only partial hedges against inflation because of limits on the size of the adjustments permitted. When high inflation appears or threatens, many capital suppliers shift their funds away from housing.

The situation is very different in markets for income properties (all types of property except owner-occupied housing and vacant land). The creators and long-run owners of most of such space are *not* the ultimate users, so capital suppliers can become equity partners with the former. This partnership allows capital suppliers to justify continued investment in such properties as hedges against inflation even when nominal interest rates are quite high, since high nominal rates usually occur when actual or expected inflation is also high. In addition, high interest rates do not reduce the demand for nonresidential space as much as they do the demand for owner-occupied housing because the final users pay a much smaller proportion of their total revenues for occupancy costs.

Furthermore, many developers of income properties are willing to gamble on achieving adequate occupancy *after* they have built new projects. This practice is encouraged by long lead times between initial conception and final availability of space. During the lengthy period when each project is being developed, it is funded by borrowed money, not by payments from its ultimate occupants. Hence its backers are often not sure whether the project will be successful until long after they have invested most of the cost of creating it. Under these conditions, and if they can get favorable financing, some space creators will go on constructing more space even when there are not enough users to occupy it. Moreover, some capital suppliers who *must* invest in real estate are willing to put up such financing despite its risks.

Thus there may be chronic overbuilding in markets for income real estate even if nominal interest rates are relatively high. The shifting of capital by thrifts from housing to income property markets actually increases when nominal rates rise because the number of homebuyers who qualify for loans falls. Such chronic overbuilding was clearly present in markets for office space throughout the nation in 1984. It will spread to other types of markets if the nation continues on its economic course of running large federal deficits and maintaining high nominal interest rates while keeping financial markets partially deregulated.

Because chronic overbuilding in nonresidential markets prevents rents there from rising, it may seem to encourage more lavish use of space by occupants. This would contradict the conclusion of chapter 5 that higher real capital costs are causing most occupants to use space more intensively. Actual experience indicates that the economizing effects that higher capital costs have on space use have been, and will probably continue to be, more powerful than the opposite effects of stagnant or falling rents. This is true partly because higher occupancy costs occurred earlier and were more widespread than overbuilding. In addition, institutional practices in renting cause most occupants to *perceive* as substantial increases any changes in rents they face when making space-use decisions; hence they are motivated to use space more intensively. This tendency holds even if the rents occupants must pay are lower than those which would exist if no overbuilding had occurred.

The strength of the capital market bias favoring real estate investment would be reduced if income tax reforms initially proposed by the U.S. Treasury in 1984 and revised in 1985 were adopted in 1985 or later. Some of the Treasury's revised proposals would greatly decrease after-tax yields on individual income properties and notably cut internal rates of return. Other proposals would decrease the willingness of many taxable investors to put funds into real estate equities and would weaken the appeal of large-scale syndications. At the same time, the Treasury's reforms would slightly reduce the relative attractiveness of corporate stocks as a whole but would increase that of most types of bonds and of owner-occupied housing. Hence the allure of equity investment in income real estate would decline compared with that of alternative investments.

As a result, adoption of these proposals in their revised form would cause prices of some income properties to fall somewhat (at least in real terms) and would cut investment in the creation of new ones. The net result would be smaller flows of financial capital into income real estate than would occur without these tax reforms. The ensuing slowdown in creation of new income properties would eventually cause space-supply shortages that would stimulate more rapid rent increases. Such increases would in turn permit owners to recapture some of the values initially lost. But since most markets had large space surpluses in 1985, this readjustment would take considerable time.

Hence adoption of all the Treasury's initial proposals might gradually eliminate the capital market bias toward real estate investment described above. But this outcome is unlikely for two reasons. First, the reforms actually adopted by Congress are certain to involve less radical changes than those proposed by the Treasury. Second, even the Treasury's proposals would not eliminate the capital market advantage held by savings and loans or their tendency to invest available funds mainly in real estate. So thrifts would still exhibit the bias described earlier. Yet they are the largest source of real estate capital, providing far more than all syndications combined. Their situation will therefore cause at least some tendency for a chronic overbuilding to persist until thrifts diversify much more of their investing to other fields. That will not happen for many years, if ever.

Lower Social Priority for Homeownership

The revolution in real estate finance has notably reduced the relative social priority actually awarded to homeownership in the United States compared with that accorded in preceding decades. The erosion of priority has occurred because the real after-tax costs of capital to finance owner-occupied homes have markedly risen in relation to the real after-tax costs of capital used for other purposes, such as investing in industrial plant and equipment, rental housing, stocks, and bonds. This change is rooted in the partial deregulation of financial markets and in the loss of the once-sheltered position housing enjoyed in credit markets. The change is likely to be permanent unless Congress adopts some offsetting subsidy or other additional aids to homeownership. The nature and implications of this development, and of possible policies related to it, are discussed in chapters 7, 8, and 9.

The Problem of Housing "Affordability"

The percentage of all potential first-time homebuyers who can actually afford to purchase homes at today's high nominal interest rates and home prices is much lower than it was in the 1950s, 1960s, and even the 1970s. For example, the fraction of all households that could afford to buy the median-priced home at current interest rates (using a 25 percent downpayment) fell from 60 percent in 1970 to 44 percent in 1982, though it has risen slightly since then.[1] This fraction is even lower in certain high-cost housing areas, such as Hawaii and California.

It thus appears more difficult for newly formed households to attain a central element of the American dream: owning one's own home. According to zealous advocates of homeownership, if this problem of affordability were to continue over a long period, it might weaken now-widespread incentives for people to work hard and to save. It might even undermine long-run support for the entire free enterprise system. Moreover, the total demand for real estate capital might be greatly reduced in the future if homeownership declined because fewer households could afford it.

Defining Affordability

What makes a home affordable? This analysis assumes that a household can afford to buy a home if it can make a cash downpayment of 25 percent of the home's price and if 35 percent of its total

1. See table 8-3 in chapter 8.

gross before-tax income will pay for the annual debt service on a twenty-five-year mortgage covering both the remainder of the price at current interest rates and the property taxes and insurance. Thus the "appropriate share" of income able to be devoted to housing is arbitrarily set at 35 percent.

Housing affordability also has a time dimension. A household can afford to buy a home immediately only if it already has the 25 percent downpayment. But the larger its downpayment on a home of given price, the smaller the monthly payments it must make from current income. Hence a household can afford the current payments on a more expensive home if it makes a downpayment exceeding 25 percent of the home price. Thus, even if a household cannot afford the monthly payments on a certain home immediately, it might be able to do so after saving several years to amass a larger downpayment. Moreover, it is reasonable to expect a household to save for a time before buying a home, as most American homeowners have done in the past. Therefore, *immediate* affordability must be distinguished from affordability *within a reasonable period.* An arbitrary judgment is made that six years is a reasonable period for saving to buy a home.

Why Housing Is Less Affordable in the 1980s

Recent trends have made housing less affordable to many households because home prices and mortgage interest rates have risen faster than household incomes. The buildup of homeowners' equities, however, has more than offset the bite of higher payments for households that already owned homes before 1980. Hence serious problems of housing affordability are confined to (1) current first-time homebuyers, (2) homeowners who bought their first homes after 1979, and (3) nonhomeowners living in high-cost markets, such as much of California.

First-time homebuyers constitute a small fraction of all households in any given year, although that fraction becomes cumulatively substantial over a five- to ten-year period. Yet few first-time buyers are in dire need of aid. Their median incomes in both 1977 and 1979 were actually about 50 percent above the median income for all households. So only relatively low-income members of the three groups above are hurt by this problem.

Reasons for Public Policy Intervention

Housing must compete with all other uses for funds in deregulated capital markets. But when nominal interest rates in general rise, the demand for housing is more adversely affected because so many households can no longer afford to buy homes. Recently the nation's basic economic strategy has generated high nominal interest rates over prolonged periods. Hence, from 1979 to 1982, housing markets remained depressed much longer than usual. If this recurs, serious housing shortages might appear, although few existed as of 1985. Whether public policy should respond depends partly on whether housing should have high social priority.

One argument favoring such priority is that housing of good quality is necessary for the sound mental and physical health of the populace. A second argument is that homeownership promotes good citizenship and greater allegiance to both democracy and the free enterprise system. Furthermore, the desire to own one's own home inspires millions of households to work harder and to save more than they otherwise would. Persuasive as these arguments may seem, little empirical evidence supports them. Moreover, there is no evidence indicating just how good or available housing must be to achieve any of these goals. So housing's relative social priority must be based almost entirely on purely subjective values.

Possible Remedial Policies

Some possible tactics for improving housing affordability are either unlikely to occur or undesirable. Such policies are keeping nominal interest rates low (not likely), restoring extensive financial regulations favoring housing (undesirable because it would require subsidizing savers), and increasing the tax advantages of homeownership (undesirable because the added subsidies would mainly benefit middle- and upper-income households that do not need such aid). Several more feasible tactics are subsidizing first-time buyers, using forms of mortgage with low initial payments, building smaller homes at higher densities to cut housing prices, and shifting housing infrastructure costs from homebuyers to the general community.

Evaluating These Policies

The effectiveness of these four tactics can be assessed in part by gauging their effects on the housing situations of three prototypical households. Each has been matched with a home of a certain price. A household at the top of the lowest quartile of the 1983 income distribution ($11,400) is matched with a home (costing $50,000) at the top of the lowest quartile of the 1983 home-price distribution. A household with the national median income in 1983 ($21,750) is matched with the 1983 median-priced home (costing $70,400). Finally, a household with the median California income in 1983 ($23,466) is matched with the 1983 median-priced California home (costing $114,000) to represent potential homebuyers in high-priced markets.

The approach is to determine how long it would take each of these households to save a downpayment large enough for it to afford to buy the home with which it is matched. While saving, each household devotes 35 percent of its current income to a combination of rent and savings deposits. Home prices, household incomes, and rents are assumed to rise 5 percent a year during the period for saving the downpayment.

If these households have no savings at the start of the saving period, it would take the lower-income household 20.7 years to save the required downpayment if it had to pay rent in the meantime, 6.5 years if it could live rent-free with relatives. Clearly this household cannot afford to buy within a reasonable period the home with which it has been matched.

In contrast, the median-income household could afford to buy the median-priced home by saving for less than six years, even if it rents during that time. Moreover, past studies of actual first-time buyers show that most of their incomes were well above the median household income. Therefore, *most potential first-time homebuyers do not have problems of housing affordability when the time dimension of affordability is taken into account.* That is not the case, however, in California and other high-priced markets. The median-income California household would have to save for 21.6 years to buy the median-price California home if it rented, for 8.4 years if it lived rent-free.

Several specific policies were tested to measure how each would affect the time required for each household to save enough to buy the home with which it was matched. The most effective policies are small, high-density housing (assumed to cost 25 percent less), graduated-payment mortgages, and a 100 percent tax credit for savings. Yet no policy by itself enables either the lower-income household or the median-income California household to buy its matched home within a reasonable period, unless it lives rent-free (and even then success is doubtful).

Some Policy Conclusions

This analysis implies that *no additional federal assistance should be given to help homebuyers—even first-time homebuyers—overcome problems of housing affordability.* Other needier households, such as poor renters, should have a far higher priority access to any additional federal aid for housing.

It is true that potential first-time and other homebuyers in high-priced markets have serious problems of affordability. But housing costs are higher in these markets mainly because of stringent local restrictions against low-cost home building. Taxpayers across the nation should not have to help residents of such areas buy high-priced homes when other residents there are primarily responsible for the high housing prices.

Imbalances in the Rewards and Costs of Risk Taking

Partial deregulation has created a serious imbalance between the potential rewards and costs of certain kinds of risk-taking behavior by financial institutions, especially those oriented toward real estate; this imbalance is analyzed in chapter 10. Federal deposit insurance removes most of the threat to banks and thrifts of losing deposits if they grow rapidly or make risky investments. But financial deregulation has increased the potential rewards for such behavior. The result has been much greater net incentives for banks and thrifts to make highly risky investments, and many have done so.

These institutions can now offer as high interest rates as they wish; they can therefore grow rapidly by bidding above market levels to attract deposits. With massively increased total funds, they can leverage their initial equity capital tremendously. It is true that regulatory agencies recently have begun pressuring banks and thrifts to increase their capital. But those institutions can earn much larger fees in relation to that capital by financing many more transactions. Moreover, they can gamble on risky investments that promise high returns if successful. For example, in 1983 some large thrift institutions used highly transient short-term deposits to make many long-term, fixed-rate mortgages. They were hoping that interest rates would fall and they would receive windfall gains plus large profits from greater rate spreads. But interest rates rose in 1984, causing some of these institutions to come close to bankruptcy.

This imbalance in the rewards and costs of risk has been aggravated by federal regulatory agencies. After the near collapse of the Continental Illinois Bank and Trust Company, the comptroller of the currency said that federal authorities would underwrite all the liabilities of the ten largest U.S. banks if any encountered similar trouble. Federal regulators have rescued dozens of thrifts from disaster by merging them with healthier ones. They have also maintained the appearance of solvency for many others by furnishing the ailing thrifts with essentially fictitious "regulatory assets." Moreover, federal connections with public or quasi-public agencies, such as the Federal Home Loan Mortgage Corporation (FHLMC, or "Freddie Mac") and the Federal National Mortgage Association (FNMA, or "Fannie Mae"), create incentives for these agencies to engage in excessively risky behavior too, although there is no clear evidence that they have done so.

This situation has critical implications for the future of financial deregulation. Creating unrestricted competition in financial markets through more complete deregulation is essentially inconsistent with preserving the advantages certain institutions receive from their special connections with the federal government. The institutions enjoying such connections—including banks, thrifts, FHLMC, and FNMA—have competitive advantages over other types of institutions that make a "level playing field" in capital markets impossible.

To reduce this imbalance, the present combination of federal deposit insurance and partially deregulated financial markets needs to be changed. Federal deposit insurance could be abolished, extended to a greater range of financial institutions, retained but accompanied by a return to more stringent federal regulation, or retained in a way that would make the institutions enjoying it more sensitive to risk. The last policy should be tried first, with the others regarded as possible last resorts.

The policy of increasing risk sensitivity would require some combination of reducing the size of deposits covered by federal insurance, restricting brokered deposits, pressing banks and (especially) thrifts to increase their equity capital bases, and varying deposit insurance premiums with the riskiness of individual institutional behavior. In addition, special federal connections with FHLMC and FNMA should be removed in the long run. There is, however, no guarantee that these policies would end all of the current risk imbalance in financial markets. That goal may be unattainable.

Institutional Turmoil in the Nation's Financial Markets

Integration of the housing sector with other sectors of the nation's capital markets, consequent on partial deregulation, has created tremendous turmoil in those markets, as discussed in chapter 11. Not since the combined financial devastation and creativity of the 1930s has so much change occurred in capital markets in such an unpredictable and seemingly uncontrollable fashion. One result has been confusion and uncertainty about which specific functions can or should be performed by which particular institutions.

This integration, however, has also greatly intensified competition, increased innovation, and upset many long-established but inefficient ways of doing business. In particular, low-cost producers of key financial services have expanded their market shares. In the long run that expansion will be good for consumers, since the average costs of financial services will fall. It will be especially good for savers in formerly regulated institutions, which are now paying much higher yields to depositors. But many small institutions will either fail or be merged with larger ones.

The entire savings and loan industry—the single largest source of real estate capital—has actually been put into a precarious financial position by these revolutionary factors, chief among them inflation and changes in fiscal and monetary policy. Whenever short-term interest rates are nearly equal to, or higher than, long-term rates, the industry becomes unprofitable, and its net worth rapidly drains away. It narrowly averted a systemwide crisis in 1982, and it still is in difficult straits.

Institutional inertia will cause some of the effects described above to appear slowly, but they are clearly on the way. Hence the 1980s should be the most dynamic period of institutional change in financial markets since the Great Depression of the 1930s. Specific changes expected to occur in particular institutions are stated below.

The *thrift industry*—savings and loan associations and mutual savings banks—was still in fragile financial condition in early 1985, in spite of two years of recovery from its near collapse in 1982. The volatility of interest rates since 1979 has steadily depleted thrifts' net worth. The overall net worth of the industry measured by generally accepted accounting procedures fell from 5.3 percent of total assets in 1980 to less than 4.0 percent in 1985.[2] It would have been less than 1 percent if intangible assets such as "good will" were excluded. Reserves of the Federal Savings and Loan Insurance Corporation (FSLIC) were so depleted from rescuing bankrupt associations that it had to make a special assessment to rebuild them.

How can capital be restored to this ailing industry so it can cushion itself against future vicissitudes? They key is for the nation to adopt a mix of federal fiscal and monetary policies that will end the volatility of interest rates. If relative rate stability can be achieved for just two to four years, well-managed associations can restructure their balance sheets by increasing the maturities of their assets (mostly mortgages) and reducing the maturities of their liabilities (mostly savings deposits). This will slash their vulnerability to losing net worth in future periods of rate instability. Then private investors will be willing to put more capital into healthy thrifts through thrift mergers, acquisitions by banks and nonfinancial corporations, and direct individual investment.

If interest-rate stability is not restored, and if rates go any higher than they were in early 1985, most of the thrift industry will become insolvent in the balance-sheet sense, even if it still has positive cash flows. FSLIC's assets will be totally inadequate to remedy this outcome. But Congress will undoubtedly not allow millions of Ameri-

2. United States League of Savings Associations, *1982 Savings and Loan Source Book* (Chicago: USLSA, 1982), p. 43.

cans to lose federally insured deposits. Hence enough capital will be supplied by the federal government to maintain depositor confidence in the industry—but not enough to restore it to true viability. Only a return to interest rate stability can accomplish that.

For the foreseeable future, most thrift institutions—especially savings and loans—will retain their primary focus on real estate investment, despite a recent broadening of their powers to acquire assets. A higher share of their investments, however, will go to equity and development efforts rather than to mortgage lending. Yet thrifts will continue to hold and expand their large portfolios of residential and other mortgages, with rising percentages in the form of mortgage-backed securities (or MBSs). More and more of those mortgages will be ARMs. Most thrifts will try to increase the share of their revenues and profits that come from fees for service rather than from interest rate spreads. Many will broaden their sources of funds beyond household savings to include money raised from national investment banking and brokerage firms.

But the number of separate thrift institutions will sharply decline because of continued mergers, failures, and the movement of some firms into more diversified activities. With all these changes taken into account, all thrifts will probably attract about half of all the added savings deposits gained by banks and thrifts combined. Hence *thrift institutions will remain the largest single source of real estate capital.*

Domestic pension funds will provide a relatively small share of total housing finance in the future—certainly less than 15 percent of housing mortgage requirements, and probably under 10 percent. Their share will be small even if they put higher fractions of their resources into real estate. Pension funds will, however, contribute a much larger share of total nonresidential financing requirements—perhaps more than 25 percent.

Life insurance companies will continue to provide real estate investment capital, primarily by acting as intermediaries for pension funds. Many will diversify into real estate operations quite new to them, such as real estate syndication.

Wall Street investment banking and brokerage firms will play a much larger role in real estate financing than in the past, mainly by selling shares in both equity and mortgage funds to small-scale investors. Their functions will be the same as those performed by many specialized *real estate syndication firms*, which will also have expanded functions. Syndicators will become more important actors in both residential and nonresidential secondary mortgage markets, using new financial vehicles if tax reform hampers traditional syndication.

Independent developers will remain key actors in the creation of real estate because they possess certain advantages that large firms or institutions have trouble matching. These include entrepreneurial risk assessment, speedier decisionmaking, and more rewarding equity-based compensation schemes for top personnel. But developers will engage in more joint development ventures and nonequity project management than in the past.

The Increased Importance of Secondary Mortgage Markets

Secondary mortgage markets involve the resale of mortgages by their originators or holders to other holders, often through specialized intermediaries. Such markets are analyzed in chapter 12. Secondary mortgage markets were created to perform six basic functions: to increase the total size of capital flows into housing, to reduce greatly the cyclical instability of those flows, to increase the overall efficiency of capital allocation, to decrease the real costs of housing finance to consumers, to increase homeownership, and to help the federal government finance certain subsidized housing projects. They have effectively carried out all these functions except greatly reducing the instability of housing capital flows, which is probably impossible.

During 1977–82, 55 percent of the dollar volume in such markets involved four large federal or quasi-federal institutions: the Government National Mortgage Association (GNMA, or "Ginnie Mae"), FNMA, FHLMC, and the Farmers Home Administration.

These organizations are major movers of funds from general capital markets into housing markets. The "Big Three"—GNMA, FNMA, and FHLMC—now all buy mortgages, package them, and guarantee payments on MBSs and other securities backed by those mortgages but held by other institutions. Secondary mortgage markets have accounted for more than half of the funds flowing into residential mortgages during recent years.

MBSs represent a key way for real estate borrowers to obtain funds from fully integrated capital markets because the greater liquidity of such securities makes them far more attractive to most investors than mortgages themselves. These securities, however, still suffer from uncertain timing of principal repayment compared with most traditional bonds. Changes in existing regulations can partially reduce this drawback. Yet the uncertainty will still cause the housing industry to pay at least as high interest rates, perhaps higher, for capital as those paid by other capital users. That puts housing at a disadvantage when the general structure of interest rates rises to high levels.

Recent Trends

The ability of savings and loans to hold mortgages in their own portfolios has been greatly reduced by their precarious financial position. Hence they must dispose of a higher fraction of mortgages they originate by selling them through the secondary market. In addition, most mortgage originators are anxious to convert their mortgages into the much more liquid form of MBSs. Consequently, the share of secondary markets in housing finance will undoubtedly be much larger in the future than its average during 1950–80. Even so, annual household savings flows will remain the fundamental source of capital for real estate finance. But savings will flow into real estate through somewhat different channels than in the past, with more going through pension funds.

Given current surpluses of available space in most markets, the nation does not really need more sources of funds for commercial, industrial, and rental apartment mortgages. Yet secondary markets are likely to be created for such mortgages because investment bankers can profit from creating them.

Implications for Public Policy

What public policies toward secondary mortgage markets should be adopted? Possible policies are analyzed in chapter 13, including the following recommendations:

—retain GNMA as a federal agency and keep its activities focused mainly on aiding low- and moderate-income households;

—transform FNMA and FHLMC into fully private institutions that pay taxes, have no special connections with the federal government, and are relatively free from federal regulations;

—adopt special policies to help FNMA cope with the problem posed by its large portfolio of low-interest home mortgages (several different tactics could be used, with varying distribution of costs and benefits; the most feasible undoubtedly require some continuing connection between FNMA and the U.S. Treasury for an interim of several years);

—encourage more private firms to enter mortgage markets for housing;

—award development of secondary mortgage markets for non-housing real estate low priority as a public policy goal.

National Economic Strategy and the Future of Real Estate Finance

A basic purpose of financial deregulation is to allow "free" markets to allocate capital on the basis of price rationing, rather than other nonmarket forms of rationing as in the past. But the current national economic strategy comprises an expansionary fiscal policy, based on large federal deficits, plus a relatively restrictive monetary policy, designed to inhibit inflation. This strategy has raised the nominal and real prices of money much higher than their traditional levels. These high prices make it harder for potential home-buying households to qualify for mortgage loans. Hence this strategy biases the deregulated system of capital allocation against channeling funds into housing transactions, in contrast to its past operation.

As discussed in chapter 14, if the nation wants to keep placing high social priority on meeting housing needs, compared with maintaining federal spending or increasing productivity through greater industrial investment, then it must adopt either of two policies. The first is to return housing to a more favored position in credit markets by "rolling back" deregulation. But savers would no longer provide private subsidies to mortgage borrowers by accepting below-market interest on deposits in housing-oriented financial institutions. Therefore the federal government would have to pay for special tax benefits to such savers to make "re-regulation" work. The other policy—which appears much more desirable—is to shift the balance between fiscal and monetary policy by reducing federal deficits and easing monetary restrictions.

The future state of financing for nonresidential real estate transactions is markedly different. During the last half of the 1980s and in the early 1990s, nonresidential real estate markets are more likely to suffer from oversupplies of capital—hence chronic overbuilding—than from capital shortages. This overcapitalization will be the result of built-in biases of financial institutions toward investing in real estate, even if the nation's basic economic strategy produces high nominal interest rates. This preference cannot be remedied by changing the nation's economic strategy, but only by altering the risk-reward balance built into federal deposit insurance. As discussed in chapter 10, that is extremely difficult, if not impossible to do without abolishing such insurance altogether. Yet such abolition may be even more undersirable than living with some imbalance related to risk behavior.

2

Causes of the Revolution

FIVE major shifts in key conditions affecting financial markets have produced the revolution in real estate finance described in chapter 1. This chapter examines these causes and shows how they have reinforced each other during the past decade.

The Shift in Lenders' Attitudes toward Inflation

For thirty years before 1980, most lenders either ignored the rate of inflation or believed that whenever it went up it would soon fall back to reasonable levels. Money suppliers were therefore willing to lend at fixed, relatively low interest rates. These suppliers included households depositing their savings in thrift institutions or buying insurance policies and financial intermediaries making mortgage loans.

But inflation accelerated unexpectedly in the 1970s. The consumer price index (CPI) rose at a compound annual rate of 7.8 percent compared with 2.7 percent in the 1960s and 1.6 percent in the 1950s. The CPI reached double-digit levels three times in 1974–80, when its compound annual rise was 9.1 percent.[1] As a result loan repayments fixed in nominal terms fell in real value. Hence *the "true-cost" of mortgage borrowing declined sharply from the mid-1960s to about 1978, even though nominal interest rates were rising to record levels.*

Real rates were even lower for borrowers when the effects of

1. U.S. Bureau of the Census, *Statistical Abstract of the United States, 1981* (Government Printing Office, 1981), p. 467.

28

income tax deductions are taken into account. On mortgage loans made in every year after about 1965, borrowers in the 25 percent income tax bracket were actually paying *negative* real, after-tax interest rates.[2] In effect lenders were paying borrowers to take money because the lenders had failed to anticipate future inflation.

For borrowers this situation was a bonanza. The beneficiaries included homebuyers, developers, and speculators. By leveraging their small investments with no-cost capital during an inflationary period, borrowers raised their rates of return on equity to unprecedented levels. This profitability motivated millions of households and thousands of developers and speculators to enter the market. Their demands drove prices of real estate up faster than the rate of inflation. Hence a form of self-fulfilling prophecy developed, fueled by money borrowed from financial intermediaries, which in turn were obtaining it from savers.

Yet, while borrowers were enjoying immense profits, lenders and savers were receiving abnormally low real rates of return on their capital because of inflation. *This was a fundamentally unsustainable imbalance between borrowers and lenders.* Borrowers were benefiting too greatly at the expense of lenders for lenders to accept the situation permanently.

Consequently in 1980 the nation's financial community drastically revised its expectations concerning inflation. A second consecutive year in which the CPI increased more that 10 percent apparently convinced the financial community that relatively high inflation rates were here to stay, perhaps indefinitely.[3]

This shift in expectations caused financial institutions and other major lenders to change their behavior in two crucial ways. First, they initially demanded higher real yields on their investments. This provided a cushion against both possible future increases in inflation

---

2. Anthony Downs and S. Michael Giliberto, "How Inflation Erodes the Income of Fixed-Rate Lenders," *Real Estate Review*, vol. 11 (Spring 1981), p. 48. Computations of real interest rates assume that each loan is held for ten years and then fully repaid (except those made after 1970, which are repaid in 1980). All payments, including the final repayment, are converted back into dollars of purchasing power equivalent to those of the year in which the loan was made, and then the real return is computed.

3. The consumer price index (CPI) rose 11.3 percent in 1979 and 13.5 percent in 1980. Bureau of the Census, *Statistical Abstract, 1981*, p. 467.

and the greater volatility of interest rates that money markets had recently experienced.

Second, they changed the forms of their investments to protect themselves against a little-recognized but central trait of inflation: uncertainty about how fast future prices will rise. If future inflation rates could be forecast reliably, lenders could write loan contracts in advance specifying annual interest rates that would exactly offset future price increases. But no one can forecast future inflation rates reliably. Moreover, the higher the average inflation rate, the greater the uncertainty about what future rates will be. This is partly because higher inflation rates provide greater scope for both upward and downward price movements in the future.

Capital suppliers can protect themselves against such uncertainty only by adopting one of three investment forms that vary nominal payments with inflation as it occurs so as to keep real yields approximately constant. The first is making a loan with an interest rate that varies in accordance with some other indicator sensitive to inflation, as in *adjustable rate mortgages* (ARMs). The second is making a loan with an interest rate renegotiated often enough to catch up quickly to changing conditions, as in *renegotiable rate or rollover mortgages*. The third consists in taking *equity positions* in the properties, since their net incomes will presumably vary with inflation.

In 1980 most major financial institutions switched from making long-term, fixed-rate mortgage loans to using one or more of these investment forms. All three approaches shift most of the risks of unanticipated inflation from lenders to borrowers. This is a radical change from past practices because long-term, fixed-rate mortgages place the entire risk of future inflation upon lenders. It is true that some savings and loan associations had been offering ARMs since the mid-1970s, when these mortgages were first permitted by regulatory authorities, but ARMs remained a relatively small share of the total market until about 1980.

These two changes in lender behavior will raise the real cost of capital to borrowers in the 1980s compared with its abnormally low cost in the 1970s. Capital suppliers are demanding much higher real interest rates at the outset.[4] Moreover, real capital costs will remain

---

4. These real interest rates are computed before the fact by subtracting the current rate of increase in the CPI from the current nominal interest rate. The real

high no matter what happens to inflation. If inflation rates soar higher than anticipated, these investment forms will adjust nominal repayments to keep real yields roughly constant. Hence any underestimation of actual inflation by lenders in the 1980s will not greatly favor borrowers, as it did in the 1970s. High inflation in the 1980s would actually produce high real interest rates, the opposite of what happened in the 1970s.

Moreover, the reappearance of relatively low inflation rates will not immediately cause most sophisticated lenders to abandon these new investment forms. The CPI increased only 3.9 percent in 1982, 3.8 percent in 1983, and 4.0 percent in 1984. Yet most nonresidential lenders did not go back to making long-term, fixed-rate mortgages at low rates during these years. In 1983 some savings and loan associations did make such loans for housing and for some nonresidential properties, for reasons discussed in chapter 5, but few other lenders followed suit. Nearly all believed inflation could easily accelerate again to much higher levels.

After all, six years elapsed from the time inflation first hit double-digit rates in 1974 until the financial community decided in 1980 that high inflation rates were likely to prevail. The lag was partly because inflation rates fell sharply right after hitting their first peak in 1974. By 1976 they had dropped to 5.8 percent, but then they rose steadily until 1979, when they soared above 10.0 percent again, mainly because of the doubling in world oil prices.[5] If high inflation took that long after its first appearance to convince capital suppliers that it would become dominant, low inflation will probably require a similarly long period after its first appearance to convince them that it has regained its dominance. This skepticism is encouraged by continuation of huge federal deficits, which create long-run pressure to ease the real burden of federal indebtedness through depreciation of the currency. Most capital suppliers are therefore likely to continue the two key changes in their behavior described above for many years.

---

interest rates discussed earlier were computed after the fact but differ only slightly from the ones used here. By definition, it is impossible to compute after-the-fact interest rates for loans of any duration at the time of making those loans.

5. Bureau of the Census, *Statistical Abstract of the United States, 1984* (GPO, 1983), p. 495.

The Shift in Favored Credit and Tax Positions for Housing

During the period from World War II until about 1980, housing enjoyed favored credit and tax positions in the nation's financial markets. The beneficiaries of these positions included the home-building industry (builders, material suppliers, mortgage lenders, and so forth), the home sales industry (realtors, title companies, mortgage lenders, and so forth), and households purchasing new or existing homes.

The advantages enjoyed by housing rested on two pillars. The first was regulations governing financial institutions that made residential mortgage funds available at lower cost than would occur in a free money market. The second was tax benefits from investing in homeownership rather than in stocks, bonds, or small businesses. These advantages caused the flow of financial capital into housing to be larger than it would otherwise have been and presumably reduced the flow of such capital into alternative investments. Recent developments, however, have greatly eroded both pillars and have diminished the effectiveness of both advantages.

Financial Regulations Favoring Housing

Before 1980 households and developers borrowing money to buy or build homes could obtain mortgages at rates lower than would have prevailed in the absence of regulations, especially during "tight money" segments of business cycles. This favored position arose from federal ceilings placed on the interest rates that thrift institutions and banks could pay savings depositors and from the requirement that thrift institutions invest most of their assets in housing. The rate ceilings allowed thrifts to pay depositors slightly higher interest rates than banks. Households were thus encouraged to save in institutions legally bound to invest primarily in housing. This increased the relative supply of residential mortgage money and reduced its relative price.

Furthermore, during segments of the business cycle when short-term interest rates rose above federal ceilings on deposit rates, thrift institutions were prevented from paying market rates to savers. So they did not have to charge mortgage borrowers full market rates either. Savers were thus deprived of the higher interest rates that they could have earned in the absence of regulations. This arrangement in effect forced small-scale savers to subsidize mortgage borrowers. In contrast, large-scale savers could obtain market interest rates on unregulated certificates of deposit of $100,000 or more or by directly purchasing U.S. Treasury bills and other securities.

As long as average inflation rates remained low, periods when short-term interest rates exceeded deposit ceilings were relatively short, and the gap between these rates was small. Hence the total subsidies provided by small-scale savers to mortgage borrowers were small. But when inflation accelerated, short-term interest rates rose well above federal deposit rate ceilings and stayed there for long periods. This increased both the size and duration of the rate subsidies paid by small-scale savers.

Wall Street entrepreneurs quickly seized the opportunity presented by this situation. They developed unregulated money market funds offering interest rates to small-scale savers well above those provided by thrift institutions. The money market funds lent their deposits on the short-term market, mainly by buying commercial paper and bank certificates of deposit. The rapid rise of these funds from under $11 billion in 1978 to over $200 billion in 1982 shows how appealing they were.

By early 1978 thrift institutions were beginning to lose deposits to these money market funds. Federal regulators decided to help thrifts retain funds by creating a new instrument that would let them, too, pay savers rates closer to market. These "money market certificates" required minimum deposits of $10,000 for six months and paid interest one-fourth of 1 percent above the Treasury bill rate. They successfully slowed the deposit losses of the thrifts but greatly raised the average cost that thrifts had to pay for funds. That cost rose steadily from 6.44 percent in 1977 to 11.53 percent in the last half of 1981 as more and more depositors transferred money out of passbook accounts.[6]

Because thrifts could no longer avoid paying their depositors high market interest rates, they had to raise mortgage interest rates to their borrowers accordingly. The average effective mortgage rate on new loans by savings and loan associations rose from 8.82 percent in 1977[7] to 14.39 percent in 1981—up 63.20 percent.[8] Moreover, thrifts experienced an increasing financial squeeze as the cost of their

6. *Federal Home Loan Bank Board Journal*, vol. 15 (June 1982), p. 99.
7. *Federal Home Loan Bank Board Journal*, vol. 14 (July 1981), p. 92.
8. *Federal Home Loan Bank Board Journal*, vol. 15 (June 1982), p. 102.

deposits rose while the income from their large portfolio of low but fixed-rate, long-term loans lagged. Hence they had to cut back on lending. Whereas all savings and loans made $110.3 billion in mortgage loans in 1978, they made only $100.5 billion in 1979, $72.5 billion in 1980, and $53.3 billion in 1981—a drop of 52 percent in three years.[9]

Inflation had made inoperable the fundamental concept underlying thrift institutions: borrowing funds for short terms through savings deposits and lending them for long terms through mortgage loans. This concept presupposed that short-term rates would remain lower than long-term rates. But high rates of inflation *not expected to last* produce short-term interest rates higher than long-term rates. Lenders then expect more intensive demand for money in the immediate future than over the course of a longer-term loan. They also expect a faster average rate of dollar depreciation during a short-term loan than during a long-term loan, since they believe future inflation rates will fall. As long as this condition prevails, thrift institutions cannot profitably borrow short and lend long. Hence the relative advantages they formerly provided to the housing industry cannot be sustained.

Even when long-term rates rise higher than short-term rates, that rise does not return thrift institutions to "normal" profitability as long as short-term rates stay high. Then thrifts still have to pay their depositors higher rates than they earn on their asset portfolios, which contain billions of dollars of old, low-rate mortgages. The low yield on those portfolios creates an upper limit on the ability of thrifts to pay interest to hold deposits without suffering capital losses. Recognizing this limit, regulators kept in effect for thrifts at least some ceilings on deposit rates through 1982.

Even so, in 1981 and most of 1982 short-term interest rates rose so far above the average yield on thrift assets that thrifts could not match the rates offered by money market funds, which have no portfolios of old mortgages. As a result, savings and loans sustained a $25.4 billion loss of net new savings in 1981 (although their total savings balances rose 2.5 percent because of interest payments credited to savings accounts).[10] They endured another loss of $17.2 bil-

9. Ibid., p. 98.
10. Ibid., p. 96.

lion in net new savings in the first eleven months of 1982 before the use of new, no-rate-ceiling accounts dramatically changed their situation in December 1982. (Their total savings balances, however, rose by $26.7 billion, or by 5.1 percent, in the first eleven months of 1982.)[11]

Yet short-term rates are likely to be high whenever either inflation rates are high or the Federal Reserve Board follows a tight money policy (discussed further below). That was the situation of thrifts during 1981 and much of 1982, when most were operating unprofitably. Hence the net worth of the industry as a whole was rapidly being eroded.[12]

In about mid-1982, the Federal Reserve eased its monetary policy; after that, short-term rates fell well below both long-term rates and the average yield on thrift institutions' portfolios. The decline stopped thrifts' loss of equity capital for as long as short-term rates remain low.

To help thrifts cope with their worsening financial plight, federal regulators carried out a series of deregulations from 1979 to 1982. They authorized several new accounts offering higher rates to small-scale savers, and almost every imaginable type of mortgage instrument. Thrifts began featuring different combinations of variable rates, short terms, increasing principals, and other elements that shift some of the risk of future inflation onto borrowers. Regulators have also broadened the kinds of assets thrifts can buy, thus permitting them to enter other businesses, such as consumer finance. These changes recognize the realities caused by rising inflation, but they also reduce the favored credit market position formerly enjoyed by housing.

Some homebuilders advocate restoring that favored position by returning to low ceilings on deposit rates and by imposing both ceilings and reserve requirements on all competitive instruments (such as money market funds). But that would force savers to accept yields below market rates. Moreover, when market interest rates are high, to get mortgage rates low enough to stimulate the housing industry thrifts would have to reduce savings rates far below the

11. *Federal Home Loan Bank Board Journal*, vol. 16 (January 1983), p. 50.
12. Andrew S. Carron, *The Plight of the Thrift Institutions* (Brookings, 1982), p. 5.

market. But Congress is not likely to compel small-scale savers to accept abnormally low returns in order to benefit mortgage borrowers, realtors, and homebuilders. The alternative is to provide a huge new federal subsidy to housing so that savers would not have to accept below-market rates. Adoption of any such subsidy seems both unlikely and undesirable in this era of large cutbacks in federal domestic spending.[13] Thus housing's loss of regulatory shelters in credit markets is almost certain to be permanent.

Tax Benefits Favoring Housing

Tax advantages for investing in homeownership rather than in rental housing, stocks, bonds, or small businesses made up the second pillar supporting the favored position of housing. Many people think housing's greatest tax advantage is the ability of homeowners to deduct mortgage interest and property taxes from their taxable incomes. But persons who make most other investments can also deduct interest and even more expenses from their taxable incomes. They must, however, then pay income or capital gains taxes on any remaining profits. Homeowners get these important deductions without paying taxes on the imputed net incomes they earn by renting their homes to themselves. This freedom from taxes on the net incomes from their investments constitutes the largest indirect subsidy to homeowners. In addition, profits from the sale of owner-occupied homes are free from all capital gains taxes if equities are rolled over into new units within twenty-four months after the sale. In addition, $125,000 in capital gains are exempt from any taxation for persons aged fifty-five and over.

These positive tax advantages of homeownership were made *relatively* even more attractive by some tax penalties for investing in corporate and other businesses during inflationary periods. The most important penalty was excessive income taxes from overestimating "true" net income during rapid inflation. Net taxable business income is computed after deductions for depreciation of plant and equipment. But past accounting practices required those deduc-

13. Congress did pass a subsidy to savers in thrifts and banks called an "All-Savers" certificate, presumably intended to aid both thrifts and housing. It did benefit thrifts somewhat, but not housing. The subsidy was adopted for only one year.

tions to be based on the actual original costs of the plant and equipment, not their current replacement costs. During periods of rapid inflation, actual replacement costs soared far above original costs. Hence the depreciation allowed did not cover the true costs of replacing the plant or equipment when it wore out or became obsolete. Because businesses were systematically understating their "true" costs when computing profits, they overstated their "true" profits. Yet federal and state income taxes were based on those overstated profits. Thus, inflation interacted with tax laws to impose excessive income taxes on many businesses. This presumably discouraged people from investing in both corporate equities and noncorporate businesses.

There are no comprehensive data on the total size of this penalty to business. One accounting authority, however, estimated that corporate taxes were increased by as much as 25 percent above what they really should have been.[14] Several econometric studies have calculated that housing received significantly larger financial capital investment during the 1970s than it would have in the absence of its relative tax advantages.[15]

The Economic Recovery and Tax Act of 1981 greatly reduced this penalty by changing the methods of computing depreciation allowances. Much shorter depreciation periods were assigned to most assets, and other tax advantages were extended to businesses. These changes greatly reduced the relative tax advantages of investing in homeownership, even though they did not alter homeowners' specific tax benefits. So the second support for housing's favored investment status has also shrunk in size and effectiveness.

The Shift in Federal Monetary and Fiscal Policies

The third transformation affecting real estate finance in the 1980s was the radical shift in the nation's monetary and fiscal policies compared with those of the 1970s and earlier. Until 1979 a key goal

14. Duane R. Kullberg, "Inflation and Its Impact on Financial Executives," speech presented at the Midwestern Area Conference of Financial Executive Institutions, Lake of the Ozark, Mo., May 30, 1980.
15. Patric H. Hendershott, "Real User Costs and the Demand for Single-Family Housing," *Brookings Papers on Economic Activity*, 2:1980, pp. 401–52.

of both policies was to smooth out typical short-run business cycles. On the monetary side, the Federal Reserve Board often manipulated the supply of credit to raise or lower interest rates so as to affect the economy's real growth rate. It sought to slow growth during "booms" and to speed growth during recessions, although these attempts did not always succeed.

On the fiscal side, federal administrations also tried to stimulate the economy during the recessions by increasing federal spending. They used both "automatic stabilizers," such as unemployment compensation, and discretionary actions, such as public works programs, to do so. Such spending, plus the normal drop in tax receipts, often created large budget deficits during recessions, as in 1975. During booms the progressive federal tax system had a dampening effect on growth because rising nominal incomes pushed both households and firms into higher tax brackets.

In 1979 the Federal Reserve drastically changed its monetary policy. Alarmed by rising inflation, it decided to direct monetary policy almost exclusively toward slowing inflation in the long run by limiting growth of the money supply. It chose money-growth "targets" that required gross national product (GNP) in nominal (current dollar) terms to increase much more slowly than in the recent past. At first much of this slowdown in nominal GNP would consist in lower real growth rather than lower price increases, with attendant higher unemployment, excess capacity, and business failures. In theory, once real growth had declined significantly, the rate of general price increase would fall too. Faced by weak demand and intensified competition, firms could no longer raise prices as rapidly and would more strongly resist large wage increases. Faced by mounting unemployment and stronger employer resistance, workers could no longer win wage increases as large as those won in the recent past. Hence the rate of inflation would gradually be forced down by a prolonged recession.

Enduring slow economic growth is not a very attractive prescription for curing inflation. But it is the only medicine almost sure to work—if the patient can stand the pains of treatment for a long enough period. The Federal Reserve abruptly shifted to this new policy in October 1979. By doing so, it essentially abandoned its previous attempts to counteract swings in the business cycle or to moderate interest rates in the short run. Since then, long-term interest rates have exhibited unprecedented volatility, often changing more in one week than they previously had in several years. This volatility increased the financial community's uncertainty about future interest rate movements.

Shortly after the Reagan administration took office in early 1981, it radically changed past fiscal policies as well. Abandoning past federal efforts to ameliorate short-run swings in the business cycle, the administration instead adopted three basic goals: (1) a massive increase in defense spending, (2) great cuts in federal domestic spending, and (3) drastic reductions in federal tax rates. Achieving those goals simultaneously under prevailing economic conditions, however, required huge federal budget deficits, even though President Reagan had decried such deficits in his election campaign and continued to do so. Hence the Reagan administration proposed several federal budgets involving record peacetime deficits. The *real* level of federal spending actually rose during each year of Reagan's term at a compound rate faster than that prevalent during President Carter's term.[16]

Large federal deficits stimulate growth in nominal GNP, so this fiscal policy is very expansionary. Fiscal expansion is quite desirable during recessions, as in 1981–82, but it is not desirable during periods of rapid private sector growth, as in 1983–84 and, possibly, in 1985. During rapid growth in the private sector, massive federal deficits would have two negative effects. One is intense competition in credit markets between the federal government and the private sector. Such competition would drive up interest rates, thereby reducing prospects for further growth. The other is creation of such strong excess demand that inflation accelerates to undesirable levels, also causing high interest rates. So the administration's expansionary fiscal policy would probably raise interest rates quite high around 1984–85, if the private sector were also prosperous then. Interest rates did increase substantially in 1984, although not to the high levels prevalent in 1981–82.[17] But, in response to weakening private growth in early 1985, the Federal Reserve eased its monetary policy again, as it had in 1982, and rates began to decline.

Fearing this combination of fiscal and monetary policy, the finan-

16. Bureau of the Census, *Statistical Abstract, 1984*, pp. 315, 493.
17. Council of Economic Advisers, *Economic Indicators, December 1984*, p. 30.

cial community was reluctant to cut interest rates in 1981–82, despite recessionary conditions that usually reduce long-term interest rates. Why should lenders in 1982 have committed funds for long periods at rates they believed were lower than those likely to occur two to three years later? It was clearly more prudent to hold funds in short-term instruments and to wait for those higher long-term rates to appear, especially when short-term rates were high. This reluctance held long-term interest rates at quite high levels, despite the recession, until late 1982, when the Federal Reserve at least temporarily eased its tight money policy.

After 1981 there was a direct conflict between the Federal Reserve's restrictive monetary policies to slow inflation and the administration's expansionary fiscal policies to achieve its three goals. This conflict kept both short-term and long-term interest rates quite high on average. Whenever expansionary forces caused the economy to begin growing in something like a "normal" business-cycle recovery, the demand for money rose rapidly as usual. This rising demand collided with the Federal Reserve's restrictions on money-supply growth, causing short-term interest rates to increase sharply. That increase tended to suppress further growth before the expansion could become a normal three- to four-year recovery. Moreover, uncertainties about future interest rates and inflation induced by large proposed federal deficits kept long-term interest rates from falling even when overall economic growth stopped altogether.

Because most real estate activities depend heavily on borrowed funds, they are quite sensitive to interest rates. So the high-rate climate produced by the radical shifts in monetary and fiscal policies after 1979 was extremely unfavorable to real estate activities. This climate persisted until late 1982, with a short hiatus when rates fell temporarily in 1980.[18]

The Shift in Regulation of Financial Institutions

The fourth radical shift since 1979 is the partial deregulation of financial institutions. It has rapidly reduced past barriers preventing each specialized type of institution from performing functions tradi-

18. Council of Economic Advisers, *Economic Indicators, January 1982*, p. 30.

tionally done by other types. Some aspects of deregulation were described in the preceding section, but several others are also important.

The Situation before Deregulation

The structure of regulations governing financial institutions in place before 1979 was created as a result of the Great Depression of the 1930s. In that decade millions of citizens suffered terrible economic losses from the collapse of the stock market, the failure of thousands of banks and thrift institutions, foreclosures on millions of defaulted mortgages, and other traumas involving financial institutions. To prevent repetition of such disasters, Congress created both comprehensive laws controlling financial activities and specific federal agencies to oversee their application.

A central principle of Congress's approach was that different organizations should specialize in different financial functions. Banks, therefore, were forbidden to engage in stockbrokerage, insurance, or real estate brokerage; insurance companies could not run banks; thrift institutions could not offer demand deposit accounts; and so on. These prohibitions had two important purposes. One was to encourage certain social goals, such as homeownership, by developing specialized institutions that would direct their efforts almost exclusively to achieving those goals. The second was to prevent major conflicts of interest from arising within individual firms.

For example, if a bank acted as both a mortgage lender and a real estate broker, it would have strong incentives to make generous loans in order to complete property sales on which it collected commissions. As a result its staff might be less rigorous in underwriting such loans, or in appraising the properties concerned, than would be appropriate for fiduciary managers of the deposits on which those loans were based. Similar conflicts of interest might arise if a single firm could conduct both banking and stockbrokerage, or insurance and either real estate or stockbrokerage, or many other combinations of specialized functions.

Congress apparently believed that the average patron of each financial institution should not have to pass prior judgment on the quality of that institution's management in order to have confidence that the institution's assets would be prudently handled. Such judgments would require knowledge and expertise far beyond the capabilities of the average citizen. Therefore federal agencies were established to supervise the behavior of financial institutions. In addition, each such institution was restricted to certain functions among which inherent conflicts of interest were presumably minimal. Finally, some financial institutions were provided with federal deposit insurance, as further discussed in chapters 6, 8, and 10.

Responses to Inflation

This system performed reasonably well until several factors began to undermine it in the late 1970s. One was sustained inflation at rates higher than normal. Such inflation made the basic economic function of thrift institutions untenable. Whenever short-term interest rates remained higher than long-term rates for extended periods, thrift institutions could not continue to borrow short through savings deposits and to lend long through mortgages. Either they had to be allowed to carry out other activities, too, or they would become bankrupt.

Bankruptcy was not an acceptable alternative. For one thing, thrifts contained over $500 billion in savings deposits, most of it insured by a federal agency.[19] That agency would have to pay off any losses involved. Even more important, failure of any sizable part of this industry would undermine public confidence in the entire financial system. That would harm the whole economy and might even weaken continued public support for the basic political and social system. Thrifts therefore had to be given the right to engage in activities formerly restricted to other institutions. This broadening of functions was necessary even if thrifts managed to survive the crisis of 1981–82 without widespread bankruptcy. Without such expanded powers, they might in the future find themselves in the same financially desperate situation.

Diversification of Functions

But permitting thrifts to "invade" the functional territories of other institutions upset the entire assignment of carefully separated

19. *Federal Home Loan Bank Board Journal*, vol. 15 (December 1982), p. 54.

functions to different organizations. It would be unfair to let thrifts perform functions formerly restricted to other institutions without similarly expanding the powers of those other institutions, especially because thrifts are so large and numerous. Those other financial institutions also demanded that Congress broaden their powers.

Other pressures had long been building to allow each type of financial institution to perform functions primarily assigned to other types. One was a shift in perspective among many corporate executives concerning their own businesses. Rather than regarding their firms as performing some particular substantive function such as selling insurance or financing homes, many began to conceive of their function as *managing assets so as to maximize financial returns*, regardless of what those assets were or how they were used. This view had emerged from the business-school training of many executives.

Moreover, expanding their permissible functions supported the desire of many large firms to keep increasing their net incomes as rapidly and as steadily as possible to raise or support their stock prices. Whenever a firm specializing in some field discovered that that field as a whole was not likely to grow rapidly in the future, its managers were tempted to shift into some other, more rapidly expanding field to maintain or improve earnings growth. Such a change often appeared more likely to maintain growth than did trying to expand market share in a stable or declining field. For example, Sears, Roebuck and Company decided to focus on financial services when it concluded that consumer retailing would no longer support its desired growth rate, especially since it already had such a large market share in retailing.

This expansionary thinking was encouraged by possibilities for synergy from combining previously separate functions. Merrill Lynch and Company realized that its nationwide network of brokers in contact with wealthy individuals and organizations could sell many products other than corporate stocks. Hence it founded a subsidiary to create and market partnership interests in real estate syndications. Sears had much earlier concluded that its many retail stores and enormous list of credit-card customers formed an appropriate basis for selling insurance, so it purchased a large insurance company and set up sales offices in many of its retail outlets. Aetna Life and Casualty recognized that its large staff of experienced real estate underwriters could operate separate accounts able to buy real estate equities and sell ownership shares to pension funds, so it developed a whole series of such accounts. Thus the desire to use existing resources as efficiently as possible led many financial institutions to expand into fields new to them.

At the same time, corporate stock prices that were unusually low in the late 1970s in relation to earnings created opportunities for some firms to buy others at bargain prices. The purchases were done through mergers or takeovers, both voluntary and involuntary. Many large firms were able to acquire others through tender offers for far less than the current market values of the assets involved if the assets were sold separately. This situation gave financial institutions seeking to enter new fields an efficient means of doing so.

The expansionary business climate also made previous legal boundaries separating different financial functions much more difficult to sustain in practice. More and more new conglomerates were created to perform a myriad of different mixes of activities. If the Almighty Amalgamated Holding Company buys both the Bustling Bank and the Inventive Insurance Company, what business is the Almighty really in? And how can those two subsidiary firms be prevented from continuing to do what they have done for years?

Yet another factor pressing executives in financial institutions to diversify into related fields was the volatility of many specialized financial markets in the 1970s. When profits from stockbrokerage fell in the mid-1970s while those from real estate brokerage began to soar, Merrill Lynch decided to enter real estate. Sears expanded from its base in insurance into both commercial and residential real estate brokerage for a similar reason. When sales of life insurance slowed in relation to inflation in the late 1970s but the stock market and investment banking were doing well, Prudential Insurance Company decided to acquire a large stockbrokerage firm.

This proclivity among financial institutions to invade neighboring territories was stimulated by two additional factors: improved technology for electronic transfer of funds and ingenious institutional innovation. These factors are discussed in the next section.

Loss of Faith in Government's Effectiveness

The last factor encouraging financial deregulation was rising skepticism about the effectiveness of federal government action in general. This loss of faith in government underlay the emergence of a relatively conservative political climate in the late 1970s and early 1980s. Presidents Carter and Reagan both campaigned vigorously against the federal bureaucracy. When airline deregulation lowered fares, a precedent was set for cutting back the proliferating regulations that many citizens perceived as reducing private efficiency and freedom of action. Hence other efforts to deregulate were at least initiated in many areas.

All these forces came together at the end of the 1970s and in the early 1980s. They created immense pressure on Congress and the administration to reduce regulations limiting the activities that each type of financial institution could undertake. Such reduction was well under way at the time this book was written in early 1985. It is true that many restrictions on financial institutions still existed, and the near failure of the Continental Illinois Bank and Trust Company in 1984 generated many fears that financial deregulation might have gone too far. But even if deregulation does not go much farther than it had by 1984, it still has changed the nation's financial markets significantly.

Technological Change and Institutional Innovation

Recent technical developments, both in the transfer of funds and in communications in general, have been intertwined with the partial deregulation of financial institutions. New electronic technology has greatly enhanced the abilities of once-specialized institutions to expand into other financial activities. Using computers, electronic fund transfer, and automated remote teller stations, financial institutions can almost instantly shift funds from one use to another. It does not matter where those uses are located geographically, whether within the United States or abroad; nor does it matter what specialized investment skills these uses require. Each specialized firm can take advantage of higher marginal profit possibilities in some other specialized field in a way not previously possible—if doing so is not prohibited by regulation.

For example, a firm taking in life insurance premiums could use those funds to make investments in commodity markets, real estate, stocks, corporate bonds, or anything else. Similarly, a retail firm with high cash flows could finance home sales or consumer credit, and a savings bank—if permitted by law—could invest its deposits in Eurobonds and oil drilling. The desire of every financial institution to use its available funds in the most profitable ways to benefit its investors and itself thus created pressure for fewer regulations on what each institution could do.

In addition, financial innovators were able to invent new processes capable of overcoming traditional and legal barriers more easily. In the early 1970s Wall Street innovators had developed money market funds, as noted earlier. These accounts depended on their managers' ability to shift funds among different investments every day and to keep track of daily balances in hundreds of thousands of individual accounts. Only computers and electronic fund transfers could accomplish these tasks. As a result, money market funds were ready to take advantage of soaring short-term interest rates when they occurred in the late 1970s and early 1980s.

Another innovation was electronic "sweeping" of centralized money-management accounts. Whenever a basic account received a dividend, deposit, or interest payment, that amount was automatically shifted to a higher-yield investment by weekly or even daily computerized examination of the account. This service encouraged each investor to keep most of his or her investments in a single master account managed by some firm capable of handling almost any type of asset. It therefore provided a great fund-raising advantage to firms simultaneously operating on a large number of investment frontiers.

But banks, thrifts, and insurance companies were prohibited from engaging in many types of investment activities. That prohibition put them at a competitive disadvantage compared with brokerage firms and investment bankers. They therefore had a strong incentive to press for removal of such regulatory barriers.

Another technical advance likely to exert much more influence in the future than it has up to now is the use of automated teller stations, both remote and in or near staffed offices of the parent institution. These devices make it possible for a financial institution to provide a surprising number of financial services around the clock at many locations convenient to consumer households yet at relatively low cost. Operating a network of such stations does not require the high real estate and personnel costs of operating many local branch offices. Hence a financial institution that has not established local branches throughout the nation, or throughout any particular region, could nevertheless provide certain key household financial services there within a relatively short period of starting to do so.

The single most important key to the success of such a financial institution might be prior name recognition among potential customers, rather than prior establishment of local contacts or branches. Many large nationwide financial or other institutions have such name recognition. These institutions include insurance companies, retailers, banks, and brokerage firms. They have the potential for establishing far-flung networks of automated teller stations very quickly—especially if they already supply credit cards and related services to a nationwide clientele.

One electronic innovation directly relevant to real estate finance consists of computerized mortgage-origination networks. The basic idea is to expose a potential homebuyer who needs a mortgage to instant information about what types of mortgages are available, and with what terms, in his or her area or even nationwide. This can be done through a computer terminal in the real estate broker's office, or in the regional office of a firm specializing in third-party counseling about mortgage availability and desirability. Several such networks have been established in relatively restricted regions. They embody different arrangements for the potential borrower's actually applying for and getting a loan commitment.

Possible questions of conflict of interest may arise from such networks because real estate brokers have vested interests in completing transactions to obtain commissions, so they might gloss over possible credit problems. In contrast, lenders are supposed to act as fiduciaries for the persons whose funds they are managing, so they should underwrite loans cautiously. It is likely, however, that some type of computerized information network will arise to increase the efficiency of the loan-seeking process, thereby aiding potential homebuyers.

The last electronic development important to financial markets in general is the immense increase in both the speed and comprehensiveness of global communications. Satellites, television recorders, home computers, and a myriad of other electronic devices are being added to existing telephone, television, and radio networks. Radio is being expanded to cover more and more of the globe. As a result events in one part of the world that before were not known elsewhere for days, weeks, or even longer are now recognized everywhere almost immediately. Furthermore, a much higher percentage of the population than ever before is exposed to at least some knowledge of such events. And far more people than before are capable of undertaking financial transactions in response to such events, often almost immediately upon learning about them.

How Long Will the Revolution Last?

Not all revolutions have lasting effects. Therefore it is reasonable to ask how long the five radical changes described above will continue to affect real estate finance.

Neither technological changes in fund transfer and communications nor partial deregulation of financial institutions can easily be reversed in the future. That is true even though some "re-regulation" might occur and further deregulation could be halted, especially in the wake of the Continental Illinois Bank failure. Effects of the revolution springing from these causes are therefore likely to be permanent.

Because the loss of the formerly sheltered position in credit markets that housing enjoyed has been caused in part by financial deregulation, this loss, too, will probably endure for a long time. Moreover, housing is not likely to regain its formerly sheltered credit position because of the high subsidy costs required. No one is willing to bear those costs voluntarily, and Congress is not willing to impose them on anyone. Stirring rhetoric about restoring the nation's "unwritten covenant" to permit middle-class households to own their own homes may resound,[20] but rhetoric does not pay for subsidies. Yet the same conditions of high inflation and high interest rates that would stimulate political demands for restoring housing's former advantages would also tremendously increase the subsidy costs of doing so. Congress might pass new subsidies to help first-

20. George Sternlieb and James W. Hughes have eloquently stated this view in "The Evolution of Housing and the Social Compact," *Urban Land Magazine*, vol. 41 (December 1982), pp. 17–20.

time homebuyers overcome the affordability problem discussed in chapter 9, but those subsidies are not likely to take the form of restoring housing's privileged credit position.

Yet both the expectations of capital suppliers toward inflation and federal fiscal and monetary policies certainly can change in the future. As of early 1985, capital suppliers had begun expecting somewhat lower inflation than they did in 1980, and monetary policy had already moved toward more accommodation than it had exhibited from 1979 through 1982. Therefore, to the extent that specific effects of the revolution are grounded on these factors, they are quite impermanent.

How long capital suppliers will continue to expect relatively high inflation depends on what happens to both inflation and federal deficits. When this book was being written in early 1985, the annual rate of increase in consumer prices had plunged from over 13 percent in 1980 to 4 percent.[21] Some savings and loan associations had returned to making long-term, fixed-rate mortgage loans on homes, and occasionally on nonresidential properties. Nevertheless, over 75 percent of all newly made home mortgage loans were ARMs. In addition, many sophisticated investors making fixed-rate loans with formal terms of twenty to thirty years regarded them on average as equivalent to ten-year loans. The typical home-buying household moves in about ten years, then selling its home. Since a 1982 Supreme Court decision made "due-on-sale" clauses in mortgages legally enforceable, lenders can compel owners to repay their mortgages whenever they sell, rather than allow buyers to assume the payments. This shortening of the likely lifetime of what appears to be a twenty- to thirty-year loan greatly reduces the risk of loss of real capital value from inflation.

Even so, most capital suppliers do not believe that making long-term, fixed-rate loans is a prudent strategy for any large share of an institution's total assets. Uncertainty about future inflation rates remains too great to risk repetition of the financial squeeze experienced in 1980–82. Hence most capital suppliers will not make such loans in any great volume until inflation rates have fallen to low levels (below 5 percent) and have stayed there for several years.

Monetary and fiscal policies have already changed somewhat. In

21. Bureau of the Census, *Statistical Abstract, 1984*, p. 493.

August 1982 the Federal Reserve Board modified its rigid commitment to fighting inflation by tightly controlling the money supply. This change in policy was a crucial stimulus to the ensuing economic recovery and to a remarkable surge in stock prices. The Federal Reserve had apparently concluded that economic recovery in the United States was vital—not only to restore our economic growth but also to avert an international banking crisis. I believe it has made sustaining that recovery its highest policy priority.

Yet Chairman of the Board of Governors of the Federal Reserve System Paul Volcker has repeatedly denied that any fundamental change has been made in the Board's long-term commitment to combatting inflation by restraining money-supply growth. Interest rates did rise again significantly in 1984, although not to nearly as high levels as they had attained in 1980–82.

Whether monetary policy will keep nominal interest rates high throughout most of the late 1980s depends on how the Federal Reserve Board resolves the dilemma it is likely to face because of continued large federal deficits. If it does not allow further growth in the money supply than in the early 1980s, both short-term and long-term interest rates will rise because of intensified competition for limited funds. This is especially likely during periods of private sector expansion. If the Federal Reserve does allow such money-supply growth, long-term interest rates may rise immediately because of anticipated future inflation. In either case, high interest rates will negatively affect real estate markets. This situation is discussed further in chapter 14.

Even if monetary policy shifts to stimulating faster real growth by accepting higher inflation, that would not produce the same low or negative real interest rates for borrowers as occurred in the 1970s. This time, capital suppliers are warily anticipating future inflation, as described above. The major financial effects of the revolution will therefore prevail in the remainder of the 1980s whether monetary or fiscal policies are altered in the near future. These effects are the subject of the next chapter.

3

Two Main Effects
of the Revolution

THE TWO main effects of the revolution in real estate finance have
been *higher interest rates* than in the past and *integration of the
nation's capital markets*. This chapter discusses how these effects
arose from the five causes described in chapter 2 and from other
forces.

Increased Uncertainty and Volatility in Financial Markets

During the past decade both uncertainty and volatility have
greatly increased in U.S. financial markets. This state of flux has
been caused partly by the factors described in chapter 2 and partly
by other factors. What is unquestionable is that it has contributed to
higher real interest rates than in the past.

Why has general uncertainty increased? The basic reasons can be
summarized as follows.

—*Many of the long-stable underlying foundations of financial
activity have recently been changing to an unprecedented degree.*
Financial deregulation radically altered, within just a few years,
many key federal rules governing financial institutions that had
remained mostly unchanged for decades. Devaluation of the U.S.
dollar in 1971 shifted the world completely off the gold standard
and onto floating exchange rates for the first time. Since 1945, economic expansions within the general business cycle had lasted three
to four years, recessions eleven to eighteen months. The business

cycle suddenly departed from that pattern in 1979–82. Federal budget deficits had normally been high during peacetime only during recessions. But they reached record levels during the "double-dip" recessions of the early 1980s and became even larger during the subsequent recovery.

—*Economic conditions gyrated much more during the 1970s than in the two preceding decades.* A recession in 1970 was followed by an economic boom through 1973. In 1973 worldwide crop failures led to soaring food prices, and in 1974 the price of oil shot up to several times its previous level. Another economic boom during 1977–79 culminated in a further doubling of world oil prices after the Iranian revolution. This oil price hike was followed by an even longer dual recession during 1980–82. Throughout this period, the rate of inflation accelerated to an average of more than triple its average in either the 1950s or the 1960s. But it did so through a series of rapid surges and declines rather than through a steady increase.

—*Improved communications and technology for fund transfer raised the potential for volatility in financial markets.* Worldwide electronic communications through radio, television, and satellites transmitted more news that might affect financial markets to more people with greater speed than ever before. Calamities that once might have gone unobserved elsewhere for weeks are now instantly known around the world. These technical changes also enhance investors' ability to respond through financial transactions to any news they believe will affect economic conditions even for short periods. Thus, massive shifts of funds can occur as thousands of investors simultaneously seek to be first in taking advantage of some newly revealed event. Financial markets have therefore become more likely to experience more rapid movements in funds and security prices than before.

—*Greater international interdependence has reduced each nation's sense of control over its own economic destiny.* The enormous increase of world trade since 1945 has raised the importance of traded goods and services within almost every economy of the free world. This makes each economy more susceptible to adverse effects from international developments beyond its own control. Moreover, citizens of many developed nations fear that much of their traditional industrial activity either has shifted or will shift overseas, captured by nations with lower labor costs. This fear is partly related to the slow growth of total employment in many European nations during the 1970s, and to very high unemployment rates there during the early 1980s.[1]

—*Interest rates, exchange rates, and security prices all exhibited much greater volatility in U.S. financial markets after 1970, and especially after 1979, than in the preceding two decades.* For example, the prime bank interest rate was 6.80 percent in 1977, more than doubled to 18.87 percent in 1981, and then fell almost by half to 10.70 percent in early 1983. Sometimes long-term interest rates have moved more within a few days than they have in entire previous decades.[2]

Effects of Greater Uncertainty and Volatility on Interest Rates

Greater uncertainty and higher volatility have affected most of the basic components of interest rates. Those components are usually considered to include the following:

—*a time preference reward* compensating the lender for deferring the immediate gratification of spending the capital involved on consumption;

—*a default risk premium* compensating the lender for the possibility that the borrower will not fully repay the principal and interest, or, in case of foreclosure, that the collateral will be worth less than the amount owed;

—*an inflation risk premium* compensating the lender for any loss in the capital's purchasing power caused by currency depreciation between the initial payment to the borrower and receipt of final repayment;

1. From 1975 through 1981 France, West Germany, Italy, and the United Kingdom all had increases in total civilian employment of less than 6.0 percent, compared with 27.7 percent in the United States and 10.7 percent in Japan. The lower increases in the European industrial nations were partly caused by lower population growth there. From 1970 through 1982 total population growth equaled 6.60 percent in France, 1.70 percent in West Germany, 6.80 percent in Italy, 0.98 percent in the United Kingdom, 13.40 percent in the United States, and 13.6 percent in Japan. Data are from U.S. Bureau of the Census, *Statistical Abstract of the United States, 1982–1983* (Government Printing Office, 1982), pp. 857–59, 873.

2. Bureau of the Census, *Statistical Abstract of the United States, 1984* (GPO, 1983), p. 521.

—an *interest rate risk premium* compensating the lender for possible long-run declines in the market value of the loan before its maturity if interest rates in general rise;

—a *volatility premium* compensating the lender for possible short-run declines in the immediate liquidation value of the loan owing to large and unpredictable day-to-day changes in interest rates.

All but the default risk premium are primarily determined by general economic conditions rather than by the particular investment involved. Moreover, all but the time preference reward, which is probably determined mainly by cultural factors,[3] are likely to be increased in size by greater uncertainty.

Thus the revolution described in the preceding chapters has raised interest rates far above what they had been in most earlier decades of this century. Table 3-1 compares interest rates by decade for the entire period 1900–84, with nominal rates adjusted to take account of both inflation and income taxes. The interest rates shown are for corporate bonds with twenty-year maturities because data are available for these rates back through 1900. Income tax rates used for computing after-tax interest rates were about midway between the lowest and highest marginal tax rates for each year.

Real interest rates—both before and after taxes—were higher during 1982–84 than at any time since 1900 except the early 1920s and the early 1930s. (In both brief periods, a surge in bond rates was accompanied by *falling* consumer prices.) As a result, both real capital and financial capital are now much costlier to borrow or use than in most prior periods. The many specific ways in which higher interest rates have affected real estate markets are discussed in later chapters dealing with the major effects of the financial revolution.

Integration of Capital Markets

Before partial deregulation occurred, the nation's capital markets were divided into a large segment concerned mainly with housing and another large segment concerned mainly with other types of

3. American households are likely to require much higher time preference rewards to achieve a given level of saving out of their incomes than Japanese households, other things being equal. At least this is a reasonable inference from their

Table 3-1. *Nominal and Real Average Annual Yields of Twenty-Year Bonds, 1900–84*

Percent

	Before income tax			After income tax (average bracket)[a]	
Period	Nominal yield (1)	Change in CPI (2)	Real rate (col. 1 − col. 2) (3)	Nominal (4)	Real (5)
1900–09	3.55	0.80	2.75	3.55	2.75
1910–19	4.18	6.56	−2.38	3.61	−2.96
1920–29	4.64	0.11	4.53	3.62	3.51
1930–39	3.61	−1.96	5.57	2.73	4.70
1940–49	2.55	5.65	−3.10	1.57	−4.08
1950–59	3.09	2.05	1.03	2.16	0.11
1960–69	4.84	2.42	2.42	3.39	0.97
1970–79	7.85	7.10	0.75	5.49	−1.61
1980–83	12.88	8.31	4.57	9.02	0.71
1982–83	13.11	4.67	8.44	9.18	4.50
1984[b]	13.04	4.10	9.94	9.13	5.03

Source: U.S. Bureau of the Census, *Historical Statistics of the United States*, pts. 1 and 2 (Government Printing Office, 1975), pp. 211, 1004, 1095. These consumer price index rates of change do not exactly correspond to those given in other tables because this source was printed in 1975 and used a different series.

a. Income tax rates used were about midway between lowest and highest marginal tax rates for each year.

b. Eight months.

investment. The latter included nonresidential real estate, corporate stocks, corporate bonds, state and municipal bonds, federal government bonds, private placements, and investment banking. These two segments were themselves subdivided into smaller, more specialized parts. The two segments were not completely cut off from each other; many transactions involved flows of capital from one to the other. Nevertheless, housing finance was greatly separated from other types of finance because the institutions providing most of it—thrifts—were regulated under special rules controlled by their own specialized federal agencies, as discussed earlier.

Partial deregulation has removed many of the institutional and legal barriers that formerly separated these two segments. In addition, electronic fund transfers and communications have made it

---

respective saving behaviors, since American savings rates are much lower than Japanese, and the differences cannot be explained by variations in economic conditions within these two nations.

possible for newcomers to enter either segment of the market much faster and more efficiently than in the past. Even so, fully integrating the nation's capital markets will require both the removal of many remaining barriers and a lengthy process of changing long-established institutions and patterns of behavior. That process is well under way, and it will undoubtedly continue over the next decade or longer.

Accurately forecasting the future course of capital market integration is extremely difficult. One reason is the complexity of the revolution in finance. Many forces affecting financial markets have changed radically within a short period, and many others are still being transformed. The final result is hard to foresee while such changes are still in process. In addition, the eventual outcomes greatly depend on future political decisions. Particularly critical is choosing whether to continue recent deregulation toward a more market-oriented financial system or to halt or even reverse this trend in favor of greater reliance on government regulations. No one can reliably predict which course will be chosen.

Nevertheless, it is important to try to forecast future changes in financial institutions. How those institutions evolve will greatly affect the cost and availability of the capital necessary to finance future real estate activities. Moreover, examining the implications of both further deregulation and a return to more regulation may help policymakers decide which way to go.

When deregulation rapidly integrates two large but formerly separated segments of a single market, certain results are likely, regardless of what activities are involved. They include the following:

—intensifed competition; a fall in average operating costs, especially in the segment that was most heavily regulated; and an increase in the use of standardized low-cost operating methods;

—a change in the average size of firms, with more vertical integration;

—increased innovation throughout the market, with greater diversity of functions among individual firms.

The ramifications of these changes will be different in the short run and in the long run. The remainder of this chapter applies these general conclusions to the current integration of real estate and other capital markets and considers the timing of market integration.

Intensified Competition and Its Effects

Because firms in each once-separated market segment can now enter the other segment, too, competition will be intensified in both. If one segment had been more regulated than the other, the firms in this part will be more strongly affected because they will have been more sheltered from both innovation and competition.

Greater competition will gradually shift each specific financial function toward those organizations able to perform it most efficiently; as a result, the average cost of production will probably fall. Increasing the size of any market tends to increase the degree of specialization of activities in it, and greater specialization usually reduces average costs. High-cost producers will be forced to reduce costs, to lose market share, or to get out of the business.

The pressure to reduce costs will cause nearly all firms performing the same service to adopt any techniques that are clearly the most efficient. For example, more and more firms that need to raise capital will try to control institutions with access to federal deposit insurance. Other replicable means of cutting costs will become similarly widespread.

These changes do not preclude moving into new functions, however, as long as institutions can perform the new functions efficiently. Thus some savings and loan associations may start making consumer loans and providing household checking services in competition with banks and finance companies. But only those associations that can handle these new tasks efficiently, or effectively combine them with other functions, will be able to compete with institutions experienced in performing these tasks.

The larger size of the combined markets will also cause a proliferation of more specialized institutions and an increase in organizational diversity. An important exception will be those functions involving large economies of scale. For example, large stockbrokerage organizations have established nationwide networks of salespersons already in contact with affluent potential purchasers of properties. They also have large legal staffs that can speedily carry out the complex registration procedures required for offering securities nationwide. Hence these organizations may be able to sell real estate partnerships more efficiently than the localized syndicators who have traditionally dominated small-scale equity markets. Such a takeover from local syndicators began happening on a large scale in 1982 and 1983.[4]

Effects on Firm Size and Organization

More intense competition will also tend to eliminate middlemen whose services can be better performed by vertically integrated organizations. This outcome will be encouraged by constant technological improvements in each organization's ability to handle complex information from scattered sources. As a result, more vertical integration of functions will occur, and the average size of organizations in these markets will increase.

For example, Sears, Roebuck and Company, the nation's largest retailer, has expanded from its previously established base in the insurance business to real estate brokerage. It did so by purchasing the single largest firm in that business, Coldwell Banker, and by urging its acquisition to buy many local realtor firms. Sears hopes to achieve efficient synergy by offering its real estate customers discounts on furniture and home furnishings at its retail stores. It may also be able to make low-cost home financing readily available to them through its access to capital markets.

Such vertical integration is socially desirable if it actually reduces average costs and product prices over the long run by cutting out profits formerly earned by intermediate distributors. Such reductions are possible if vertical integration produces genuine economies and if the integrated firms face strong competition at all market levels (perhaps from other vertically integrated firms). But vertical integration is socially undesirable if it is a temporary tactic in a long-run strategy of reducing competition. Limiting competition can occur if the vertically integrated firms at first cut prices below cost so as to drive competing, nonintegrated firms out of business. Price-cutting integrated firms can then become either monopolists or oli-

---

4. Large networks of brokers, however, also force these firms to incur high costs in distributing nearly *all* products, even though some products could be more efficiently distributed in other ways. The firms must pay high commissions to their brokers for going through them; they cannot easily avoid such commissions because it is the individual brokers who have built up contracts with affluent investors, not the firms themselves. This issue is discussed in "Merrill Lynch's Big Dilemma: Its' Strong Broker System Is a Costly Handicap in a Deregulated World," *Business Week*, January 16, 1984, pp. 60–67.

gopolists in the final product markets, raising prices above the initial level, increasing profits, and reducing consumers' welfare.

The shift in integrated markets toward larger firms will force many smaller institutions either to merge or to disappear. This result is especially likely in real estate financial markets, long dominated by thousands of small thrift institutions. Not all small firms, however, will be eliminated from real estate capital markets. Those markets are so extensive and diverse that many small firms will continue to find highly specialized niches in which they can operate efficiently and profitably. Moreover, the increased specialization of functions within now merged capital markets will generate many new firms, including some that will remain small.

Even if a few giant "financial department stores" such as Sears, Merrill Lynch and Company, Prudential Insurance Company of America, and Shearson-American Express emerge, the form is not likely to become heavily dominant in the nation's overall financial markets. There are too many different possible combinations of activities, with the effectiveness of each influenced by the individual talents of its operators, to permit any one form to become truly dominant.

Greater Innovation

Another important result of market integration will be much greater innovation of all kinds, including development of new products and new institutional forms. Regulated markets tend to develop standardized, even ossified, institutional forms and operating procedures conforming to the existing regulations. Moreover, those regulations have often been designed to benefit the industry's suppliers rather than their customers. So the suppliers are not anxious to change existing rules.

Deregulation has a dual effect on such well-established procedures. First, it removes the legal rules to which practices conformed, opening the possibility of trying many other methods previously prohibited. Second, it puts a large number of new players into each part of the market. These newcomers include firms that were formerly in another part of the market, newly formed firms, and "invaders" from entirely different fields. Such new players are not inhibited by habitual ways of doing things and are willing to try entirely new approaches. Their brashness tends to shake up the former establishment in each market.

The next decade is therefore going to be a period of great institutional and product innovation in real estate markets. Deregulation is just the first of a long series of sweeping changes likely to occur. The greatest among these will concern the functions that offer the highest profit potential. These activities will clearly attract the most attention from both long-established firms and newcomers. Sales commissions paid on real estate transactions have traditionally been much larger, in relation to market prices, than have sales commissions paid on security and stock transactions. Therefore real estate finance is likely to experience more innovation in the near future than other parts of capital markets.

The Timing of Change

Because institutional inertia will slow but not stop the process of change, those organizational forms that eventually survive may not emerge immediately. At first there will be a flurry of innovations and shifts in direction to accomplish the organizational and other changes that can be carried out quickly.

But established organizations always exhibit tremendous inertia. They especially resist profound changes in the very nature of their functions. Hence many will only gradually shift their activities toward what will eventually be their long-run "equilibrium" mix. That is why most thrift institutions will for a long time continue to focus on real estate activities rather than on commercial lending, stock-brokerage, or other quite different undertakings.

As a result, many will at first underestimate the degree of change likely to prevail over the long run. The initial persistence of previously established institutional forms and procedures will be mistaken for an ability of those forms and procedures to survive permanently. Not all previously dominant institutional forms or procedures will vanish—some will prove equally efficient in the new, merged and deregulated capital market.

Yet deregulation and the consequent merger of real estate capital markets with all other capital markets has radically changed the whole environment of real estate finance. The revolution is likely to make quite different institutional forms and procedures more efficient over the long run than those which dominated the past, particularly because the latter were developed in a highly regulated and sheltered environment. The ways in which coming changes will affect specific real estate finance institutions are discussed in chapters 10, 11, and 12.

4

The Fundamental Structure
of Real Estate Financial Markets

To ANALYZE the effects of the revolution in real estate finance, it is first necessary to sketch the structure of the financial markets concerned. The description presented in this chapter is a broad one intended only to provide background perspective for later chapters. More detailed analyses of key elements of real estate financial markets are set forth in appendix A.

Distinguishing between Real and Financial Capital

At the outset it is important to distinguish between real capital and financial capital and between annual flows and existing stocks of both types of capital.

Real capital comprises actual physical resources such as building materials, land, and labor. Annual flows of such capital are the amounts of physical resources consumed each year in the construction or repair of various structures, whereas existing stocks are the inventory of such structures. Annual flows of real capital are counted as investment in measuring gross national product (GNP).

Financial capital comprises money and other forms of debt that are promises to provide real resources sometime in the future. Annual flows of financial capital are the expenditures of such promissory instruments made each year. They may be based on purchasing annual flows, on existing stocks of real capital, or on trading financial capital instruments without any underlying changes in real capital. Existing stocks of financial capital are the total assets formed by such debt instruments held by their owners. *Net* annual financial capital flows among financial and other sectors, and among their largest components, are measured in the Federal Reserve Board's flow of funds accounts. Only net flows are included because most economists believe that only net flows affect interest rates.

Net elements in those accounts are usually computed by subtracting the total stock of certain assets at the start of a year from that stock at the end of the year. Mortgage flows are an example. This net measurement omits flows of such assets that occurred entirely within the year. For instance, assume that Mr. A pays off his outstanding mortgage debt of $100,000 to his bank on January 31. The bank immediately lends that $100,000 in a mortgage to Mr. B. But Mr. B decides to repay his $100,000 loan on December 1 of the same year. The bank then lends the same amount plus another $50,000 to Mr. C. At the end of the year, these transactions have increased the total amount of mortgage loans outstanding by $50,000, from $100,000 to $150,000. But the bank has originated $250,000 in mortgages in that year through those same transactions. This distinction shows why *mortgage originations* within any given year almost always exceed *net mortgage flows* for the same year as measured by the Federal Reserve.

The number of existing properties of all types sold in the United States each year greatly exceeds the number of new ones built plus existing ones remodeled. Therefore, the annual flows of financial capital required to conduct normal levels of activity in real estate markets are much larger (measured in either current or constant dollars) than the annual flows of real capital involved. This study emphasizes financial capital flows, although real capital flows are discussed when relevant.

The Structure of Real Estate Financial Markets

The primary social function of real estate financial markets is to move capital from those who save it out of their current incomes to those who will invest it in real estate. Real estate financial markets are just one component of the nation's overall financial markets, but this chapter focuses mainly on this one part. Although real estate financial markets are extremely complicated, their general operation can be illustrated relatively simply, as in figure 1-1 (page 6).

The figure depicts the five major actors in these markets: savers, savings depository institutions, secondary market transformers, mortgage originators, and final capital users. (Some institutions perform multiple functions, as discussed later.) The solid arrows show how money flows from savers to final capital users through the other actors, who are all financial intermediaries. For each solid arrow (usually moving from left to right) there is an opposite flow of debt or equity instruments shown by other types of arrows. Thus savers put money in depository institutions and receive some evidence of deposit in return (flows 1 and 2 in the figure). Examples are an entry in a passbook account, a money market certificate, a vested interest in future pension payments, and the cash value in a life insurance policy. At the right-hand side of the diagram, mortgage originators lend money to final capital users and receive mortgages in return (flows 12 and 14 in the figure). The way these markets operate can be briefly described by discussing each of the key actors in turn.

Savers are mainly individual households, which put some of their current incomes aside in myriad forms. At any given moment, some saving is also done by business firms, nonprofit organizations, and even some state and local governments. But most savers will later borrow at least as much as they save, and perhaps more. Hence, when all major sectors or economic actors are considered as a whole, only the household sector is a consistent net saver over time.

Most household savings are placed in various types of *savings depository institutions*, which in turn invest those funds in productive uses. The major types are commercial banks, savings and loan associations, mutual savings banks, life insurance companies, credit unions, trust companies and bank trust departments, pension funds, and real estate equity syndicators.[1] Syndicators differ from all the others because they issue equity shares rather than debt to savers.

---

1. Contributions to pension funds are usually deducted from household incomes in advance according to set formulas, as part of employment contracts. Yet these contributions are savings just as much as discretionary deposits in bank savings accounts, since they shift current income into financial intermediaries and create assets held by the households concerned.

Some households also invest directly in real estate without going through financial intermediaries. They usually buy either mortgages, mortgage-backed securities (MBSs), or real estate equity in their own homes or in other properties. These flows are also shown (as flows 3–5) in figure 1-1.

Most savings depository institutions must invest their funds to earn enough income to pay the interest or other benefits they provide to attract households' savings. These institutions can be divided into three groups on the basis of their investment behavior in real estate markets. *Mortgage originators* lend money directly to final real estate capital users; *nonoriginators* also provide debt funds, but only indirectly; and *equity syndicators* furnish equity funds to developers or owners or perform those functions themselves.

Successful *mortgage originators* must have specialized expertise in real estate lending plus detailed knowledge of local real estate markets; hence the costs involved are large. Many institutions that want to hold mortgages as assets, especially small depository institutions, find it more efficient to buy them from other originators than to bear these costs themselves. Nonoriginators include most pension funds, many small life insurance companies, credit unions, and many trust companies and bank trust departments. Those depository institutions that are also originators are commerical banks, savings and loan associations, and mutual savings banks. Many originators, however, also buy mortgages originated by other institutions from time to time.

Mortgage originators include not only those depository institutions that lend directly to final borrowers, but also some actors who make loans but do not retain them. Mortgage banking firms are the primary example. Moreover, many depository institutions that originate mortgages subsequently sell rather than hold many of them. Savings and loan associations and mutual savings banks have increasingly followed this pattern, for reasons discussed later.

Secondary market transformers buy mortgages from originators and transform them into different types of investment more attractive to certain depository institutions. One such transformation is holding the mortgages in a portfolio that is purchased with money obtained by selling bonds and notes (flow 9 in figure 1-1). This allows financing long-term debt (mortgages) with short-term debt (notes and short-term bonds), which is more attractive to many investors than mortgages themselves. The Federal National Mortgage Association (FNMA) is the chief follower of this strategy.

Another transformation occurs when groups of mortgages are packaged as backing for a new security, or MBS, that derives its income from those mortgages. This security is then sold to investors, who perceive it essentially as a bond rather than a mortgage (flows 3, 8, and 11 in the figure). The Government National Mortgage Association (GNMA) is the leading practitioner of this strategy, the Federal Home Loan Mortgage Corporation (FHLMC) uses it extensively, and FNMA has begun to do so as well.

The secondary mortgage market as a whole includes far more than the activities of these transformers. One of its basic purposes is to shift funds from depository institutions that want to hold mortgages they did not originate to final borrowers by way of mortgage originators. (Several other important purposes of the secondary market are discussed in chapters 12 and 13.) This channeling of funds is accomplished when the originators sell mortgages to (1) secondary market transformers, (2) nonoriginating savings depository institutions, (3) originating savings depository institutions that want to hold more mortgages than they create themselves, or (4) saving households.

The last key group comprises *final real estate capital users* who invest in real properties funds received from others. This group includes those developers who retain equity in their projects, persons buying properties, and owners refinancing properties. As figure 1-1 shows, these final capital users often obtain equity funds from syndicators (flow 15), as well as debt funds from lenders (flow 12), in order to complete their transactions. Final capital users also frequently add their own equity contributions to the funds they have obtained from others. They use those total funds to buy real properties, to renovate or repair them, to develop new ones, to buy non–real estate goods or services, or for some combination of the foregoing.

These final uses are not shown in the diagram or analyzed in this chapter, although they are considered later in the book. Many other important aspects of real estate financial markets cannot be shown in this simplified chart. For example, it does not depict repayment of loans and subsequent reinvestment of those funds, matters that will be discussed later. Nevertheless, it provides a useful perspective for viewing real estate finance markets.

Household Savings: The Underlying Source of Real Estate Capital

As shown in figure 1-1, most institutions holding large amounts in mortgages receive their basic funding from household savings. Some—especially commerical banks and life insurance companies— also receive deposits from sources other than households. Nevertheless, the flow of personal income through households into these institutions is clearly the main support for additional mortgage lending, as will be shown below. Indeed, household savings flows are the basis for most financial investments in the U.S. economy.

The magnitude of this capital source can be determined through an analysis of household finances. Data have been taken from the Federal Reserve Board's flow of funds accounts for the period 1971– 81.[2] Figure 4-1 diagrams the flow of personal income through households, steered by various decisions relating to saving, borrowing, and investment in different types of financial assets. Each step in the diagram shows the percentage of personal income it involves, calculated as the annual average percentage during 1971–81. This diagram allows tracing of the conversion of personal income from initial receipt by households into specific forms of investment. (Personal income itself averaged 81 percent of GNP during 1971–81, although it was over 82 percent in both 1980 and 1981.)[3] Most policies intended to make a larger share of personal income available for real estate investment would presumably involve changing these percentages.

The first division of total personal income shown in figure 4-1 is that into taxes (14.7 percent), consumption (79.4 percent), and sav-

2. Board of Governors of the Federal Reserve System, *Flow of Funds Accounts, Second Quarter 1982, Annual Revisions* (The Board, September 1982); and *Flow of Funds Accounts, Assets and Liabilities Outstanding, 1957–1980* (The Board, September 1981).

3. U.S. Bureau of the Census, *Statistical Abstract of the United States, 1984* (Government Printing Office, 1983), p. 450.

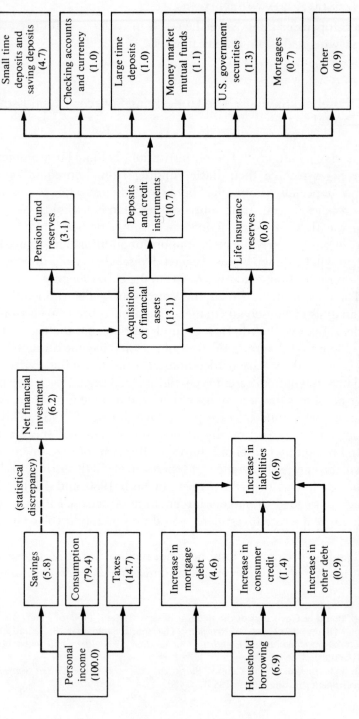

Figure 4-1. *Household Savings Flows as Percentage of Personal Income, 1971–81*[a]

Source: Board of Governors of the Federal Reserve System, *Flow of Fund Accounts* (The Board, various issues).
a. The numbers in parentheses indicate the percentage of total personal income.

ings (5.8 percent).[4] Although taxes averaged 14.7 percent over the eleven-year period, they were above 15.0 percent in 1979 and 1980 and 16.0 percent in 1981. The share of personal income used for consumption was relatively constant around its average of 79.3 percent.

Savings as a fraction of personal income averaged 5.80 percent over all eleven years, but savings were notably higher during 1971–75 (6.94 percent) than during 1976-81 (5.24 percent). This difference may be related to the lower fraction of personal income going into taxes in the first period (14.06 percent) than in the second period (15.13 percent). Thus one way to increase the flow of income into saving might be to reduce personal taxes, especially those on income earned from savings.

But other factors are also associated with the lower level of savings in the second part of the 1970s. Higher inflation rates in the last part of the decade could have discouraged savings for three reasons. First, households had to spend higher fractions of their incomes to maintain previous real living standards because their real incomes were declining. In addition, consumers often bought durable goods in advance of normal need, rather than add to their savings, because they thought future prices of such goods would rise. Finally, rapid increases in home prices created a huge buildup of homeowners' equities on household balance sheets. That decreased households' need to improve those balance sheets by saving out of current incomes.

This analysis implies that lower inflation rates in the remainder of the 1980s are likely to be accompanied by higher savings rates out of personal income than those in the late 1970s. Personal savings rose, however, to 5.7 percent of personal income in 1981 but then fell to 5.3 percent in 1982, 4.3 percent in 1983, and 5.2 percent in 1984.[5] The exact reason that savings have declined despite higher real interest rates is not clear.

Before savings from personal income are transformed into the acquisition of financial assets, they are supplemented by borrowing.

4. These numbers do not add to exactly 100.0 percent because they are rounded averages of eleven annual averages.

5. Council of Economic Advisers, *Economic Indicators, May 1985*, p. 6. In the fourth quarter of 1981 personal savings were even higher (6.35 percent of personal income), although they averaged 5.7 percent for that entire year.

The flow of funds accounts indicate that *net* financial investment averaged 6.2 percent of personal income—slightly higher than savings of 5.8 percent, because of a statistical discrepancy. In addition, households borrowed enough to increase their financial liabilities by an amount equivalent to 6.9 percent of their personal incomes. This provided them with annual average financial purchasing power equal to 13.1 percent of personal incomes. Over 85.0 percent of this borrowing consisted of mortgage loans (averaging 4.6 percent of personal income) and consumer credit (averaging 1.4 percent).

This 13.1 percent of personal income is the fundamental source of capital flows into financial institutions that provide funds for real estate—and for most other types of typical household investment (such as stocks and bonds). This savings flow does not supply the main basis for corporate and other business investments, however, since such investments are financed predominantly from business savings out of net earnings.

Most of this 13.1 percent of personal income (82.0 percent, or 10.7 percent of personal income) went into deposits and the purchase of credit market instruments. The largest amounts of deposits were in small time deposits and savings deposits, which captured 4.7 percent of personal income. Those deposits went into commercial banks, savings and loan associations, mutual savings banks, and credit unions. Large time deposits, checking deposits plus currency, and money market funds each captured an average of about 1 percent of personal income during 1971–81. But the relative shares of these instruments varied greatly from year to year. For example, money market funds rose from zero in 1976 to 4.5 percent of personal income in 1981. Small time and savings deposits attracted 8.5 percent of personal income in 1976 but only 1.9 percent in 1981. Large time deposits experienced net withdrawals by household in 1975 and 1976 but attracted 2.1 percent of personal income in 1980. Another way to increase capital flows into real estate would thus be to maximize the relative attraction of those forms of deposits most likely to be reinvested in real estate.

Pension funds are often mentioned as a potential source of future real estate capital because they are growing rapidly and have relatively long-term liabilities. Pension funds received an annual average of 3.1 percent of personal income flows in 1971–81. Their share was rising steadily throughout this period, however, and closed at

3.7 percent in 1981. If their rate of increase were extrapolated through 1991, pension funds would capture an average of 4.3 percent of personal income from 1981 through 1991, with a high of 4.9 percent in the last year. That seems a reasonable basis for making future projections later in this study.

Other Sources of Real Estate Capital

Real estate markets draw financial capital from several other sources besides household savings flows, sources that are not shown in figure 1-1.

—*Income earned by real estate investments held by depository and other financial institutions.* Such income includes interest payments on mortgages and earnings from real estate equities. These flows are generated mainly by the use of real property by its occupants. They can be reinvested in real estate or in other uses.[6]

—*Investments by foreigners in U.S. real estate.* These include investments by individuals, pension funds, insurance companies, and operating companies.

—*Use of homeowners' equity to finance housing sales.* Equity is used mainly through "take-back" financing by homesellers in the form of purchase-money mortgages.

—*Investments in real estate by corporations that are not financial intermediaries.* These include renovation and modernization using capital consumption (depreciation) allowances, purchases of new plants and offices for direct use, and speculative purchases of land or buildings.

Past contributions of most of the sources listed above to flows of real estate capital are discussed in detail in appendix A.

6. Repayments of mortgages are also an important source of real estate capital, but they generally come out of household savings; hence they are not counted as a separate source here.

5

More Intensive Use of Space and Greater Emphasis on Equity Ownership

THE REVOLUTION in real estate finance has altered almost every aspect of real estate markets to some degree. This chapter describes two key effects concerning the physical use of space in individual properties and the division of ownership of these properties between developers and capital suppliers.

Pressure to Use Space More Intensively

The higher real cost of capital in the 1980s has raised the "true cost" of each square foot of new space compared with two other costs. One is the cost of *creating new space* in past periods, especially in the 1970s. This increase changes past behavior patterns of using new space, heightening pressures to use such space more intensively than before. The other is the cost of *using existing space* created when capital was less expensive. The relative appeal of older space will therefore rise.

Even so, higher real capital costs have also increased the cost of using existing space, even though it was built earlier with less expensive money. The market price of older space has risen because of greater demand for it deflected from much more expensive new space. Older space does almost always remain less costly than new space because it is more obsolete, both technically and in fashion,

72

but higher costs of older space will also cause behavior in using space to differ from that of the past.

These changes have had—and will continue to have—the following specific effects on space use.

—Users of new structures will allocate less space per occupant than was the case in earlier periods, other things being equal.

—Many occupants of existing structures will use space there more intensively, allocating fewer square feet to each use than they would have if real capital costs had been lower.

—Firms will shift more activities not requiring high-cost space to locations with lower-cost space.

—More firms and households will renovate older space, built earlier with less costly capital, rather than occupy costlier new space.

—Fewer persons who might have formed separate households will do so.

—A higher proportion of newly formed households than in the past three decades will rent rather than buy their own homes.

These effects are examined in more detail below, following discussion of another pressure on space users.

Combined Effect of Higher Real Capital Costs and Higher Real Incomes

An opposite pressure on space use will arise from rising real incomes among households, business firms, nonprofit organizations, government agencies, and others. Whenever real incomes rise (including profits or surpluses retained by those other than households), space use per person or function also tends to rise. This tendency follows from the basic economic principle that rising real incomes cause people to consume more of almost everything they positively value. Real incomes tend to rise in periods of economic expansion, which have predominated in the U.S. economy since 1945.

Thus the use of space by these entities that is *actually observed* will be a net result of downward pressure from higher real capital costs and of upward pressure from rising real incomes. Other forces will also influence the observed results. One example is technologi-

Table 5-1. *Median U.S. Household Income,*
Selected Years, 1965–82

Year	Median household income (1982 dollars)	Median income of husband-and-wife families with wife in paid labor force (1981 dollars)
1965	n.a.	24,885
1967	20,650	n.a.
1970	21,711	28,753
1974	21,916	n.a.
1978	22,288	n.a.
1980	20,745	29,667
1981	n.a.	29,247
1982	20,171	n.a.

Source: U.S. Bureau of the Census, *Statistical Abstract of the United States, 1982–1983* (Government Printing Office, 1982), pp. 459, 466.
n.a. Not available.

cal change, such as the compression of office machinery into smaller modules. Nevertheless, shifts in real capital costs and real incomes are likely to have the largest and most pervasive influence because these two forces are ubiquitous in real estate markets.

During 1967–82 median real household income actually *fell* 2.3 percent (table 5-1). Even real incomes of husband-and-wife families with the wife in the paid labor force—"two-earner" families presumably more prosperous than most other households—went up only 0.15 percent a year compounded from 1970 to 1981. Thus, at least until after the recession of 1982, rising real incomes did not put much pressure on households to consume more space. This result contrasts sharply with the period 1950–70, during which median family income in constant dollars rose at a compound rate of 3.1 percent a year.[1]

No reliable evidence exists for the percentage changes in space use that are likely to result from a 1 percent change in either capital costs or real incomes. Therefore only rough conclusions can be drawn about which of these two pressures will dominate under dif-

1. Data are from George Sternlieb, James W. Hughes, and Connie O. Hughes, *Demographic Trends and Economic Reality* (New Brunswick, N.J.: Rutgers Center for Urban Policy Research, 1982), p. 68.

ferent circumstances. These conclusions can be based on the following principles, each of which presumes that other things will remain equal.

1. Users likely to experience relatively slow real income growth will feel less pressure to expand the space they occupy, and more pressure to economize on space use, than users likely to experience rapid real income growth.

—Business firms will be likely to expand space use near the end of economic expansions and to contract it during recessions.

—High-level executives will be under less pressure to reduce the size of their offices than will lower-level clerical workers.

—Middle- and upper-income households, and two-earner households, will be more likely to expand space use than will low- and moderate-income households or those with only one wage earner.

2. Intensive competition will encourage more economizing than its absence.

—Most government agencies will economize on space use less than most private firms in semimonopolistic industries, and both will economize much less than private firms in highly competitive industries.

3. Users who occupy large areas per person or production process will feel greater pressure to economize than those who occupy small areas.

—Industrial warehouses will experience more increases in rationalized space allocation than will office firms employing thousands of workers in open office areas.

4. Users compelled to change their occupancies will feel greater pressure to economize than those who have no explicit reasons to do so. The latter can merely continue their existing behavior without facing any need for making space-related decisions, whereas the former must confront such decisions.

—Newly formed households will be under much greater pressure to occupy small housing units than will households already living in relatively large units.

—Organizations that must greatly expand or contract their activities are more likely to become more space-economizing than those which merely continue at the same level of activity.

5. Users who occupy quite expensive space will feel greater pres-

sure to reduce their usage than those who occupy relatively inexpensive space.

—Thus, occupants of new, centrally located downtown office buildings and retail stores will economize more than will occupants of older, more peripheral office, loft, or retail space.

6. Users for whom occupancy costs are a relatively small part of total expenses will feel less pressure to economize on space than those for whom such costs are a large part of their expenses.

—Business firms will in general be under less pressure to economize on space use than will households faced with occupancy decisions because occupancy costs are typically a much smaller share of total business costs than they are of total household expenses.

—High-income households will be under less pressure to economize on space than will low-income households.

Specific applications of the above principles are analyzed in the remainder of the chapter.

Some Implications of More Intensive Space Use

The era of "small is beautiful" has finally hit development of *new* real estate. As a result, new housing units, new hotel rooms, new retail shops, office space per worker (net of office machines) in new buildings, and new industrial space per worker will all become smaller, on average, in the near future compared with the recent past. Exceptions will be firms that experience extraordinarily rapid gains in real income (profits or retained nonprofit surpluses) per worker.

This trend toward smaller units has already become evident in housing, with units as small as 400 square feet now being sold in many regions. The median size of new single-family housing units built did actually rise in 1983, to 1,565 square feet from 1,520 square feet in 1982, after falling for three previous years. Nevertheless, the number and proportion of small units—often much smaller than any previously built new units—has risen dramatically compared with the 1970s. Thus, from 1971 through 1978, the fraction of all newly built, privately owned single-family homes containing less than 1,200 square feet fell from 34 percent to 18 percent. But from 1978 through 1982 it rose again to 25 percent.[2]

Even most users of *existing* space will shift toward smaller areas per person or production process whenever they have to rearrange their accommodations for some reason. Those who do not face any explicit need for such rearrangement, however, are more likely to be dominated by inertia and to retain their existing patterns of space use. Economizing on space in existing properties will therefore manifest itself only gradually over time.

Just a small decline in existing office space consumption caused by such economizing would free enormous amounts of space, depressing the demand for new space. For example, if the average area per worker occupied by office workers in the United States dropped by just 5 square feet (about 2.2 percent), over 185 million square feet of office space would be vacated. That area probably equals a full year's "normal" absorption for the entire nation.[3]

Pressure for more economical use of space will also affect users' choice of locations within each metropolitan area. More large users of space will subdivide their activities and move those not requiring expensive space to less expensive space. For example, many retailers are storing their inventories in warehouses instead of in their shopping center outlets.

In most communities rental rates per square foot are notably higher in downtown office buildings than in suburban or other outlying buildings. Economizing on space will also be greater in newly built structures than in older ones, and most downtown areas contain more new office buildings than do areas between downtowns and the suburban periphery because of the recent boom in new downtown office construction.

---

2. Data on sizes of new single-family homes are taken from U.S. Bureau of the Census, Construction Reports, *Characteristics of New Housing, 1971–82* (Government Printing Office, 1971-82). Cited in William C. Apgar, Jr., "Trends in the Size of New Homes" (Cambridge, Mass.: Joint Center for Urban Studies of MIT and Harvard University, April 1984), fig. 4.

3. These calculations assume that there are 8.5 billion square feet of occupied office space, that the average worker occupies 225 square feet, and that average annual absorption of office space for the entire nation in recent years has been over 175 million square feet.

For both these reasons the suburban share of added demand for office space, relative to the downtown share, will be larger in the future than it has been up to now. In most metropolitan areas suburban office space will therefore grow in the future more rapidly than downtown office space, both relatively and absolutely.

Nevertheless, suburban office vacancy rates are likely to remain higher than downtown vacancy rates, as they have been for some time. Higher vacancy rates there will occur because it is easier to create new office space in the suburbs than downtown. Suburban office buildings are typically smaller, occupy less costly land, and face less stringent zoning and other local regulations than do downtown buildings. Hence it takes less capital to build them. There are also far more reasonably well-located potential office sites in the suburbs of each metropolitan area than in its downtown. Thus future supplies of office space will expand faster relative to demand in the suburbs than downtown—even though demand will also grow faster in the suburbs.

Because older structures have lower real capital costs built into them than do new ones, it will frequently be more economical to renovate or expand existing properties than to build new ones. Hence redevelopment and renovation will rise as a proportion of all real estate activity, especially in built-up areas. This conclusion applies to all types of real estate, including single-family homes, apartment projects, shopping centers, and office buildings. In time, the shift of demand at the margin toward existing properties will raise their prices relative to new ones.

Some Effects on Housing Other Than Smaller Unit Size

The real costs of homeownership will remain higher in the 1980s than in the 1970s even if inflation abates. Higher costs will prevail because of (1) higher real interest rates on borrowed funds; (2) lenders' use of mortgage instruments that raise nominal payments if inflation escalates; and (3) slower real appreciation of home values (discussed later in this chapter), with consequent smaller resale profits with which to offset occupancy costs.

As a result, a higher fraction of households seeking shelter will rent rather than buy because they cannot afford homeownership.

This increase will raise the demand for rental housing compared with that for home purchase. Residential rents will start escalating faster than the consumer price index (CPI) as a whole for one of the few times since 1960. This escalation has already begun, despite the negative effect of the 1981–82 recession on rental demand.[4] September-to-September data show that the rent component of the CPI rose 42 percent faster than the overall index from 1981 to 1982 and 93 percent faster from 1982 to 1983. It rose 29 percent faster from August 1983 to August 1984.[5]

After rents have risen faster than living costs for a while, it will become economically feasible in more locations to develop new rental housing. Such development had already begun by 1984, encouraged by the bias of capital markets toward real estate investment (discussed in chapter 6). It would accelerate if nominal interest rates were to decline, thereby adding to the increased attractiveness of such investment because of faster depreciation under the Economic Recovery and Tax Act of 1981, even after modification by the 1984 tax act.

New rental housing will also be financed, however, with higher real capital costs than those for older, existing housing. Hence *all* new housing will be costlier to occupy in relation to household incomes than it was in the 1970s. The real cost of housing is a key factor influencing the rate at which additional households are formed. When real housing costs are low, as in the 1970s, many people can afford to end shared living arrangements and to occupy their own housing units. Then a rapid increase in housing demand is generated by any given increase in population. But when real housing costs are high, fewer people can afford to end shared arrangements, so a much smaller added demand for housing is generated by the same increase in population.

As a result, the rate of additional household formation in the

4. Rental vacancy rates typically rise sharply during recession as households double up to reduce housing costs.

5. From September 1981 to September 1982 the overall consumer price index (CPI) rose 5.0 percent, and its residential rent component rose 7.1 percent. From September 1982 to September 1983 the respective increases in the CPI were 2.9 percent and 5.6 percent; from August 1983 to August 1984 they were 4.2 percent and 5.4 percent (the latter for residential rents). Data were provided by the Bureau of Labor Statistics.

1980s will fall well below its 1970 levels, even though it would be higher than those levels if purely demographic factors prevailed. An average of 1.69 million net additional households were formed annually during the 1970s, but this number will probably decline to around 1.40 million in the 1980s.[6] Hence the overall demand for new housing units will be lower in the 1980s than in the 1970s, even if inflation and nominal interest rates fall well below their record levels at the beginning of the decade. How much lower that demand will be depends in part on whether high or low inflation predominates in the remainder of the decade.

This future change in housing demand is consistent with future changes in financial capital flows. The declines in relative advantage afforded housing as an investment described earlier are likely to lower the share of total financial capital flowing into housing in the 1980s compared with that in the 1970s. From 1970 through 1979, mortgages on homes in structures containing one to four units absorbed 24.2 percent of net funds raised in nonfinancial sectors of U.S. capital markets. This was by far the largest single use of such funds. U.S. government borrowing by both the Treasury and other agencies absorbed the second largest fraction (15.4 percent). The next largest shares went into corporate bonds (9.4 percent), consumer credit (9.0 percent), bank loans not otherwise classified (8.5 percent), state and local government obligations (7.5 percent), commercial and industrial mortgages (6.4 percent), and multifamily residential mortgages (3.1 percent). The share of total financial capital flowing into home mortgages in the 1970s (24.2 percent) was lower than that during 1950–65 (28.1 percent), but much higher than that during 1966–70 (16.0 percent). But this share began dropping as the 1980s started, to 20.1 percent in 1981 and to 14.2 percent in 1982. It rose back to only 21.1 percent in 1983, even though savings and loan associations made their up-to-then all-time-high total of mortgage loans, exceeding the previous record in 1978 by 23 percent.[7]

6. For specific computations of future household formation rates, see Anthony Downs, *Rental Housing in the 1980s* (Brookings, 1983), pp. 153–64.

7. Data are from Board of Governors of the Federal Reserve System, *Federal Reserve Bulletin*, vol. 70 (August 1984), p. A40; and *Federal Home Loan Bank Board Journal*, vol. 17 (March 1984), p. 52, and vol. 15 (May 1982), p. 48.

Increased Importance and the Changing Nature of Equity Ownership

The most important initiators of activity in real estate markets have traditionally been borrowers of funds. They include most developers of new properties and purchasers of existing ones. Both groups always try to use as much "OPM" ("other people's money") as they can, thereby increasing the purchasing power of their own funds through what is known as leverage. The revolution in real estate finance, however, has greatly affected such behavior because capital suppliers are now demanding a much greater share of the profits from real estate investment than they received in the 1970s, as noted in chapter 2.

Part of this demand is the vastly increased desire among capital suppliers *to own part or all of the equity* in the properties they finance rather than to advance "pure" loans on those properties. This desire stems from the belief of capital suppliers that inflation rates will remain higher in the 1980s than they were before the 1970s. Hence capital suppliers need to protect their assets from being eroded by currency depreciation. Long-term loans with fixed interest rates provide no such protection, unless those interest rates are extraordinarily high (and seldom if then). But sharing in that part of each property's net receipts that is likely to rise along with inflation does provide such protection. Hence capital suppliers want either to own outright some or all of the real properties they finance or to attach "quasi-ownership" clauses to loans made on such properties. This trend means that the traditional initiators of new real estate development and other transactions will be able to retain a much smaller share of total equity in their projects than they have in the past.

One result of these developments is that *equity ownership of real estate will be less profitable in the 1980s than in the 1970s,* even if real properties produce operating profits just as high as those in the 1970s. This conclusion applies to all types of real estate, from owner-occupied homes to multiuse commercial projects. One reason is the higher real interest rates initially demanded by capital suppliers. Those rates shift some of the operating profits from real properties toward capital suppliers and away from the borrowers who traditionally owned such properties. Yet the major transaction-initiating investors in real estate have always been, and will undoubtedly remain, dependent on obtaining most of the required capital from others. If these investors cannot capture profits from their ownership as great as those in the past, they will be less willing to bid up property prices in response to any given amount of anticipated inflation.

Equity ownership of real estate will also be less profitable than in the past because it will represent a larger fraction of total capital involved in each transaction. Except for owner-occupied homes, the very meaning of *real estate equity* is different from what it was before 1980. It formerly referred to the small fraction of total project cost put up by the developer or purchaser, who borrowed the bulk of the required capital from a long-term lender at a fixed rate of interest. The equity owner was therefore in a highly leveraged position that provided two advantages. First, it generated high yields on the initial equity investment during periods of inflation. If the owner of a property has invested only 10 percent of its cost and borrowed the rest, a 10 percent rise in the property's market value represents a 100 percent increase in the initial equity investment. Second, high leveraging similarly multiplied the tax benefits of depreciation deductions based on all the improvements, since tax benefits could be used entirely by the owner of the much smaller equity interest.

But the insistence of most long-term capital suppliers on obtaining some equity in the properties they finance drastically reduces the positive effect of leveraging on equity yields. Because more of the total value of each project consists of equity ownership, the ratio of overall debt to such ownership is greatly reduced. For example, if the combined equity investors in a property have put up all the funds in the form of equity, a rise of 10 percent in the property's market value is only a 10 percent increase in their equity investment. The rate of return on equity is cut to one-tenth of what it would have been if equity had made up only 10 percent of total capital, as in the example cited in the preceding paragraph. (That example did not take account of debt service costs, however, so that the net difference in profitability is less than this simple arithmetic implies.) Even if equity ownership does not constitute 100 percent of required capital, its increase from the "thin" percentages formerly supplied by developers and purchasers will greatly reduce the profitability of equity ownership.

From the perspective of developers and purchasers, this is a highly undesirable change. But from the perspective of capital suppliers, it is very desirable because their real investment yields may be higher than the depressed real returns they received from fixed-rate mortgage loans made in the 1970s. Even so, this change, combined with higher real interest rates, will decrease average real rates of return on real estate equities in the 1980s below their unsustainably high levels in the 1970s.

Consequently, the real values of most real estate properties are not likely to appreciate as rapidly during the next decade as during the past one. Lower profits from owning real properties will reduce the demands for both buying and creating them among those developers and investors who have traditionally initiated nearly all real estate transactions. Although the nominal values of real properties will rise because of inflation, their real value may or may not rise, depending on the particular supply and demand situation in each market.

It is true that capital suppliers who obtain equity positions should achieve higher profits from investing in real property than they did in the 1970s. This favorable prospect will *increase* their demand for such ownership. But such capital suppliers have not traditionally been the initiators of either new development or the sales and refinancing of existing properties in real estate markets. Hence the shift of demand for real estate ownership from the traditional initiators to capital suppliers will probably cause a net decline in activity in real estate markets compared with the 1970s. If that occurs, real values of real estate will not appreciate as rapidly as in the past.

This tendency will be partially offset by a movement of capital suppliers into more active initiation of new development and other transactions. Institutions that formerly were content to lend money to developers and investors will start to become developers themselves, or to pressure others more forcefully to initiate transactions. For example, the Prudential Insurance Company of America has already begun large-scale real estate development on its own account. Other insurance companies, using pension fund money, have created equity investment funds that buy new projects from developers or enter into joint ventures with them. Hence traditional capital suppliers are already playing far more active roles in stimulating transactions than they did in the past.

Nevertheless, these large institutions cannot become as entrepreneurial as traditional developers and investors have been, for reasons discussed in chapter 11. Hence their increased incentive for initiating transactions will not fully offset the decline in that incentive among independent developers and investors. Real estate will remain an alluring investment for many traditional investors, so that the levels of activity in real estate markets will remain significant. Yet such investment will not have the compelling attraction to developers in the 1980s that it did in the 1970s.

In addition, if the average inflation rate in the 1980s falls below that in the 1970s, the demand for real estate equity as a hedge against inflation will also decline.[8]

A final factor supporting a forecast of slower appreciation in real values is the possibly chronic overbuilding in income property markets because of an excess supply of funds seeking real estate investments. This oversupply of funds is the subject of the next chapter. Paradoxically, such an abundance of money initially inflates nominal property values above what they would otherwise be, and above what is justified by the true earning power of the properties involved. But in the long run overbuilding decreases property values by reducing average occupancy levels, slowing rent increases, and cutting average operating profitability.

These conclusions do not mean that investment in real estate equities will no longer be profitable. On the contrary, equity investment will remain attractive to many, especially to traditional capital suppliers. Yet such investment will definitely be less profitable than it was in most of the 1970s. This decline is probable over the entire decade, even though the slowdown in value appreciation described above was counteracted in part by the 1983 flood of capital into real estate markets. That inflow, too, is analyzed in the next chapter.

8. It is by no means certain that the average rate of inflation will actually be lower in the 1980s than in the 1970s. Lower inflation seemed likely as of early 1985, but changes in basic economic policies by the Federal Reserve Board, Congress, and the administration could lead to a resumption of relatively high inflation.

6

The Real Estate Bias of Capital Markets

UNDER the rules of the game prevailing in early 1985, and after the partial deregulation described earlier, U.S. capital markets appear somewhat biased in favor of overinvesting in real estate. Hence they will tend to allocate more financial capital to real estate investments than the amount that would produce equal marginal returns with other investments. This chapter considers the nature, causes, and effects of this bias.

The Concept of Bias in Capital Markets

Economic theory predicts that capital markets will allocate financial funds so as to equalize net after-tax marginal yields from different types of activities. If one activity has higher than average yields at the margin, investors will shift more money into it to gain those yields. The law of diminishing marginal returns, however, will eventually come into play. Greater investment in that activity will increase supply relative to demand. The increase in supply will in turn reduce net profits from operations and therefore decrease yields to investors. When marginal yields from the activity equal those available from other activities, on the average, further shifting of capital to this activity will cease.

Conversely, if some other activity has lower than average yields at the margin, investors will shift money out of it in pursuit of better yields elsewhere. Eventually, smaller supply relative to demand will increase marginal yields until they reach the average. Otherwise that activity will cease to be conducted altogether. When all activi-

85

ties have equal yields at the margin, equilibrium will exist, and no further shifting of capital flows among activities will occur. In theory, such equilibrium represents the socially most efficient allocation of financial capital among available activities.[1]

In reality, such a theoretical equilibrium is continually being disturbed by changes in conditions that alter relative yields among different activities. These changes are inherent in our dynamic world. In addition, deliberate public policies can cause certain activities to receive more, or fewer, capital inputs than those which would equalize all yields at the margin.

For example, public policy may permit investors in a specific activity to reduce their taxable incomes, or income taxes, by some fraction of their investment and not extend similar benefits to other activities. Then investors will put more capital into that activity than the "pure equilibrium" amount. It is true that such excess investment will depress the marginal yield of that activity below yields from other activities. But investors will add their income tax benefits to those depressed yields in calculating their total yields from that activity. Thus they will keep putting more money into that activity even after its marginal yield has fallen below average. Conversely, special taxes or other penalties on investment in certain activities will reduce capital flows into them below the amounts under "pure" equilibrium.

Governments have long used such policies to "bias" capital markets in favor of activities regarded as having high social priority. The most widely recognized bias of this kind is toward investment in homeownership by individual households, as described in chapter 2. Even though recent tax-law and other policy changes have reduced this bias, it still increases financial capital flows into homeownership compared with other possible household investments. Other similar biases favor investment in the creation of new multifamily rental housing and of new oil and gas wells.

These effects of public policies on capital allocation are considered biases or "distortions" by most economists because they alter the allocation that would arise under pure equilibrium. However, if

1. Logical proofs that free-market equilibrium represents the socially most efficient allocation of resources can be found in many standard economic works. Whether the many unrealistic conditions required for this conclusion to hold render it meaningless in practice I leave to the reader to decide.

society chooses through its political processes to favor investment in certain activities more so than would occur under purely market-dominated conditions, the consequent allocation of resources may improve society's overall welfare. Hence the concept of bias is meaningful only in relation to pure equilibrium. A biased capital allocation is therefore not necessarily less socially desirable than an "unbiased" one.

But some biases affecting capital allocation are unintentional results of policies adopted for entirely unrelated purposes. In such cases the concept of bias or distortion often implies lower social welfare than would arise without such effects, other things being equal. From the viewpoint of society as a whole, those distortions may indeed be worth accepting to gain the advantages for which the policies were designed. But usually the persons who designed such policies were unaware of the distortions in capital markets that the policies would produce; hence they did not take those distortions into account when deciding whether the policies were worthwhile. Pointing out such distortions may cause political decisionmakers to conclude that such policies have net negative effects and should be changed.

Types of Bias in Capital Markets

Existing capital market biases can be classified in several different ways, depending on:

—whose behavior is influenced: household investors or financial institutions;

—what choices about where to invest capital are influenced: those among different institutions or those among different types of activities;

—what kinds of influence are used: tax advantages, provision of services below actual cost, legal prohibitions against certain types of behavior, and so forth.

This analysis classifies such biases first by whose behavior is involved, then by what choices are involved, and finally by what kinds of influence are used. Although I have tried to make the following list of kinds of bias as complete as possible, it surely is not wholly comprehensive.

Biases Affecting the Behavior of Household Investors

Biases affect the type of institution in which households invest.

—Individual retirement accounts (IRAs) permit households to deduct up to $2,000 per employed worker each year from federally taxable income for funds deposited in such accounts (proposals made in early 1985 would raise the amount deductible to $2,500 per employed worker). Furthermore, income earned in these accounts is free from income taxes until withdrawn. Hence it can be reinvested tax-free for many years. Institutions that can receive such deposits include banks, thrift institutions, insurance companies (in special accounts), and stock brokerage firms.

—Keough accounts are similar to IRAs but are only for self-employed persons and have much higher annual deposit ceilings. The same types of institutions that offer IRAs can also offer these accounts.

—Federal deposit insurance can be offered only by banks and thrift institutions. It covers individual accounts of up to $100,000 and guarantees that depositors will not lose their funds even if the institutions in which they have deposited become bankrupt. The full cost of providing such insurance privately (if that would be possible at all) would be much larger than the premiums that the federal insuring agencies charge these institutions. Hence this constitutes a below-cost service to individual depositors.

—Contributions from current earnings to pension funds are not taxed as income, and pension funds can reinvest those funds without paying income taxes on the resultant earnings until the earnings are distributed to individual retired persons. This arrangement encourages workers to take a portion of their wages as pension fund contributions.

—Some federal agencies guarantee their investments in various ways, thereby causing household investors to perceive those investments as more secure than others not having such guarantees. Examples are shares in Government National Mortgage Association (GNMA) mortgage pools, since the mortgages themselves are guaranteed by the Federal Housing Administration and since timely payment of interest and principal is guaranteed by GNMA.

—Some federal and quasi-federal agencies have either explicit or implicit relations with the U.S. Treasury that cause household investors to perceive securities issued by them as more secure than those issued by other institutions without any such connections. Examples are the Federal National Mortgage Association (FNMA) and the Federal Home Loan Mortgage Corporation (FHLMC). The legal connections between them and the Treasury are probably much less extensive than most investors realize. Nevertheless, those investors believe that the federal government would never permit these agencies to become bankrupt, and this perception affects investor behavior in financial markets.

Biases affect the type of activity in which households invest.

—Homeownership provides significant income tax benefits, as described in chapter 2; hence households are encouraged to invest in homeownership.

—Equity shares in real estate syndications offer income tax advantages by allowing investors to deduct depreciation and other costs from federally taxable income. These shares require investing in various types of income real estate, including office buildings, shopping centers, hotels, rental apartments, resorts, motels, and industrial buildings.

—Oil and gas investments permit deduction of depletion and some exploration expenses.

—Other more exotic activities—such as operating vineyards, raising prize cattle, and the like—also provide incentives for investing in them.

Biases Affecting the Behavior of Financial Institutions

Biases affect the type of activity in which institutions invest.

—Savings and loan associations can deduct certain reserves against their taxable income for investing in "qualified real estate assets." The higher the percentage of assets so invested within a certain range, the larger the reserve deduction permitted. This relation encourages savings and loans to focus their investments on real estate, including mortgage loans, construction loans, and equity investments.

—Some institutions are permitted to invest in only certain types of activities and are prohibited from investing in others, or are permitted to invest only limited fractions of their total capital in others. For example, commercial banks are not allowed to invest in real estate equities, except for buildings in which they operate or for foreclosed properties they own temporarily. Their trust departments, however, can own real estate under separate legal entities. Insurance companies cannot own commercial banks and in many states can invest only limited fractions of their assets in real estate equities.

Biases affect the rates of return on investment from certain activities conducted by financial institutions and, therefore, the ability of these institutions to increase their capital investment in those activities.

—Some specialized institutions pay lower tax rates on their net incomes than others because of varying rules about reserves and other specialized aspects of their operations. Such net-income-tax advantages constitute a bias even when their size is not related to how these favored institutions allocate the funds entrusted to them among the activities they are permitted. By increasing net profits for these institutions, such advantages encourage greater capital investment in them, hence greater expansion of their activities, than would otherwise occur. This is true of mutually owned or nonprofit organizations as well as of publicly owned ones. Although the public cannot invest in the first two categories, such organizations have larger net receipts for reinvestment in themselves than they would without such advantages. An example in place until tax-law changes in 1984 was the relatively low average income tax rate levied against life insurance companies compared with that levied against other financial institutions.[2]

It is beyond the scope of this book to draw statistically defensible conclusions about the overall effects of these biases—and possibly others—on capital allocation in the United States. The estimation would require extensive data collection and analysis concerning the relative tax status and earnings performance of *all* the nation's principal types of financial institutions.

---

2. During 1978, the last year when savings and loan associations as a group were earning sizable positive net incomes, the average rate of federal income taxes they paid (as a share of net income) was higher than that paid by commercial banks, life insurance companies, or pension funds. Because so many associations had negative earnings much of the time from 1980 through 1982, however, their loss carry-forwards have enabled many to avoid paying income taxes altogether, even after they started having positive earnings.

Nevertheless, capital market behavior since further deregulation of banks and thrift institutions in late 1982 and early 1983 has convinced me that there is a significant overall bias encouraging investment in real estate beyond the amount justifiable by the actual yields of such investment. My reasons for this conclusion are presented in the remainder of the chapter.

The 1983 Flood of Capital into Real Estate Markets

Although the revolution in real estate finance sharply increased the real *cost* of capital in the short run, it had an opposite effect on the *availability* of capital to real estate. Consequently, real estate markets were flooded with financial capital in 1983 and early 1984. Thousands of equity investors sought to buy properties, and many financial institutions sharply increased their real estate lending. At least for a while, this escalation of demand counteracted some of the negative effects that higher real capital costs had on property appreciation. This development was caused by an unplanned focusing of relatively low-cost capital on real estate investment.

Certain biases described above had reduced the relative cost to some financial institutions of two particular ways of raising investment funds compared with all others. One was using the federally insured savings accounts offered by banks and thrifts. The other was real estate syndication. Both derived their comparative cost advantages from unique connections with federal institutions or policies. Both also directed more of the money they raised into real estate than into any other form of investment. Moreover, both were likely to have greater positive effects on the demand for real estate properties in the short run—especially during 1983 and shortly thereafter—than in the long run.

Federally insured savings accounts are a relatively low-cost means of raising money because of the unique security they offer. Such insurance guarantees that savers will not lose their deposits, no matter how bad the economy or how incompetent the management of the savings institutions involved. Only the federal government can offer such a secure guarantee: no one else can tax or print money to cover liabilities if necessary. Therefore savers are willing to accept lower interest rates on accounts carrying federal insurance than on those without it. Or, if two institutions offer the same rates to savers but only one has federal deposit insurance, that one can attract far more funds for the same promotional cost.

The allure of federal deposit insurance was clearly demonstrated in late 1982 and early 1983. Deregulation then permitted banks and thrifts for the first time to offer interest-bearing checking accounts with no ceilings on rates. That made these accounts directly competitive with relatively unregulated money market funds, which had attracted billions of dollars from bank and thrift savings accounts in the preceding few years. Total assets in money market funds had grown from under $20 billion in 1978 to about $230 billion in 1982. Even though these funds did not have federal insurance, the absence of ceilings on their rates enabled them to outbid banks and thrifts for savers' deposits. But once the money market funds had to compete with federally insured accounts that also had no rate ceilings, they began to lose assets.

As soon as these new accounts became available at banks and thrifts in December 1982 and early 1983, a flood of money poured into them. Net new savings at all savings and loan associations had been −$25.4 billion in 1981 and −$16.9 billion in the first eleven months of 1982. This flow reversed to $10.4 billion in December 1982 and $28.9 billion in the first quarter of 1983. Another $33.9 billion was added in the remainder of 1983.[3] Commercial bank savings accounts had gone up $22.5 billion in the first eleven months of 1982 (including interest paid by the banks themselves), but they soared by $51.6 billion in December 1982 and another $123 billion in the first quarter of 1983. They added another $41.5 billion in the remainder of 1983.[4] At the same time, the assets of money market funds declined from about $230 billion to around $165 billion.

The immense inflows suddenly reversed the lending postures of banks and, especially, thrift institutions. The latter had been losing deposits and net worth through 1981 and most of 1982, so they had

3. *Federal Home Loan Bank Board Journal*, vol. 16 (January 1983), p. 51; vol. 16 (October 1983), p. 43; and vol. 17 (March 1984), p. 50.

4. Board of Governors of the Federal Reserve System, *Federal Reserve Bulletin*, vol. 69 (January 1983), vol. 70 (January 1984), and vol. 70 (August 1984), p. A17. Total deposits in commercial banks did not go up nearly as much because many persons shifted funds from time or demand deposits to savings deposits to obtain the new higher interest rates.

been relatively stingy about making mortgage loans or other real estate investments. Almost overnight thrifts were inundated with new deposits on which they were paying high savings rates. They had to put that money to work earning interest as quickly as possible. Although their asset-acquisition powers had just been broadened by financial deregulation, their existing expertise was still concentrated on real estate investment. So most thrifts directed these funds to real estate markets, as they had done in the past.

Their investment attitudes in those markets were instantly transformed from miserliness to open-handed generosity and eagerness to do business. Savings and loans began to offer high loan-to-value ratios to borrowers and to plunge into joint ventures with developers, homebuilders, and land speculators in order to put their funds to work. Because thrift institutions are the single largest source of real estate capital in the nation, this lightning-fast reversal of their attitude had an enormous influence on the financial climate prevailing in most real estate markets.

Commercial banks did not similarly pour most of their big inflows of funds into real estate because they are mainly engaged in making short-term business loans. But many liberalized the terms on which they offered mortgage loans and entered into more joint ventures with real estate developers than in the preceding few years. Furthermore, they refrained from foreclosing on most of the many billions of dollars in construction loans they still had outstanding on new nonresidential buildings created from 1978 to 1982. Because of the overbuilt condition of most real estate markets, many of these buildings were not yet producing enough profits either to pay full interest on those loans or to attract long-term financing. Hence these loans were prolonged far beyond the normal duration of construction mortgages. So banks were making large *implicit* equity investments with some of the new funds they had received in late 1982 and early 1983.

At the same time, the other lowest-cost method of raising capital was also producing record amounts of funds to be channeled into real estate investment. The allure of real estate syndication to investors and financial institutions alike had been greatly increased by the Economic Recovery and Tax Act of 1981, which shortened the period for computing depreciation on real estate investments to fifteen years.[5] This accelerated depreciation enhanced the tax-shelter benefits of owning syndicated partnership interests in real properties, especially if these partnerships were heavily leveraged. That same law also permitted individuals to set up IRAs, described above. IRAs became a substantial new pool of money that needed investment opportunities. In addition, the sharp drop in interest rates in late 1982 and early 1983 motivated many investors to shift out of the bond market into real estate equities. Moreover, other investors, who had profited from the stock market rally in late 1982 and early 1983, decided that stock values had peaked; they too shifted into real estate equities. All these factors combined in 1983 to produce a strong demand for limited partnership interests in real estate syndications.

Three types of financial institution leapt forward to meet this demand. One was small-scale, local syndicators who had always been putting together deals with funds supplied by investors whom they knew personally, such as doctors, dentists, and other professionals. A second comprised much larger professional syndication firms that had grown up since the early 1970s. They operated nationwide, had sizable, well-trained staffs, and were capable of financing much larger transactions than the first group. These firms included JMB Realty Trust, McNeil Real Estate Fund, Fox-Cascarden Financial Corp., and several others. The third type comprised large investment banking and brokerage firms that entered syndication partly to take advantage of their national networks of broker-salespersons. These included Merrill Lynch and Company, The E. F. Hutton Group, Shearson-Lehman/American Express, Goldman, Sachs and Company, and many others. Their broker-salespersons were already in contact with thousands of affluent investors and thus were able to sell large dollar amounts of partnership interests with amazing speed. As a result, a record amount of capital was raised through both public and private syndication offerings in 1983.

From the viewpoint of these institutions, real estate syndication offered two great advantages. First, it was a unique way to raise capital at low cost. Second, it permitted syndicators to profit from

5. That period had previously varied from twenty-two years to forty years depending on the particular method of calculating depreciation used. The 1984 tax law extended this period to eighteen years for most investments other than in low-income rental apartments.

large "front-end" fees collected immediately from the initial capital raised. Hence they could "cash in" without having to wait until the properties in which they had invested proved profitable. Their ability to collect such fees was enhanced both by the strong demand for real estate equities and by the low cost to them of raising capital through syndications.

That low cost existed because the investors who supplied the capital gained major benefits from syndication, benefits for which the fund raisers themselves did not have to pay. The investors received tax-shelter benefits that raised after-tax returns to them, but the resultant costs fell on other federal taxpayers. Just as with federally insured savings accounts, the federal government was conferring a special advantage upon a particular form of investment. This advantage permitted financial institutions using that form to raise funds at less than the full cost of providing the benefits that the investors themselves received. No other investments provided fund-raising institutions with capital under such advantageous terms.

It is true that other capital market biases favor other institutions and types of investment, as indicated above, but several factors differentiate these other biases from federally insured savings accounts and real estate syndication. These two forms of investment provide *larger* cost advantages to the financial institutions using them. Hence those institutions can offer higher prices when seeking assets in which to invest their funds, such as apartment projects, shopping centers, and office buildings. Therefore, during 1983 syndicators consistently outbid traditional investors such as insurance companies in the competition for real estate equities.

In addition, in 1983 the advantages of both these low-cost fund-raising methods had recently been improved by changes in federal laws or regulations. Real estate syndication was made more attractive by the 1981 tax law. The appeal of federally insured savings accounts was magnified when their interest rate ceilings were first abolished in late 1982 and early 1983. Both forms experienced large initial surges of increased funds in 1983 as investors responded to these changes. Similar *increases* in investment will probably not recur in the future unless other legal changes make these investment forms more attractive.[6] Hence they are not likely to generate

6. For example, the interest they earn could be made free from federal income taxes, although that is not likely to happen.

another big surge of new money into real estate investment such as the one in 1983.

Nevertheless, the effect was certainly impressive in 1983 and 1984. The flood of cash searching for real estate equities created intense competition among buyers for high-quality existing properties. That competition generated a strong upward pressure on property prices. Prices rose sharply, and cash-on-cash yields fell.

Yet the operating profitability of those same properties was suffering both from overbuilding and from high real interest rates (if the properties had recently been financed). Moreover, generous lending by thrifts to developers of new properties often added to existing supplies despite overbuilt conditions, further cutting operating profits for both new and existing properties. Thus, in 1983 and 1984, real estate markets exhibited the paradox of rising property prices and falling operating profitability.

Will the Bias Favoring Real Estate Investment Continue in the Long Run?

Several factors indicate that the real estate bias will continue in the long run. First, federal deposit insurance will almost certainly neither be abolished nor be extended to other types of financial institutions. Its use may be made somewhat more sensitive to market conditions, as discussed in chapter 11. Even so, federal deposit insurance will continue for the indefinite future to provide a fund-raising advantage to banks and thrifts. That advantage probably will not generate huge surges of added funds comparable to the one in 1983, for reasons noted above. Yet thrifts will continue to capture a larger share of household savings than they would otherwise because of their combination of market-oriented interest rates and federal insurance.

Second, most thrift institutions aided by such insurance will continue to focus their investments on real estate to obtain the tax advantages of doing so. Other reasons for such continuation of their past practice are discussed in chapter 10. Hence the savings flows that thrifts will enjoy will still be channeled mainly into various types of real estate investment. These will include mortgages, equities in commerical and industrial real estate and apartments, joint ventures with developers, syndications, and land speculation.

Third, more and more individuals will seek tax-shelter investments as inflation pushes them into higher marginal tax brackets. This will happen even if inflation occurs much more slowly in the 1980s than in the 1970s, as long as it averages 4 percent or more. At that rate of inflation, millions of individuals each year will find themselves moved into the maximum bracket, especially if Congress raises taxes to reduce swelling federal deficits. Additional millions will discover that their marginal tax brackets, although lower than the maximum, have nevertheless become high enough to make tax-shelter investments attractive.

Possible Effects of Comprehensive Income Tax Reform

Many economists and tax experts have long advocated fundamental reforms to reduce the increasing complexity and perceived unfairness of the U.S. income tax code. Most proposed reforms involve cutting tax benefits now enjoyed by investors in income-oriented real estate, so the profitability of such properties would be greatly affected. In November 1984 the U.S. Treasury tentatively proposed comprehensive changes affecting almost the entire income tax code. It submitted a revised version of these changes to Congress in May 1985. At the same time, Congress was considering two other comprehensive tax reform proposals. It had not acted, however, on any of these proposals when this book was written in early 1985, and nearly every specific change proposed was bitterly opposed by one or more interest groups.

Hence it was not possible to predict which of the many changes proposed would actually become law. Yet adoption of even a few of the proposed changes could affect the capital market bias toward real estate described above. Therefore it is desirable to explore briefly how some of the most important proposed tax reforms might affect future real estate investment.

This analysis focuses on the Treasury's tentative proposals because they were the most comprehensive offered, and because the Reagan administration backed the revised version of them.[7] It is convenient to divide these proposals and their effects into four categories, as indicated below.

7. U.S. Department of the Treasury, *Tax Reform for Fairness, Simplicity, and Economic Growth: The Treasury Department Report to the President*, vols. 1 and 2 (Treasury Department, 1984).

Changes Directly Affecting Profitability of Individual
Real Properties

Properties owned by tax-free investors such as pension funds would not be directly affected. The profitability of those properties owned by tax-paying investors, however, would be influenced by many of the suggested changes. These reforms include indexing depreciation payments against inflation; a lower rate of annual depreciation; lower tax rates; taxation of capital gains at income rates; and the abolition of industrial revenue bonds, so-called builder bonds that allowed homebuilders to defer income taxes on homes sold; the investment tax credit, and special rehabilitation tax credits. Simulations of how these proposals would affect the profitability of individual properties reveal the following.

—Annual after-tax yields on equity would fall sharply.

—Internal rates of return (IRRs) would also be lower by similar amounts.

—To restore yields and IRRs to their pre-tax-reform levels, rents on apartments, office buildings, shopping centers, and other income properties would have to be raised. Simulations using typical project cost, rent, and expense relationships, and assuming 5 to 6 percent annual inflation, reveal that base rent increases of 5 to 10 percent would be necessary to counteract the specific tax reforms proposed by the president in May 1985.

—However, whether rents would *actually rise* in the short run depends on the balance of supply and demand in each market. Most U.S. nonresidential markets were heavily overbuilt in 1985. So it would take several years of lower new space construction to achieve the required offsetting rent increases.

—Capital gains taxes would be *lower* than at present if inflation became at all sizable. Adjusting the depreciated basis of each property upward would reduce taxable gains at sale, more than offsetting use of a higher tax rate on such gains.

Changes Affecting Willingness to Invest in Equity Real Estate

These proposed reforms include limiting total deductions from each investment to the amount actually at risk therein and limiting the total amount of interest that could be deducted by any one taxpayer to net investment income plus $5,000. If adopted, these proposals would reduce the tax-shelter attractions of real estate syndications. Syndicators of all types would have to shift emphasis from tax-shelter investment to long-term equity investment. The real estate investment trust might be revived as a means of enabling small-scale investors to share in pooled real estate equities. This investment form cannot, however, provide the same tax shelter as syndications. Thus the total volume of funds invested in real estate equities through this form would probably fall.

Yet capital would continue to flow into real estate through savings and loan associations. Their competitive advantage, consisting in federal deposit insurance combined with no-ceiling interest rates on their accounts, would attract additional billions of dollars. The proposed tax reforms would remove another advantage thrifts have derived from large, deductible reserves of bad debt. But this loss would be offset by large loss carry-forwards from the early 1980s and by a possible drop in interest rates. Most of the funds attracted by savings and loans would continue to go into real estate investments. Because thrifts have always supplied far more capital to real estate than have syndicators, total capital flows into real estate would not be greatly reduced by the Treasury's proposed reforms. Thus the capital market bias described earlier would persist.

Changes Affecting Investments Competitive with Real Estate

Competitive investments include corporate stocks, corporate bonds, municipal bonds, short-term securities, and owner-occupied housing. Preliminary estimates indicate that the stocks of corporations extensively using machinery and other physical capital would decline in value because lower depreciation allowances, higher capital gains tax rates, and the abolition of the investment tax credit would reduce their profitability. Stocks of service and other corporations using little machinery or equipment would not lose value. The shielding of 10 percent of their dividends from taxation would partly offset higher capital gains taxes. The net result would probably be a moderate overall decline in the stock market, at least initially. Thus stocks would not draw much capital away from real estate.

Corporate bonds would gain in value because the rates at which they were taxed would decline. Municipal bonds would decline in value because lower marginal tax rates would make their tax-free advantage less valuable even if interest rates fell slightly. However, their supply would fall, since industrial revenue and mortgage revenue bonds would be outlawed.

Owner-occupied housing would gain in *relative* investment attractiveness because it would retain most of its tax advantages (except deductibility of property taxes), whereas most other investments would lose many of theirs. Second homes owned for pleasure or as investments rented to others, however, would lose in value because much of their interest deduction would be disallowed.

On the whole, income real estate would likely lose some of its *relative* attractiveness as an investment, compared with the alternatives, because it would be more thoroughly stripped of tax-sheltering benefits than would other investments. Hence there would be an initial decline in the market values of many existing properties. This would produce losses (or smaller gains) when those properties were sold by their current owners compared with what would happen without such tax-law changes. Just how large these losses would be depends in part on the next type of effect. But many owners would hold onto their properties longer, hoping that rents would eventually rise and restore these capital losses.

Changes Affecting General Economic Conditions

To cut individual tax rates and to exempt more low-income households from income taxes completely, the Treasury's initial proposals would shift about 5 percent of the 1984 tax burden on households to businesses. This would raise the total business tax burden by over 22 percent. Households would spend more out of their increased after-tax incomes, but businesses would invest less. Whether this would cause any net change in total spending—hence in overall economic growth—depends on assumptions about the propensity of households to consume compared with the propensity of businesses to invest. The best guess is that total economic growth would not be much affected.

Borrowing to finance investments of all types, however, would be less desirable under the Treasury's proposals because lower tax rates would reduce the value of interest deductions. If the demand for debt therefore declined, and the supply either rose or remained the same, interest rates would fall, although no one can reliably forecast by how much. The prevailing view is that general interest rates would probably not be affected much.

The Most Likely Outcome

The Treasury's initial proposals of reform would have both short-term and long-term overall effects. In the short run, development of additional income real estate would decrease considerably, and the market values of many existing properties could decline. Rents in most markets would not be affected immediately because large over-supplies of space exist today (except in rental housing). But in the longer run, such a slowdown in the creation of new properties would reduce supply in relation to demand, causing rents to rise. This outcome would eventually allow most properties to regain their initial values or even to appreciate in value. But a lower total share of U.S. capital flows would go into the *creation* of real estate than in the past decade.

Although important tax reforms will undoubtedly be adopted in 1985 or 1986, they will probably embody somewhat scaled-down versions of the Treasury's proposals. Even if all those proposals became law, real estate and other markets would surely adapt to them in the long run. After all, people and firms will still want to occupy buildings—and will have to pay enough to justify investment in the creation of such space. Hence there will still be good reason for long-term investors to own income real estate. The transition to that new market, however, would be a period filled with both uncertainty and sudden changes in the values of existing properties.

Consequently, adopting some version of the Treasury's proposed tax reforms would probably decrease the capital market bias favoring real estate. The weakening of this bias would reduce the problem of chronic oversupplies of space that plagued many markets in early 1985. But the real estate bias of capital markets will not be fully eliminated as long as savings and loans continue to enjoy competitive advantages in capital markets because of federal deposit insurance. Eventually, even savings and loans might diversify greater shares of their investments away from real estate. But until they do, capital markets will remain at least somewhat biased toward investing more funds in real estate than is justified by the "pure," market-determined balance of supply and demand of space.

Distinguishing a Bias Favoring Real Estate from Objective Factors

These possible causes of a continuing bias toward real estate investment should be distinguished from other factors also likely to stimulate greater real estate investment—but not because of market biases. Changes in economic conditions unrelated to market distortions may make real estate investment attractive. For example, if people expect inflation to accelerate, they may want to buy more real estate as a hedge against inflation. If capital flows into real estate rose for that reason, it would not be evidence of market bias.

The prospect of future inflation higher than in 1950–70 will probably motivate millions of households and many pension fund managers to invest more heavily in real estate equities—other than in homeownership—than they did then (although perhaps not more than they did in the late 1970s). Appraising, buying, owning, and managing specific real properties is very difficult for most such investors. Those activities require detailed knowledge of local real estate conditions plus investment of much personal time. Hence most such equity seekers will prefer attaining equity interests by purchasing shares in syndications put together by specialists. This preference will create a steady market for future syndication, even if its tax-shelter benefits are reduced by further legislation. But that market will not be based on *biases* favoring real estate investment as much as on *objective conditions* favoring it.

Yet the size of that market will be increased by the outcome of a definite capital market bias: the attraction of tax-exempt IRA and Keogh accounts. These accounts have been expanding rapidly in recent years. Tax sheltering itself is not beneficial to tax-exempt accounts. Nevertheless, more and more real estate syndications are being designed to emphasize long-run capital gains in equity positions rather than tax sheltering. These equity-oriented syndications will capture a rising share of the total syndication market, especially if the existing tax-shelter benefits of syndication in general are reduced.

Presumably, one of the effects of these accounts will be to raise the rate of total personal saving above what it would have been in the absence of the accounts. That effect represents a "bias" in capital markets because the tax exemption enjoyed by these accounts is not available for most other types of investments. Hence some of any future increase in real estate investment caused by rising IRA and Keogh accounts presumably would occur at the expense of future consumption, rather than at the expense of alternative investments. That result may be quite beneficial to society as a whole, but it still must be considered part of a bias as defined in this analysis.

This example illustrates the difficulty of untangling the effects of biases in capital markets from those of purely "objective" changes in economic conditions or expectations. Nevertheless, I believe a significant net bias in favor of real estate investment is likely to persist throughout the 1980s unless sweeping changes in tax laws not foreseen in early 1985 take place before 1990.

Possible Chronic Overbuilding of Commercial and Industrial Space

If capital markets are notably biased in favor of real estate investment, more financial capital will be put into real estate than is justifiable from the economic yields of such investment alone, in relation to yields from alternative investments. This overinvestment could result in the *overbuilding of space* in relation to demand. Such overbuilding occurs whenever developers and capital suppliers create more new structures than occupants are willing to consume at the rents or prices set high enough to produce competitive yields on the capital invested. Such conditions happened in markets for office space in many large U.S. cities during 1981–82 and 1983–85. Consequently, office vacancy rates soared to above 20 percent in some cities, and to above 15 percent in the downtowns of thirty-one of the largest metropolitan areas combined as of March 1985.[8]

8. Coldwell Banker, *Office Vacancy Index of the United States*, March 31, 1985, pp. 10, 11.

It is important, however, to distinguish between cyclical and chronic overbuilding, particularly in commercial, industrial, and rental apartment space. *Cyclical overbuilding* is one of the three normal phases in the nonresidential property cycle. It typically occurs when new structures started during the boom portion of a business cycle come onto the market. Because of the long lead times required for their development, these structures are not ready for occupancy until after the general economy has entered the subsequent recessionary portion of the business cycle. But then growth of the demand for space has slowed or stopped, so that the large new supplies of space create unbalanced vacancy that puts downward pressure on rents.

Excess space created during such *overbuilt phases* of the normal nonresidential cycle usually disappears, however, during the subsequent *gradual absorption phases*. Then actual shortages of space appear that generate new *development boom phases* in such cycles.

In contrast, *chronic overbuilding* would exist if capital markets continued to finance new space construction even when current markets were clearly overbuilt. Rents would then be depressed below the levels necessary to provide competitive yields. In that case excess space created during the development boom phase and extending into the overbuilt phase would not be removed by the expansion of the general economy. Although that expansion would absorb much formerly vacant space, further new development would keep adding to the available supply faster than growth in demand would absorb it. As a result, rents would remain relatively depressed over the entire business cycles. Hence yields on investments in such property would not attain levels competitive with those on alternative investments at any time during the business cycle.

Has this happened in recent times—say, since 1945? It did not happen before partial deregulation of financial institutions in the early 1980s. Until then, possible chronic overbuilding was largely prevented by cyclical credit rationing in real estate–oriented financial institutions. Short-term interest rates typically rose sharply in the boom phase of the general business cycle. As a result, many depositors in thrift institutions shifted funds to U.S. Treasury bills or other investments offering higher rates than the legal ceilings on thrift rates. Similarly, policyholders of life insurance companies borrowed against their policies from those companies at the low rates permitted in their policies so they could reinvest at higher rates elsewhere. This "disintermediation" cut the funds available to thrifts and insurance companies for real estate investment at the peak of the boom in the general economy. Hence the development boom phases of the nonresidential cycle did not generate large enough space surpluses to depress rental markets throughout the subsequent general economic recovery.

Moreover, during general business recessions nominal interest rates fell to low enough levels so that housing demand rose sharply. Millions of households unable to qualify for mortgage loans during the preceding period of high interest rates were then able to borrow at prevailing lower rates. Hence new housing development and sales of existing units absorbed the increased capital made available to thrifts and insurance companies by the return of deposits to their coffers. In addition, these institutions were content to invest their capital in the form of fixed-rate mortgages on housing because they did not anticipate that inflation would rise in the future.

These inherent limits on the overbuilding of commercial and industrial space have been radically reduced by the revolution in real estate finance. Because thrift institutions have no ceilings on deposit interest rates, they no longer lose funds during periods of high interest rates. (Instead, they lose money on operations, thereby weakening their solvency.) Insurance companies do still suffer from more policy loans during periods of high interest rates, even though they have raised the interest rates permitted on such loans. But this possible loss of capital for investment in nonresidential and rental apartment properties has been offset by much larger flows into equity syndication that are fueled by tax-law changes and expectations of higher inflation. On the whole, the amount of money available for real estate investment during the development boom phase of the nonresidential property cycle is higher than before, compared with the total capital supply.

Equally important, housing markets are absorbing smaller fractions of all available financial capital than before, particularly during the recession and early recovery portions of the general business cycle. Their share is smaller for two reasons. First, nominal interest rates have remained relatively high throughout the general business cycle, for reasons described earlier. Hence fewer households can qualify for mortgage loans to buy new or existing homes. Because less capital is required for owner-occupied housing, more is available for nonresidential and rental apartment transactions. But markets for owner-occupied housing are much larger than all other real estate markets combined. Hence shifting even a relatively modest percentage of total capital from the former can cause a huge percentage increase in total capital available to the latter.

Second, capital suppliers now fear increased future inflation more than they did before partial financial deregulation occurred. (Greater inflation was one of the key causes of such deregulation.) Therefore they want to invest greater shares of their available capital as equity rather than as loans. But equity investment by capital suppliers is almost impossible in owner-occupied housing, whereas it is quite feasible in other types of real estate. Hence capital suppliers feel a relatively stronger attraction than before to invest in nonresidential and rental apartment markets.

Recent Evidence of Possibly Chronic Nonresidential Overbuilding

From 1979 to 1981 the changes described above made possible the continued availability of financial capital for investment in nonresidential and rental apartment properties, whereas owner-occupied housing markets slumped sharply. As a result of this and other factors, the United States experienced the largest private nonresidential property development boom in history during 1978–81. Table 6-1 shows millions of square feet of new commerical and industrial space placed under construction contract each year from 1960 through most of 1984. An average of 965 million square feet of such space was contracted for annually in 1978–81—more than in any single preceding year except 1973. Although such new space placed under contract dropped 22 percent below that average in 1983, it rose to annual rates of 937 million square feet in 1984 and 1,029 million square feet in the first four months of 1985. This occurred despite high vacancy rates in such space in 1983 and 1984, as discussed further below.

Table 6-1. *Contracted Commercial and Industrial Floor Space, 1960–85*

Millions of square feet a year

Year	Space contracted	Year	Space contracted	Year	Space contracted
1960	461	1969	883	1978	977
1961	443	1970	743	1979	1,059
1962	500	1971	727	1980	904
1963	534	1972	854	1981	919
1964	599	1973	1,010	1982	690
1965	680	1974	840	1983	756
1966	769	1975	555	1984	937
1967	694	1976	592	1985[a]	1,029
1968	779	1977	739		

Source: F. W. Dodge, as reported in Council of Economic Advisers, *Economic Indicators*, various years.

a. Average annual rate for first four months.

The relative continuity of financing underlying this boom is not evident from looking at data on mortgage lending alone. As shown in table 6-2, during 1979–80 net gains in constant-dollar mortgages dropped 38 percent for commercial and industrial mortgages, but only 5 percent for mortgages for one- to four-unit family housing. But these data understate actual financing of commerical projects. Many investors frightened by the surge of inflation in 1979–80 shifted from debt to equity investments, which do not appear in table 6-2.

Possibly chronic nonresidential overbuilding is indicated by the experience in 1983–84 shown in both tables. After the recession of 1974–75, net increases in commercial mortgages remained low, both absolutely and as a share of the total for two years (1975–76), before rising again during 1977–79. But after the 1982 recession commercial mortgages quadrupled in constant dollars in 1983, accounting for 33.5 percent of total mortgage gains—by far their largest total and highest share in modern times. They held a 28.0 percent share in 1984 as well, and their absolute gain in constant dollars was only 4 percent smaller in 1984 than in 1983—by far the biggest year for such lending in this entire period.

These large increases in nonresidential building occurred even though most markets still had sizable vacancy rates. Coldwell Banker's index of downtown office occupancy, based on data from thirty-

Table 6-2. *Changes in Total Mortgages Outstanding, 1971–84*
Billions of constant 1972 dollars[a]

Year ending Dec. 31	One- to four-unit family	Multi-family	Farm	Commercial	Total	Percentage change in commercial
	Annual changes in net mortgages outstanding, by type of property					
1971	28.1	9.7	1.78	10.5	50.0	21.1
1972	38.3	9.2	2.50	15.3	65.3	23.4
1973	66.8	15.6	5.50	22.7	110.6	20.5
1974	27.8	6.1	4.30	13.9	52.1	26.7
1975	33.4	0.8	4.00	9.5	47.7	20.0
1976	49.1	3.0	4.5	9.1	65.7	13.8
1977	71.8	4.9	6.3	13.0	96.0	13.6
1978	70.0	6.7	6.9	15.6	99.2	15.7
1979	67.4	5.3	9.9	15.7	98.4	16.0
1980	64.3	3.6	−0.2	9.7	77.4	12.5
1981	40.1	−0.4	5.0	12.4	57.0	21.7
1982	23.6	1.9	2.5	6.8	34.7	19.5
1983	46.6	5.0	1.3	26.7	79.5	33.5
1984	58.8	6.2	0.7	25.6	91.3	28.0
Average	49.0	5.5	4.0	14.8	73.3	20.2

Sources: Board of Governors of the Federal Reserve System, *Federal Reserve Bulletin*, various years; and U.S. Bureau of the Census, *Statistical Abstract of the United States* (Government Printing Office, various years).
a. Current prices deflated with GNP deflators.

one large metropolitan areas, showed a continuous rise in vacancy from under 5.0 percent in early 1981 to 15.3 percent in early 1985.[9] Downtown office vacancy exceeded 10 percent throughout 1983— the same year in which commercial mortgages (in 1972 dollars) increased by *48 percent more* than their highest previous annual gain. Suburban office vacancies in thirty areas were even higher, exceeding 18 percent from mid-1983 to early 1985 (the only years for which suburban data are available). Not all commercial mortgages are for office space, but new office projects continued to be started throughout this period despite high vacancy. Moreover, Coldwell Banker's index of industrial vacancy also showed continuous increases from 3.5 percent in late 1980 to 5.1 percent in late 1983,

9. Ibid.

although vacancy then began declining slightly until mid-1984, when it began inching upward again.[10] While industrial vacancy was at a much lower level, its continued rising during 1983 and 1985 shows that investors in nonresidential properties were not stopped from creating new space by a clear relative surplus of existing space.

Whether this remarkable surge in commercial and industrial building in the face of high existing vacancies is evidence of a new tendency toward chronic overbuilding, or just another cyclical phenomenon, cannot yet be clearly determined. I believe, however, that the revolution in real estate finance has created a built-in tendency toward the former possibility. If so, vacancy rates will remain higher than usual throughout the expansion portion of the general business cycle that began in early 1983. Hence rents in most cities will not rise as much as most developers and investors have anticipated and perhaps will not even keep up with inflation. Actual yields on properties created recently and in the near future will be depressed below those anticipated and those available from alternative investments.

Will Chronic Overbuilding Encourage More Lavish Use of Space?

If chronic overbuilding occurs as described above, and if nonresidential rents either rise very slowly or decline, tenants might seem likely *to increase their consumption of space* because its cost per square foot will have fallen relative to other costs. But the analysis in chapter 5 argued that occupants—whether tenants or owners— would tend *to use space more intensively* than in the past because of the higher real cost of capital in the 1980s. How can these seemingly contradictory predictions be reconciled?

Experience indicates that economizing on use of nonresidential space because of higher real capital costs has up to now predominated over using such space more lavishly because of flat or declining nonresidential rents. This is clearly the case with retail shopping

10. Coldwell Banker, *Industrial Vacancy Index of the United States*, March 31, 1985, p. 1.

centers and industrial buildings and with the movement of some low-intensity office uses out of expensive downtown buildings to outlying locations. It is less clearly the case with space use in hotels and *within* individual downtown or outlying office buildings. Although total space occupied per office worker seems not to have declined much, it has not increased either—and more space is being taken up by office machinery such as personal computers and word processors. Moreover, the dominance of economizing over more extensive use of space is likely to persist for some time, even if nonresidential rents fail to keep up with the general price level.

One reason that far more nonresidential tenants have economized on space than have used it more lavishly is that rising occupancy costs occurred both earlier and more comprehensively than did sluggish rents. Nonresidential rents rose rapidly in the late 1970s because of actual space shortages and because of inflationary increases in construction costs. Such cost increases were partly due to higher interest rates, which affected every new structure. In contrast, the overbuilding caused by heavy flows of capital into real estate markets did not really begin to affect rents until 1982 and later. Moreover, not every building was affected. Some were in markets that had not been overbuilt, others were entirely leased by one institutional tenant, and others had unique locations or other attributes that enabled them to keep rents from declining.

Another relevant factor was the continuance of pressures on most firms to economize on costs in general because of the 1982 recession, exactly when the surplus of space began to affect nonresidential rents. Typically, cost-cutting pressures that emerge during recessions are sustained into the beginning of the following expansion even when business volume grows. That lag is one reason that profits rise sharply early in each business cycle. In this case, most firms were still engaged in holding costs down when rents began to stabilize or even to fall. Hence they did not start using space more lavishly, even though their rents were lower than if no overbuilding had occurred.

More important, markets for nonresidential space normally operate with certain *lags in tenant perception* concerning rent levels. These lags cause most tenants to feel strong pressure to economize on use of space whenever they are making critical decisions about occupancy. Tenants in office and industrial buildings normally reassess their space use mainly when their existing leases are up for renewal or when rapid growth or shrinkage in their operations requires them to change their current occupancy before then. Nonresidential leases usually run for five or more years, sometimes with options to renew for even longer periods at stated rents. Thus, whenever renewal time arrives, the rents that are being paid were negotiated several years earlier. During periods of general inflation those rents are usually well below the market rent that then prevails, even with escalation clauses tied to inflation taken into account.

As a result, tenants almost always perceive the change in rents facing them at lease-renewal time as a substantial increase, even if the change is to a lower rent than would have prevailed in the absence of space surpluses. This perception is particularly likely for the first few years of a general rent slowdown caused by overbuilding. Then even stagnant rents seem high to tenants accustomed to paying rents negotiated five or more years earlier.

Another factor reinforcing such perceptions is the tendency of building owners to grant rent concessions as periods of "free rent" at the outset of occupancy, or as extra-large space-preparation expenditures, rather than as lower base rents throughout the occupancy. Thus owners will offer a 10 percent rent concession on a five-year lease with a base rent of $18.00 per square foot by granting six initial months of free rent, rather than by charging an average rent of $16.20 over the entire lease period (even though the latter would provide them with a higher discounted present value). Then, when the lease comes up for renewal, the nominal base rent remains at $18.00 rather than the lower actual average. Moreover, much of the free-rent period often occurs while the space is being refurbished, before the tenant actually occupies it. Hence the tenant becomes accustomed to thinking of the full base rent as the price actually paid for occupancy.

For all the reasons above, stagnant or declining nonresidential rents caused by chronic overbuilding in 1983 and later have not yet offset the tendency of higher capital costs to intensify use of space by most occupants. Nor is this likely to happen in the mid-1980s, even if chronic overbuilding continues. Only if the lag of perceived rents behind other costs persists well into the late 1980s will it significantly encourage more lavish use of nonresidential space.

Why Chronic Overbuilding Is Less Likely in Owner-occupied Housing

Although chronic overbuilding may occur in nonresidential property and rental apartments, it is far less likely in owner-occupied housing. Two major checks will inhibit chronic overbuilding in the latter: high nominal interest rates, and a much closer relation in the home-building industry between the financing of new space creation and the actual occupancy of new space by its ultimate users.

As noted earlier, nominal interest rates appear likely to remain much higher than in the past. Such rates reduce the number of households that can qualify for the loans required to buy homes. Hence the demand for transactions in owner-occupied units will remain limited unless nominal interest rates fall sharply.

In contrast, high nominal interest rates since 1979 have not greatly restricted the development of new nonresidential space or the sales of such space already in existence. This is clear from tables 6-1 and 6-2. It is true for the following reasons.

—Occupancy costs are a much smaller share of total current income for tenants in nonresidential buildings than they are for homeowners. Hence when higher interest rates increase current occupancy payments, this increase does not cause nearly as many potential occupants to withdraw from nonresidential space markets as from homeownership markets.

—Nominal interest rates are high partly because institutional capital suppliers expect high future inflation rates. Under such conditions they want to make equity or quasi-equity investments to hedge against future inflation. This investment is quite easily accomplished in the financing of nonresidential properties and rental apartments, but it is not feasible in the financing of homeownership. Hence such institutions tend to shift funds from the latter market to the former when nominal rates are high.

—Investors expecting high future inflation tend to project rapidly rising future rents and ultimate sales values in computing the desirability of making particular investments. This projection increases their willingness to invest in properties that have poor immediate income prospects because of current overbuilding. In essence these investors assume that future inflation will bail them out of any adverse short-run market conditions. Hence they remain willing to finance nonresidential properties and rental apartments, in spite of both poor current profitability from such properties and high nominal returns available from alternative investments that offer less protection from long-run inflation.

The second check on chronic overbuilding of owner-occupied units is the relatively short lead times required to construct housing compared with that required for most nonresidential projects. The home-building industry does not usually build up large inventories of vacant units well in advance of their sale to ultimate occupants. Many builders do not construct any new units (except for a few models) until they have closed sales with their eventual buyers. Others build some units on speculation, but few get very far ahead of actual sales because most operate on very thin financing. Therefore, whenever potential homebuyers stop buying, homebuilders soon stop creating new units.

In nonresidential markets, however, the economic linkage between final space users and the process of creating new space is much weaker. It takes much longer to move from conceiving of a new nonresidential project to getting it actually built and occupied. This process requires at least two years, and often five to ten years. Hence the entire industry is geared to providing much more and longer-lasting project funding "up front," well ahead of occupancy receipts, than is the case with owner-occupied housing.

Before the recent revolution in real estate finance, many suppliers of long-term mortgage credit would not commit funds to proposed projects until enough tenants had signed up to occupy most of the planned space. But now developers are far less reliant on such sources of long-term funding. They often get construction financing from banks without having either long-term funds or tenants. Banks have become more willing to assume the greater risks in such transactions. One reason is that in 1983 banks were flooded with money they wanted to lend, as noted above. Moreover, they believe that nonresidential space demand will keep rising in the future—soon rescuing them from short-run overbuilding. But bankers are not nearly as willing to finance homebuilders' inventories of vacant space, partly because of the past history of many bankruptcies in that industry.

Real estate syndications contain an even more tenuous linkage between the initial financing of new projects and their ultimate occupancy. The high-bracket investors seeking a tax shelter who invest in many syndications do not expect to receive any cash returns for years. They can immediately benefit from reducing their income taxes, so they do not need any quick return on their capital. Hence, if the buildings these investors are financing do not rent as quickly as promised, that does not lead them to pressure the syndicators into more effective action. This lack of financial pressure combines with the long lead times typical of new nonresidential projects to divorce, to an amazing degree, creation of new space from its ultimate occupancy by actual users.

For all these reasons, the chronic overbuilding that seems likely to plague nonresidential markets (and possibly rental apartments) in the future is much less likely to occur in owner-occupied housing markets. It is true that savings and loan associations will continue to receive big inflows of savings because of federal deposit insurance. Moreover, they will continue to invest a large share of whatever other funds they have available in financing owner-occupied housing transactions whenever demand warrants. They are eager, however, to shift as many funds as possible away from homeownership into whatever other forms are available. Because those markets are much smaller than markets in homeownership, any sizable shift will tend to flood nonresidential and rental apartment markets with funds.

What If Nominal Interest Rates Were to Fall?

If nominal interest rates fell sharply, perhaps because of a change in the nation's basic economic strategy (discussed further in chapter 14), would this tendency toward chronic overbulding still obtain? Several important differences from the situation described above would be the result.

Large drops in nominal interest rates would probably occur only if certain other changes took place, so those changes can also be assumed to happen. One such change would be a decline in capital suppliers' expectations about future inflation. A second would be short-term rates lower than long-term rates, permitting thrift institutions to make profits again. A third would be lower federal deficits in the late 1980s, absorbing a smaller share of gross national product and freeing more resources for private investment and consumption of various types. These conditions plus lower rates would produce the following results.

—Demands for home mortgages would soar because millions more households could afford to buy new or existing homes. This condition would last for at least a few years, although household formation will decline in the 1990s because of slower population growth.

—Capital suppliers would be more willing to invest in the form of debt rather than equity, although lingering fears of future inflation would probably make many continue to avoid long-term, fixed-rate mortgages. Capital suppliers would therefore be less reluctant to finance homeownership and less eager to put funds into nonresidential markets.

—Savings and loan associations and other thrifts would be more able and willing to continue emphasizing home mortgages and would be under less pressure to diversify into other forms of real estate and non–real estate investments.

—Demand for equity interests in syndications would decline in relation to that for other types of investments. Nevertheless, syndications would probably still attract a significant share of household funds.

—More proposed nonresidential transactions would become economically feasible because of lower capital costs. But the relative gain in total attractiveness of nonresidential projects from lower rates would be much less than that of homeownership projects.

—A larger share of total capital flows would go into real estate— and into all other forms of private investment—than when huge federal deficits were absorbing the largest portion of such flows.

Overall, the flows of both financial and real capital into real estate would probably both increase in total size and shift toward greater homeownership financing than when rates were higher. As a result, any current tendencies toward *chronic* overbuilding in nonresidential markets would be greatly reduced and perhaps eliminated altogether. "Normal" tendencies toward *cyclical* overbuilding would remain, however, because they are rooted in the long lead times inherent in most nonresidential projects.

Will nominal interest rates fall sharply in the mid- or late 1980s?

No one can answer that question with much certainty. But nominal rates will certainly remain relatively high unless the nation changes the basic economic strategy prevalent in the mid-1980s, as discussed in chapter 14.

In conclusion, investing in nonresidential real estate was extremely profitable in the late 1970s because of a combination of inflation, the availability of fixed-rate mortgage loans at low real rates, a general economic boom, and rapid growth of office space use in particular. But the same markets that experienced extremely rapid rent increases and value appreciation then are likely to experience chronic overbuilding in the mid- and late 1980s, as long as the nation continues to follow an economic strategy involving high nominal interest rates. So much financial capital will be looking for real property to buy or lend against that developers will be tempted to build more new space than users can effectively absorb.

The consequent oversupplies of space—although not present in all metropolitan areas—will dampen future rent and value increases where they occur, especially compared with those of the late 1970s. This is much more likely to occur with nonresidential properties than with owner-occupied housing.

It is true that the evidence for such chronic overbuilding observable so far in the 1980s might also be consistent with a purely cyclical phenomenon. Such a cyclical effect would not have the long-range effects described above. But analysis of likely future market conditions makes chronic overbuilding seem a more probable outcome. Such overbuilding would certainly surprise many investors who are expecting another real property appreciation boom like that of the late 1970s.

7

The Concept of Housing Affordability

RAPID increases in home prices during the late 1970s and in nominal interest rates during the early 1980s have made homeownership less affordable for typical households than at any time since World War II. This chapter explores the meaning of "housing affordability" and its relation to real estate capital flows. Chapter 8 examines recent changes in housing affordability, and chapter 9 explores possible public policy responses to the problem of housing affordability.

What Is Affordable Housing?

According to the dictionary, a person can *afford* something if he or she can "bear [its] cost . . . without serious harm or loss."[1] Therefore, a household can afford to buy a home if it can both *make the downpayment* and *carry the monthly costs* without serious harm or loss.

Federal Housing Administration mortgage insurance has permitted downpayments of less than 5 percent of the purchase price to encourage more widespread homeownership. Lenders are willing to accept such small equities when their principals are guaranteed by the federal government or by private mortgage insurers. Without such guarantees, lenders normally require downpayments of 20 percent to 30 percent. They want each borrower to have a sufficient

1. *Merriam-Webster Dictionary* (New York: Pocket Books, 1974), p. 30.

117

equity stake to discourage default. They also want a large margin between the amount of each loan and initial market value of the property. Then, if foreclosure is necessary, the sale price of the property will surely cover the full amount of the loan, even if the market value of the property has declined somewhat. In my analysis I will assume a conventional loan, without mortgage insurance and requiring a downpayment of 25 percent.[2]

How much of a household's total net worth can be devoted to a housing downpayment without its incurring "serious harm or loss"? In 1977 initial home equities—which equal downpayments—amounted to 20 percent or more of total net worth for 75 percent of first-time buyers and 60 percent of repurchasers, and 50 percent or more of total net worth for 28 percent of first-time buyers and 18 percent of repurchasers.[3] Hence most households have far more assets than their downpayments. To simplify my analysis, however, I assume that a home-buying household is willing to devote *all* of its savings to making a downpayment on a home. A household can therefore "afford" a downpayment of whatever size it has the cash to make.

How large a share of total monthly income can a household spend on monthly housing costs without suffering serious harm or loss? I will refer to the maximum such share as "the appropriate housing share" of income. There is no purely scientific way to determine its size. For many years 25 percent was considered the appropriate housing share. This ratio was based on a definition of "income" as total gross household income before taxes, and of "housing costs" as monthly payments for mortgage principal, mortgage interest, property taxes, and insurance (these elements are referred to as PITI). Most European housing policies, however, assume that households should devote a much smaller fraction of their incomes to housing, closer to 15 percent. Furthermore, when U.S. housing prices began

2. This downpayment equals a loan-to-value ratio of 75 percent. The national average loan-to-value ratio for conventional loans made by savings and loan associations was 72.9 percent in 1982 and 73.5 percent in the first eight months of 1983. Data are from *Federal Home Loan Bank Board Journal*, vol. 16 (October 1983), p. 48. Hence I am requiring a slightly *smaller* downpayment than were most lenders in 1982 and 1983.

3. U.S. League of Savings Associations, *Homeownership: Realizing the American Dream* (Chicago: USLSA, 1978), p. 69.

rising faster than household incomes during the late 1970s, strong pressures arose to increase this 25 percent rule of thumb.

One approach to determining the appropriate housing share is based on lenders' experience with mortgage defaults. Lenders have concluded that households devoting more than 35 percent of their gross (pretax) incomes to *all types of debt repayment combined* incur an unacceptably high risk of default. Hence, few mortgage lenders would make loans requiring the borrowers to spend over 35 percent of their income for debt repayment, including PITI. Moreover, the two major secondary mortgage lenders—the Federal National Mortgage Association (FNMA) and the Federal Home Loan Mortgage Corporation (FHLMC)—will normally not accept loans on which more than 28 percent of the household's gross income is spent on PITI. Most lenders abide by this standard most of the time, except in a few markets with very high housing costs, such as California and Hawaii. There lenders often permit borrowers to devote 35 percent of their income to PITI, and FNMA and FHLMC usually accept this practice.

A second approach to determining the appropriate housing share of income is based on how much households actually spend for housing. The median fraction of income devoted to housing costs in 1980 was 19 percent among homeowners who had mortgages on their homes and 13 percent among those without mortgages. These housing costs included mortgage payments, property taxes, utilities, heating, insurance, water, and trash collection.[4] The fraction of income devoted to such costs was much higher among poorer households. Thus the median percentage spent on these costs by homeowners with mortgages was 56 percent among households with incomes of $3,000–$6,999, 37 percent among those with incomes of $7,000–$9,999, but 17 percent or less among those with incomes of $25,000 or more.

These data encompass millions of households that bought their homes many years ago when prices and mortgage rates were much lower. More relevant is the experience of recent homebuyers. U.S. League of Savings Association surveys showed that current home-

---

4. Data are from U.S. Bureau of the Census, *Annual Housing Survey, 1980*, pt. C: *Financial Characteristics of the Housing Inventory* (Government Printing Office, 1981), p. 4.

buyers devoting over 25 percent of their income to PITI plus utilities accounted for 38 percent of all homebuyers in 1977 and 45 percent in 1979.[5] Apparently, households today are spending much higher fractions of their incomes to carry their home purchases *at the outset of their carrying periods* than in the past. Because they are doing so voluntarily, and lenders are accepting such behavior, they must be able to afford such homes.

Many first-time homebuyers have previously been renting, so whatever fractions of their incomes they have been spending on rent could presumably keep going to housing costs. The median fraction of income devoted to gross rent in 1980 was 27 percent for all renters. But this includes many with incomes clearly too low for them to afford homeownership. More germane is the behavior of renters who are not poor. The median fraction spent for rent was 25 percent among renters with incomes of $10,000–$14,999, 20 percent among those with incomes of $15,000–$19,999, and 17 percent or less among those with incomes of $20,000 or more. Thus most 1980 renters with relatively high incomes were not paying very high fractions of their incomes for rent.

Considering all the factors above, I will assume in most of the ensuing analysis that *during the 1980s a home-buying household can afford to devote 35 percent of its total gross pretax monthly income to paying its monthly PITI.* This is a relatively high fraction compared with past experience. Therefore I will use lower fractions when calculating "affordable" housing prices in earlier periods. Each homeowning household, however, can deduct both mortgage interest and property taxes from its federally taxable income. The actual share of total income devoted to these housing costs *after taxes* is thus considerably smaller than 35 percent (as analyzed later). I will indicate when changing this ratio makes a big difference for any important conclusions.

If a household makes a 25 percent downpayment on a home, its mortgage will cover 75 percent of the purchase price. For this analysis I assume a twenty-five year, fixed-rate, level-payment, fully amortized payment at the current interest rate. The ramifications of using other types of mortgage will be discussed later. I also assume

5. U.S. League of Savings Associations, *Homeownership: Coping with Inflation* (Chicago: USLSA, 1980), p. 19.

that annual property taxes equal 1.5 percent of the purchase price of each home, and that annual insurance costs equal 0.5 percent. All these assumptions lead to the following definition.

—A household can afford to buy a home if it can make a cash downpayment of 25 percent of the home price, and if the appropriate share of its total gross pretax income will pay both the annual debt service at current interest rates on a twenty-five-year mortgage for 75 percent of the home price and property taxes and insurance totaling 2.0 percent of that price.

If the appropriate housing share is 35 percent of income, the prices that households with different incomes can afford to pay for homes under different mortgage interest rates are as shown in table 7-1. Affordability is about equally sensitive to changes in household income and interest rates. Thus a 50 percent rise in household income from $20,000 to $30,000 enables a household to purchase a home priced 50 percent higher if interest rates remain the same. A 33.3 percent fall in interest rates from 15 percent to 10 percent enables a household to buy a home priced 33 percent higher if household income remains the same. If the household devoted only 25 percent of its income to PITI, it could afford far less for a home at each combination of income and interest rates, as shown in table 7-2.

Three variables have critical effects on housing affordability once an appropriate housing share of income has been defined: home prices, household incomes, and mortgage interest rates. Other factors also vary, but their influence is far less important.

The Time Dimension of Affordability

The definition of affordability stated above implies that a household can afford a home only if it can *immediately* purchase that home under the conditions set forth. That is, the household already has the downpayment in hand and is already receiving an income large enough to cover the monthly payments as indicated. No allowance is made for any initial period of saving during which the household accumulates the required downpayment. Yet most homeowners first had to save for their downpayments, often for quite a few years. I believe most Americans would regard it as quite acceptable for

Table 7-1. *Housing Affordability under an Appropriate Housing Share of Income of 35 Percent*
Dollars

Annual household income	Maximum affordable housing price at indicated mortgage interest rate (percent)					
	10	12	13	13.5	14	15
10,000	34,617	30,742	29,066	28,285	27,540	26,148
15,000	51,925	46,113	43,598	42,427	41,310	39,223
20,000	69,233	61,484	58,131	56,570	55,079	52,297
25,000	86,542	76,854	72,664	70,712	68,849	65,371
30,000	103,850	92,225	87,197	84,855	82,619	78,445
35,000	121,159	107,596	101,730	98,997	96,389	91,519
40,000	138,467	122,967	116,262	113,140	110,159	104,593
50,000	173,084	153,709	145,328	141,425	137,699	130,742
Addenda						
Price-income ratio	3.46168	3.07418	2.90656	2.8285	2.75398	2.61484
Monthly debt service multiplier for mortgage amount	110.9643	95.89602	89.62597	86.75455	84.04215	79.05027

Source: Author's calculations. A household can afford to buy a home if it can make a 25 percent downpayment on that home and if an appropriate share of its income will cover debt service, property taxes, and insurance on that home. In this table, "an appropriate share of income" for housing equals 35 percent; "income" means total gross pretax household income; property taxes and insurance combined equal 2.0 percent of home price; the mortgage is a twenty-five-year, fixed-rate, level-payment, fully amortized traditional mortgage; monthly payments are made at the beginning of each month.

potential homebuyers to spend at least a few years saving before they purchased their homes.

Therefore, if a short initial period of saving is the only obstacle to a household's buying a particular home, the household should be considered able to afford that home. Hence housing affordability has a *time dimension*. Yet this dimension is almost never taken into account in analyses of this subject.

To consider this subject properly, it is necessary to distinguish between *immediate* affordability and affordability *within a reasonable period*. But what is a reasonable period for accumulating a downpayment? I am not aware of any well-established criteria for determining such reasonableness. Therefore, I will arbitrarily set *six years as the maximum time that a household can reasonably be expected to spend accumulating a downpayment before buying a home*. This saving period and its successful objective would permit a

Table 7-2. *Housing Affordability under an Appropriate Housing Share of Income of 25 Percent*
Dollars

ADD 25% for yours

Annual household income	Maximum affordable housing price at indicated mortgage interest rate (percent)					
	10	12	13	13.5	14	15
10,000	24,726	21,958	20,761	20,203	19,671	18,677
15,000	37,089	32,937	31,142	30,305	29,507	28,016
20,000	49,452	43,917	41,522	40,407	39,342	37,355
25,000	61,815	54,896	51,903	50,509	49,178	46,693
30,000	74,178	65,875	62,283	60,610	59,014	56,032
35,000	86,541	76,854	72,664	70,712	68,849	65,371
40,000	98,905	87,833	83,044	80,814	78,685	74,709
50,000	123,631	109,792	103,805	101,017	98,356	93,387

Addenda
Price-income ratio	2.472614	2.195832	2.076106	2.020343	1.967117	1.867734
Monthly debt service multiplier for mortgage amount	110.9643	95.89602	89.62597	86.75455	84.04215	79.05027

Source: Author's calculations. Assumptions relating to affordability are as in table 7-1, with the exception that here the appropriate share of income for housing equals 25 percent.

household formed by college graduates right after completing their schooling to purchase a first home before these household members reached the age of thirty, or one formed by high-school graduates right after completing their schooling to do so before they were twenty-five years old. In the ensuing analysis I will further assume that each household has no savings at all when it begins to accumulate the necessary downpayment.

Housing affordability can now be redefined as follows.

—A household can *immediately* afford to buy a home if it can make a cash downpayment of 25 percent of the home price, and if the appropriate housing share of its total gross pretax income will pay both the annual debt service at current interest rates on a twenty-five year mortgage for 75 percent of the home's price and property taxes and insurance totaling 2.0 percent of that price.

—A household can *afford to buy a home within a reasonable period* if it can, within six years of starting, accumulate enough cash to make a downpayment of 25 percent *or more* of the home price, and if the appropriate share of its total gross pretax income *at the time of purchase* will pay both the other elements mentioned in the preceding definition.

Introduction of this time dimension complicates the analysis of housing affordability because it requires making further assumptions about the following.

—How much of the household's income can it be expected to save during the period for accumulating the downpayment?

—If the household is renting during this period, rent would absorb some of the share of income it can devote to housing, including saving for the downpayment. How much rent would it have to pay?

—How does the household invest its savings, and what rate of interest does it obtain on them?

—What is the tax rate against interest on the household's savings?

—While the household is accumulating the downpayment, home prices, rents, and household incomes are all likely to rise because of inflation. How fast will these different elements increase?

These issues are considered in detail in the next chapter.

The distinction between immediate affordability and affordability within a reasonable period has some surprising implications. For example, table 7-1 shows that a household with an income of $30,000 a year could immediately afford to buy a home costing $87,197 if the prevailing interest rate were 13 percent. This conclusion implies that the household has already amassed the required downpayment of $21,799. But it might want to purchase a home costing $95,000 instead, on which a 75 percent mortgage would equal $71,250. But the household's current income can only support a mortgage of $66,898, given the property taxes and insurance charges for the lower-priced home. Yet if it accumulated a larger downpayment, it could reduce the size of the mortgage on the $95,000 home to a level it could afford to carry within 35 percent of its income.

This analysis shows that *a household that can immediately afford to buy a home of any given price already has some savings; therefore it can also afford a considerably more expensive home by saving for a reasonable period to accumulate a larger downpayment.* On close examination, the concept of housing affordability has become far more flexible—and less easily defined—than most past analyses have indicated.

The Relation of Housing Affordability to Financial Deregulation

Purchases of both new and existing single-family homes accounted for over 70 percent of average annual total real estate capital requirements during 1970–82.[6] Any large reduction in the number of such purchases each year would greatly decrease total future capital flows into real estate. Such a reduction would occur if many households seeking to buy new or existing homes could not afford to do so.

Moreover, housing affordability is closely related to the basic economic strategy implicit in financial deregulation. This strategy assumes that eliminating certain regulations formerly encouraging capital flows into housing will not harm American society; rather, relatively unregulated markets will best allocate society's limited capital. According to this view, building or buying housing should have no special priority over other uses of capital. The relative social priority of any activity is reasonably shown by its ability to pay interest rates for the capital it needs. Presumably, when housing needs become acute enough, those with such needs will be motivated to pay high enough interest rates to get the capital they require.

This analysis implies that financial deregulation will not cause capital shortages leading to seriously inadequate production of new housing units or to an undesirable inability of households to buy existing homes. How realistic is that implication?

The *supply side* of real estate markets contains no major obstacles to unrestricted access to capital.[7] Suppliers of capital will be attracted to the highest yields, so users of housing capital can always get funds by offering higher yields than other capital users. Moreover, because of recent deregulation the real estate industry is no

---

6. See tables 5-1 and 6-2 in those respective chapters.

7. Deregulation has actually *improved* the accessibility of capital to real estate, including housing, in two ways. The first is by permitting thrift institutions to pay market rates for savings, thereby ending the "disintermediation" that periodically caused shortages of housing mortgage funds in the past. The second is making it easier for pension funds and other institutions to invest in housing by changing regulations governing secondary mortgage markets.

longer prevented from paying high rates by legal ceilings on how much thrift institutions can pay savers.

If financial deregulation is to work without undesirable space shortages, however, there must also be no major obstacles to unrestricted capital flows into real estate on the *demand side*, even during periods of high interest rates. Is this condition realistic? The answer differs greatly in two types of markets.

The response is affirmative in markets for nonresidential properties and rental apartments. High interest rates are most likely during rapid inflation. Then many capital suppliers are seeking real estate equity ownership as a hedge against inflation. Developers of nonresidential property can therefore escape the negative effects of high interest rates by entering joint ventures with those capital suppliers. The capital suppliers can justify this use of their funds by citing high future yields based on projected rapid inflationary increases in future rents and property values.

Thus, even when interest rates are high, most potential users of capital for building or buying nonresidential properties and rental apartments are not prevented from acting by capital suppliers telling them the risk of default is too high. Such transactions can thus continue during periods of high interest rates. Nonresidential development remained at very high levels in 1980 and 1981, and again in 1983 and 1984, for this reason.

 But activity in single-family markets depends on how many households can borrow enough money to buy homes. When nominal interest rates soar, millions of households able to purchase homes at lower rates can no longer do so. The required monthly payments become such large fractions of their incomes that lenders fear they might default. Lenders will therefore not lend these households enough to purchase homes, and they drop out of the market. This housing *affordability problem* can drastically reduce total transaction levels in real estate markets, and total capital flows into real estate, as it did in 1980–82.

In the 1980s some of the market-shrinking effect of high nominal interest rates has been offset by wide use of adjustable rate mortgages (ARMs) and interest rate buydowns by homebuilders. ARMs are usually offered by lenders at lower initial interest rates than those of fixed-rate mortgages; hence more households can qualify for the former than the latter. In addition, homebuilders often help potential buyers qualify by putting up sufficient funds to reduce interest rates in the first one to three years. This cuts the initial monthly payments and permits lower-income buyers to qualify if lenders look only at the first few years of payment, which most do. In a few cases, builders dropped initial interest rates below 5 percent to attract business, but FNMA and FHLMC soon refused to purchase such mortgages, fearing that later drastic increases in monthly payments posed unacceptable risks of default. That refusal essentially killed the practice of such radical buydowns, but many builders continued more modest interest rate reductions during the first one to three years.

Another offsetting factor that would reappear if inflation were rekindled is the graduated-payment mortgage. Such mortgages permit borrowers to make much lower payments in the first years than in later years, under the assumption that both borrowers' incomes and the values of their homes will rise over time. Because qualification for such loans is made on the basis of first-year incomes and payments, more households can qualify than could for traditional mortgages with the same interest rates.

When Does Housing Affordability Become a Serious Social Problem?

All these devices, however, are not antidotes for the market shrinkage caused by high nominal interest rates powerful enough to prevent capital flows into homeownership from falling when such rates occur. Such shrinkage certainly has adverse implications for homebuilders, realtors, mortgage lenders, and other actors within the housing industry. But it is not necessarily bad from the viewpoint of society as a whole. After all, not every household can afford to buy a home without incurring a risk of default unacceptable to those lending it the required capital. Therefore, even if millions of households that want to buy homes are thus pushed out of the market by higher interest rates, their exclusion does not necessarily mean that society should come to their assistance.

Thus, *housing affordability is not a social problem merely because many households that want to buy homes cannot do so.* Many households that want to buy luxury cars, stereos, or trips to

Acapulco also cannot afford to do so. Yet society rightly refrains from springing to their aid with subsidies paid for by others. The inability of households to purchase their own homes becomes a social problem only:

—if households are blocked from such purchases by market imperfections that could be removed through cost-effective social policies;

—if so many households become unable to afford occupancy of "decent" living quarters that socially undesirable housing shortages arise;

—if a large fraction of all households seeking to achieve the American dream of homeownership are unable to do so within their lifetimes and hence become disillusioned both with the rewards of hard work and with American social and political values in general.

Thus, if high interest rates prevail only for short periods, and for a small fraction of each decade, U.S. society will not suffer excessively from the "pure" price rationing of capital. Potential homebuyers forced to defer purchases during periods of high interest rates can find alternative dwellings relatively easily or can postpone forming separate households. Most will know they will soon be back in the market for the kind of housing they desire. Such flexibility is especially true of first-time homebuyers, who usually can rent while waiting to buy. Most rental housing markets exhibit great flexibility of supply because so many renter households can double up if necessary.

But if high nominal interest rates prevail for long periods, and over a large fraction of an entire decade, then many potential homebuyers will have to defer homeownership for significant portions of their lives, even permanently. Moreover, far fewer new homes will be built than under lower interest rates. Hence housing shortages may arise that most people would regard as socially undesirable.

In the early 1980s U.S. society could surely have experienced a few years of low housing production without major hardship—if those years were followed by several years of higher "normal" production, as in 1983 and 1984. But if low housing production were to prevail during most of the decade, certain groups and areas would begin suffering from seriously inadequate housing.

Whether society should try to remedy this problem through public policies depends on the importance accorded to both adequate housing and homeownership, compared with other social goals requiring capital, and on the likely effectiveness and costs of such policies. The first factor is discussed below; the second is analyzed in the following chapter.

Arguments for Awarding High Social Priority to Housing and Homeownership

Everyone regards decent housing for all households as a desirable social goal, and Congress has repeatedly enshrined this goal as an official objective of public policy. Nevertheless, why should decent housing have any higher priority than many other desirable goals that also require real and financial capital?

One often-cited justification is the belief that physically adequate housing is necessary for the proper socialization of children and for the healthy conduct of all family life. Surprisingly little empirical evidence supports this conclusion. Few studies have found any clear link between physical or psychological maladies and quality of housing. Moreover, in many societies healthy children and well-adjusted families have grown up living in housing that most Americans would consider grossly inadequate. Even if good-quality *housing* were a requirement for healthy family life, that would not necessarily justify awarding high social priority to *homeownership*.

Another argument is that homeownership is a vital support for our democratic society. According to this view, individual homeownership encourages a majority of American households to favor private property, the free enterprise system, limited government authority, and strong local government. This argument seems plausible, but it is also hard to prove empirically. Homeowners do make up a large share of all households in many stable democracies, but other societies exist in which the fraction of homeowners is much lower than in the United States. In 1981 this fraction was 65 percent in the United States but only 30 percent in Switzerland, 37 percent in West Germany, 44 percent in the Netherlands, 47 percent in France, and 59 percent in Great Britain.[8] Even if there were indis-

8. Data are from Mark Boleat, *National Housing Finance Systems* (London: Croom Helm, 1984), cited in *The Economist*, vol. 293 (October 20, 1984), p. 61.

putable evidence that widespread homeownership is essential to stable democracies or free enterprise economies, there is no way to know exactly how large the proportion of homeowners must be to maintain those conditions, or whether any given change in that proportion would endanger the existing social structure.

A final argument for awarding homeownership high social priority is that most Americans themselves consider owning their own homes a central goal—a pillar of the American dream of a successful life. Numerous polls concerning American values confirm that most Americans want to own their own homes, and that they overwhelmingly prefer detached, single-family homes to all other types of housing.[9] George Sternlieb has argued that relatively widespread access to homeownership is part of the "middle-class contract" concerning the rewards people ought to receive for working hard, saving, and conforming to basic American social values.[10] If individual households consider homeownership to have high priority, then society as a whole ought to honor their values by deliberately channeling capital flows into housing markets, rather than leave capital allocation entirely up to "free market" forces.

Whether to award higher social priority to adequate housing than to other goals, such as continuing social transfer payments at high levels, is ultimately a value judgment that cannot be made objectively. But determining whether high interest rates will generate inadequate housing conditions can be empirically analyzed. Such analysis is the topic of the next chapter.

9. For example, see *Professional Builder*, November 1981, p. 132.

10. George Sternlieb and James W. Hughes, "The Evolution of Housing and the Social Compact," *Urban Land*, vol. 41 (December 1982), pp. 17–20.

8

Recent Trends in Housing Affordability

DURING THE 1980s changes in household incomes, home prices, and interest rates have reduced the number and percentage of households that can afford to buy homes compared with preceding decades. These changes have created what has come to be called the "housing affordability problem."

"Standard" Analysis of the Recent Decline in Housing Affordability

Data concerning key variables of housing affordability in 1950–84 are set forth in tables 8-1 and 8-2. Table 8-1 shows the levels of these variables at different dates, whereas table 8-2 shows the compound annual rates of change of the variables. These tables use *medians* of both family incomes[1] and home prices to measure changes in housing affordability because most other analyses have employed those indexes. Distortions from doing so are discussed later.

On the left side of table 8-1 is computed the maximum amount that the median-income family could *immediately afford* to pay for

---

1. Data in tables 8-1, 8-2, and 8-3 refer to families rather than households because appropriate income data for the latter were not available for all the dates shown. Most of the analysis in this book, however, refers to households because that is a broader category for covering the entire population. The family category excludes many one-person households, and family incomes are always somewhat higher than household incomes.

131

Table 8-1. *Affordability of Single-Family Housing, Selected Years, 1950–84*
Dollars unless otherwise specified

				Maximum affordable home price				Actual affordability of median-priced existing home				Mortgage payments as an average percentage of income during:		
Year	Median family income	Appropriate housing income share (percent)	Average mortgage interest rate (percent)	Monthly mortgage payment multiplier	Maximum immediately affordable home price	Ratio of affordable price to median price	Median price of existing home[a]	Mortgage amount[b]	Monthly mortgage payment	Annual mortgage payment	First year	First five years	First ten years
1950	3,319	25	4.09	188.24	12,236	1.22	10,050	7,538	40.18	482	14.53	13.11	11.59
1960	5,620	25	6.23	152.66	17,795	1.12	15,865	11,899	78.35	940	16.73	14.99	13.16
1970	9,867	25	8.22	128.03	27,318	1.19	23,000	17,250	135.66	1,628	16.50	14.52	12.48
1975	13,719	28	8.95	120.54	40,579	1.15	35,300	26,475	221.27	2,655	19.35	16.44	13.58
1980	21,023	30	12.95	89.92	52,520	0.84	62,200	46,650	524.38	6,293	29.93	n.a.	n.a.
1982	23,430	35	15.38	77.29	60,102	0.89	67,800	50,850	666.33	7,996	34.13	n.a.	n.a.
1983	24,580	35	12.85	90.52	72,037	1.02	70,300	52,725	582.47	6,990	28.44	n.a.	n.a.
1984c	26,054	35	12.17	94.78	79,323	1.07	73,800	55,350	584.00	7,008	26.90	n.a.	n.a.

Sources: U.S. Bureau of the Census, *Statistical Abstract of the United States, 1982–83* (Government Printing Office, 1982), pp. 432, 461; National Association of Realtors, *Monthly Report: Existing Home Sales*, December 1982, October 1983; author's calculations. Data refer to families, not households.

n.a. Not available.

a. Median prices for 1950 and 1960 calculated as 1.33 times the median home values as reported by decennial censuses because that was the approximate ratio of these two variables in 1970 and 1980. Prices for other years were taken from National Association of Realtors, *Monthly Report*, various issues.

b. Seventy-five percent of median price.

c. Estimated. Family income was estimated to be 6 percent above 1983; the mortgage interest rate was the average of the first six months; and the median price was for June.

Table 8-2. *Compound Annual Growth Rates of Key Affordability Variables, 1950–84*
Percent

Period	Median annual household income	Median existing single-family home price	Consumer price index (all items)	Single-family home mortgage interest rate	Monthly mortgage payment on median-priced existing single-family home
1950–60	5.41	4.67	2.09	4.29	6.91
1960–70	5.79	3.78	2.75	2.81	5.64
1970–75	6.81	8.95	6.75	1.72	10.28
1975–80	8.91	12.00	8.89	7.67	18.84
1980–84	5.51	4.37	5.92	−1.54	2.73

Sources: Bureau of the Census, *Statistical Abstract, 1982–83,* pp. 432, 461; National Association of Realtors, *Monthly Report,* December 1982, October 1983, and September 1984; author's calculations as for table 8-1. Data refer to families, not households. Data for 1984 were taken from table 8-1.

a home in each of the years shown. The definition of immediate affordability used is that given in chapter 7. Different fractions of income are used as "appropriate housing ratios" in different years to reflect changes in both lending practices and household investment patterns over time. From 1950 through 1975, the median-income family could afford to pay more than the cost of the median-priced home. Thus the ratio of maximum affordable price to actual median price (the sixth column in table 8-1) is larger than 1.0. In 1980 and 1982, that family could not immediately afford the median-priced home, even though a much higher appropriate housing ratio was used to determine how much it could afford. Lower interest rates in 1983 and 1984 once more enabled the median-income family to afford the median-priced existing home.

The right side of table 8-1 indicates what fraction of income the median-income family would have had to pay to carry a 75 percent mortgage (not counting property taxes or insurance) on the median-priced, existing single-family home in each year. As table 8-2 shows, during 1950–80 these monthly mortgage payments increased at compound annual rates about double those of the consumer price index. Yet in the 1950s and 1960s, median family incomes rose almost as fast. Hence the fraction of median family income required to make such payments in the first year after purchase (at the right side of table 8-1) remained relatively stable from 1950 through 1970, rising from 14.5 percent in 1950 to 16.5 percent in 1970.

In the 1970s home prices rose much faster than family incomes, as

Table 8-3. *Families Immediately Able to Afford Median-priced Single-Family Existing Home, Selected Years, 1950–84*
Dollars unless otherwise specified

Year	Median family income	Appropriate housing income share (percent)	Amount available for monthly mortgage payment	Mortgage interest rate (percent)	Actual median home price[a]	Monthly payment needed[b]	Annual income needed	Estimated percentage of families with needed income[c]
1950	3,319	25	69.15	4.094	10,050	56.93	2,733	61.3
1960	5,620	25	117.08	6.23	15,865	104.79	5,030	57.6
1970	9,867	25	205.56	8.22	23,000	173.99	8,352	60.0
1975	13,719	28	320.11	8.95	35,300	280.10	12,004	58.0
1980	21,023	30	525.58	12.95	62,200	628.05	25,122	39.9
1982	23,430	35	683.38	15.38	67,800	770.90	26,430	43.8
1983	24,580	35	716.92	12.85	70,300	699.64	23,988	n.a.
1984[d]	26,065	35	760.23	12.17	73,800	707.00	24,240	n.a.

Sources: Bureau of the Census, *Statistical Abstract* (various years), tables on family incomes in sections on "Income, Expenditures, and Wealth."
n.a. Not available.
a. Median home prices estimated for 1950 and 1960.
b. Monthly payment includes $1/12$ of 2 percent of home price to cover property taxes and insurance. Assumes 75 percent fixed-payment mortgage for 25 years at interest rate shown.
c. Assumes an even distribution of families within each income bracket as reported for the indicated year.
d. Estimated.

did interest rates in the last half of that decade. This increase caused mortgage payments to soar almost twice as fast as consumer incomes. By 1980 families with the median family income had to pay 29.9 percent of their incomes to cover their first-year mortgage payments on median-priced, existing single-family homes. That figure was almost double the fraction required in 1950, 1960, and 1970. By 1982 this fraction had soared to 34.1 percent—above the limit at which most financial institutions would qualify the family for such a loan. However, the fraction dropped back into the range of 26 percent to 28 percent in 1983 and 1984, when rates declined. Nevertheless, that figure was almost double the fraction required in 1950, and much higher than the percentage required in 1960, 1970, and 1975.

As a result of these developments, a smaller percentage of all families can afford to buy the median-priced existing single-family home today than in the past. This is evident from table 8-3. Hence fewer households will be able to afford buying *any* homes in the 1980s than earlier, and construction of single-family housing should be slower. Thus less financial capital, in relation to total economic activity, should be required to support housing transactions.

Qualifications to the "Standard" Analysis

Advocates of public intervention to improve housing affordability usually cite the statistics above to dramatize their case. But recent declines in housing affordability are not nearly as dire as those statistics imply, for reasons summarized in the following paragraphs.[2]

The fraction of all households that can afford to buy homes is much larger than the fraction that can afford to buy the median-priced home, because one-half of all homes sold are priced below the median. Many households seeking to buy homes, among the 60 percent that could not afford the median-priced home in 1980, could still have bought suitable dwellings among the 50 percent of all

2. Some of the points in this section were taken from Carol Anderson, "Reading the Yardsticks of Affordability," in Frank Schnidman and Jane A. Silverman, eds., *Housing Supply and Affordability* (Washington, D.C.: Urban Land Institute, 1983), pp. 21–28.

homes sold at prices lower than the median. Moreover, half the families in the nation have incomes above the median, so they can afford more costly homes than the median-income family.

It is misleading to judge a household's ability to purchase a home by looking at the relation between household income and mortgage payments for only one year. Annual mortgage payments are typically fixed for several years or longer, but the household's income rises along with inflation, and sometimes faster. Hence the share of household income required to make mortgage payments declines over time. Moreover, the faster the rate of inflation, the faster that share drops, if inflation is reflected in rapid nominal income growth.

For example, in 1970 a median-income family had to devote 16.5 percent of its income to mortgage payments in the first year after purchasing a median-priced home. But that fraction declined to 12.7 percent in the fifth year and to 9.1 percent in the tenth year. Hence such payments averaged 14.5 percent of income over the first five years, 10.4 percent over the second five years, and 12.5 percent over the first ten years.

Nearly all households recognize that the real burden of a fixed-payment mortgage will decline over time, especially if inflation is rapid. Hence more households bought homes in the late 1970s precisely when some academic experts were saying that affordability was declining. The experts apparently looked only at first-year data, but the purchasers themselves looked at the entire ten-year average period before resale of the home.[3]

This is one reason most homebuyers prefer fixed-rate mortgages to adjustable rate mortgages (ARMs) unless the former have a large cost advantage over the latter. They realize that fixed mortgage payments permit them to "inflate out from under" the burdens of their mortgage debts.

During 1980–83, however, the fraction of ARMs among all home mortgages rose sharply, exceeding two-thirds in 1983. Borrowers using such mortgages cannot rely on inflation to reduce the real burdens of their payments because those payments will rise along with prevailing interest rates. It is true that there are both legal and

3. For example, see the Joint Center for Urban Studies of the Massachusetts Institute of Technology and Harvard University, *The Nation's Housing, 1975–85* (Cambridge, Mass.: Joint Center, 1977), pp. 115–16.

market-imposed limits on how large the payment adjustments can be each year, and those limits will often prevent lenders from fully offsetting inflation by raising monthly payments, or even by adding to the total principal owed. Nevertheless, increased use of ARMs has greatly reduced the ameliorating effects of inflation on homebuyers' real debt burdens.

Comparisons based solely on median prices of homes at two dates do not take into account increases over time in both the size and quality of U.S. housing. These comparisons often overstate the rise in price of homes of identical quality in that period. During 1965–79 the median-priced new home increased in size 10 percent, from 1,495 square feet to 1,645 square feet. In addition, a typical new home built in 1978 used 34 percent less energy per square foot for heating and cooling than one built in 1973.[4] New homes today are also more likely to contain air conditioning, dishwashers, fireplaces, and other amenities. During 1970–80 the price of a new single-family home of constant quality rose 162 percent, whereas the median price of all new single-family homes sold went up 176 percent. Hence about 5.3 percent of the latter rise was probably due to improved quality.[5]

Increased tax benefits to homeowners from deducting higher mortgage interest and property taxes from their taxable incomes partly offset greater charges for these expenses. Moreover, inflation has shifted many homeowners into higher marginal tax brackets, thus enhancing these tax benefits.

Affordability analyses such as that done earlier do not take into account the buildup of homeowners' equities. During the entire post-1945 period, especially in the 1970s, homeowners benefited greatly from selling their homes at much higher prices than they originally paid for them. Homeowners realized large capital gains because their initial mortgage amounts did not rise. The resultant equity profits enabled millions of households to buy much more

4. U.S. Bureau of the Census, *Statistical Abstract of the United States, 1981* (Government Printing Office, 1981), p. 752.

5. Data are from Bureau of the Census, *Statistical Abstract of the United States, 1982–1983* (GPO, 1982), p. 749. From 1960 through the late 1970s, the average size of both new and existing homes rose steadily, although it has declined slightly and then risen slightly in more recent years. Hence this qualification would not apply to comparisons between the late 1970s and the early 1980s.

expensive homes without straining their current budgets. With those profits they made large enough downpayments to reduce the monthly payments on their costly new homes to amounts they could manage. The only households that did not benefit from such equity buildups were (1) renters, (2) homeowners who purchased their first homes after 1979, and (3) those now seeking to buy their first homes. Hence problems of affordability apply mainly to these groups, not to homeowners who bought their current homes before 1979.

Homeowners who purchased their homes before the late 1970s actually have experienced *declining* housing costs both in real terms and relative to their incomes, despite high real interest rates in the early 1980s. Until about 1980, housing became more affordable for them because of negative after-tax real interest rates in the 1970s and the equity buildups described above. According to the *Annual Housing Survey*, about 43 percent of all homeowners in 1980 had purchased their dwellings before April 1970, and 85 percent had purchased homes before 1979.[6] So *the vast majority of owner-occupants were not suffering from problems of housing affordability.*

In any one year, the percentage of all households likely to encounter problems of affordability is quite small. In 1978—the year with the greatest number of single-family home sales ever—*Annual Housing Survey* data indicate that a maximum of about half of all homebuyers were first-time buyers. Yet they formed only 3.5 percent of all households and 17.6 percent of all households that moved from one dwelling to another.[7] Surveys by the U.S. League of Savings Associations show that first-time buyers accounted for 36 percent of all homebuyers in 1977 and only 18 percent in 1979. (I have used 50 percent in this analysis to be conservative.)[8]

Data from the 1980 *Annual Housing Survey* show that 15 percent of all owner-occupants had moved into their current dwellings dur-

6. Bureau of the Census, *Annual Housing Survey, 1980*, pt. A: *General Housing Characterisics* (GPO, 1982), p. 7.
7. Data are from Bureau of the Census, *Annual Housing Survey, 1978*, pt. D: *Housing Characteristics of Recent Movers* (GPO, 1981), p. 9. I counted as first-time buyers all owner occupants who had moved during the preceding year and had either rented previously or were newly formed households.
8. See U.S. League of Savings Associations, *Homeownership: Coping with Inflation* (Chicago: USLSA, 1980), pp. 15–21.

ing the preceding two years, and about 57 percent during the preceding ten years.[9] If half of all homebuyers were first-time buyers, then they averaged about 3.75 percent annually of all households over the previous two years, and 2.85 percent annually over the previous ten years. Thus, in any year, no more than 28.5 percent of all households would have been first-time homebuyers at some time during the preceding ten years, and 15.4 percent during the preceding five years. Hence 71.5 percent of all households would probably not have encountered problems of affordability in the preceding ten years, and 84.6 percent would not have in the preceding five years.

In the past, first-time buyers had incomes higher than average; hence most are less in need of financial aid than are many poorer households, especially poor renters. The 1979 survey of 14,000 homebuyers cited earlier showed that the median income of first-time buyers was $25,230 and that only 9.9 percent had incomes of less than $15,000.[10] The median income for all households in 1979 was $16,553, and 45.5 percent had incomes below $15,000.[11] Moreover, among renting households 1979 median income was $10,000, and 72 percent had incomes below $15,000.[12] Thus in 1979 the median income among first-time buyers was 52 percent higher than that among all households, and 152 percent higher than that among all renting households. Yet 1979 was a year in which home-buying conditions were quite favorable. Over 3.3 million existing single-family homes were sold—only 2 percent below the all-time record in 1978. And 1.76 million new housing units were started, about average for the entire decade.[13]

In 1977 mortgage availability and interest rates were even more favorable to first-time buyers than in 1979. Yet median income in 1977 was 47 percent higher among first-time buyers than among all households. Only 15.7 percent of all 1977 first-time buyers had

9. Data are from Bureau of the Census, *Annual Housing Survey, 1980*, pt. A, p. 7.

10. U.S. League of Savings Associations, *Homeownership*, p. 61.

11. Bureau of the Census, *Statistical Abstract, 1981*, p. 434.

12. Bureau of the Census, *Annual Housing Survey, 1979*, pt. B: *Indicators of Housing and Neighborhood Quality by Financial Characteristics*, p. 111.

13. Bureau of the Census, *Statistical Abstract of the United States, 1984* (GPO, 1983), p. 744.

incomes below the U.S. household median.[14] Clearly, "typical" potential first-time homebuyers are far more able to meet their housing needs without public assistance than are millions of poorer households.

Calculations of affordability based on nationwide data ignore huge regional variations in key variables. National median home prices are driven upward by high prices in certain areas—especially in California, where a disproportionate share of housing transactions occurs. In 1980 California sales of single-family, apartment condominium, and cooperative units accounted for 14.7 percent of all such sales, although California contained only 10.4 percent of the nation's population and 10.7 percent of its households.[15] But the median price of single-family homes sold in California in 1980 was $98,041—57.6 percent higher than the nationwide median of $62,200.[16] In contrast, the median price in the North Central region was $51,900, and that in the South was $58,300. Family income differences between California and these other regions were much smaller than housing price differences. For example, 1979 median family income was only 7.9 percent higher in California than in the entire United States, and three of the fourteen North Central states had higher median family incomes than California. Therefore, higher fractions of households in those other regions could afford to buy homes than would appear possible from national data alone.

These qualifications have two important implications. First, *housing affordability was not a major problem until about 1980, when real interest rates rose sharply.* Until then, increases in the share of family income required to support monthly mortgage payments in the late 1970s were offset by the other factors described above.[17] This conclusion is confirmed by dramatic changes in the

14. See U.S. League of Savings Associations, *Homeownership: Realizing the American Dream* (Chicago: USLSA, 1978), pp. 48–49; and Bureau of the Census, *Statistical Abstract, 1982–1983*, p. 429.

15. National Association of Realtors, *Monthly Report: Existing Home Sales*, September 1983, p. 14; and Bureau of the Census, *Statistical Abstract, 1982–1983*, pp. 28, 48.

16. National Association of Realtors, *Monthly Report: Existing Home Sales*, September 1983, p. 14.

17. National Association of Realtors, *Monthly Report: Existing Home Sales*, December 1982, p. 4.

number of existing single-family homes sold each year. This sales figure rose from 1.60 million in 1970 to 3.99 million in 1978 and 3.29 million in 1979. Then it plummeted to 2.97 million in 1980, 2.42 million in 1981, and 1.99 million in 1982—a drop of 50 percent in four years. In 1983, fueled by lower interest rates, the number of such homes sold rose to 2.72 million, and in 1984 it reached 2.87 million.[18] Hence the affordability problem was not as bad in 1983–84 as in the two preceding years.

Second, *because affordability became a problem after 1979, its effects have been, and will continue to be, concentrated among first-time homebuyers*, including most of those who bought homes after 1979. Other types of households have been largely insulated from such problems by one of more of the factors just described. Therefore, how much affordability problems will affect future flows of real estate capital depends greatly on how important first-time buyers will be in housing markets.

The Future Importance of First-Time Homebuyers

During the 1980s, many people born during the post-1950 "baby boom" will enter the ages at which households typically have become first-time homebuyers. Nina and Claude Gruen have calculated increases during 1980–90 in the number of households with heads of various ages, assuming an overall rise of 17.50 million households.[19] I believe that a smaller total increase—of about 14.36 million households—is more likely; hence I scaled back their estimate for each age group by 18 percent. These calculations indicate that households with heads aged twenty-five to thirty-four will rise by 3.78 million (26.3 percent), those thirty-five to forty-four will rise by 5.95 million (41 percent), those sixty-five and over will rise by 3.20 million (22.3 percent), and all others will rise only by 1.42 million (9.8 percent). These estimates foreshadow a jump of 9.7 million households in the key home-buying ages of twenty-five to

18. National Association of Realtors, *Monthly Report: Existing Home Sales*, April 1985, p. 14.
19. Nina Gruen, Claude Gruen, and Wallace F. Smith, "Living Space: Households in the 1980s," in Schnidman and Silverman, eds., *Housing Supply*, pp. 61–66.

Table 8-4. *Homebuyers in Different Age Groups, 1977*
Percent

Age of household head	First-time buyers among all homebuyers	Homebuyers in age group		
		First-time	All	Repurchase
18–24	74.5	23.8	11.5	4.6
25–29	56.5	39.1	24.9	16.9
30–34	31.4	19.0	21.8	23.4
35–39	20.1	7.2	12.9	16.1
40–44	16.6	4.2	9.1	11.9
45–49	14.2	2.8	7.1	9.6
50–54	10.5	1.6	5.5	7.8
55–59	8.0	0.8	3.6	5.2
60–64	17.1	0.9	1.9	2.5
65 and over	14.4	0.6	1.5	2.0
Total	36.0	100.0	99.8	100.0

Source: U.S. League of Savings Associations, *Homeownership: Realizing the American Dream* (Chicago: USLSA, 1978) pp. 13, 57, 65.

forty-four, or 973,000 a year. But not all households in these age groups are homebuyers, and not all homebuyers are first-time buyers (table 8-4).

How many households of all types will buy homes each year during the 1980s? In 1977—a very strong year for home-buying— 3.547 million existing single-family homes and 819,000 new such homes were sold, or 4.366 million altogether.[20] These home sales represented about 5.7 percent of all 77.1 million U.S. households in 1977, or 8.7 percent of all owner-occupied housing units. Therefore, a high projection of annual total home sales for the 1980s would be equivalent to 5.0 percent of total households, averaging about 4.42 million a year.[21] A more conservative estimate would be 4.0 percent

20. Data on sales of existing homes are from National Association of Realtors, *Monthly Report: Existing Home Sales*, December 1982, p. 4. Data on sales of new homes are from Bureau of the Census, *Statistical Abstract, 1984*, p. 745.

21. This assumes an average of 87.578 million households a year, on the basis of growth from 80.400 million in 1980 to 94.757 million in 1990. The figure for 1990 is the low-growth projection given in Anthony Downs, *Rental Housing in the 1980s* (Brookings, 1983), p. 158; it is an optimistic projection because actual sales in 1980–84 averaged about 2.606 million, or 3.2 percent of the average number of households in that period. See National Association of Realtors, *Monthly Report*, September 1983, p. 4, and Council of Economic Advisers, *Economic Indicators*, September 1983, p. 19.

of total households, or 3.54 million sales a year. (The actual average in 1980–84—the first half of the decade—was about 2.606 million a year, so both these estimates are quite high.)

What percentage of total homebuyers will be first-time buyers? First-time buyers were about 36 percent of all homebuyers in 1977, but only 18 percent in 1979. Hence, over the whole decade, they might average from a high of 35 percent of all buyers to a low of 20 percent. These estimates indicate a high projected annual average of 1.55 million first-time buyers (35 percent of 4.42 million) and a low projected average of 708,000 (20 percent of 3.54 million). The mid-point of these estimates is 1.095 million first-time buyers a year, or 27.5 percent of the annual average of 3.982 million total homebuyers, as shown in table 8-5.

If there were 1.095 million first-time homebuyers annually during the 1980s, first-time buyers would account for only 1.24 percent of the average annual number of households. This percentage might rise to over 2 percent in the first half of the decade but will not exceed that level by much. During the entire decade fewer than 15 percent of all households are likely to be first-time homebuyers. That percentage is large in absolute numbers—as many as 13 million households. But it also implies that the vast majority of U.S. households will not confront problems of housing affordability during the 1980s.

Nevertheless, because sales of single-family homes absorbed over 70 percent of total real estate capital flows during 1970–83, first-time homebuyers could account for 14 percent to 25 percent of all real estate capital flows in the 1980s.[22] If circumstances reduced their numbers by the difference between the high and low estimates just stated, the total amount of real estate capital required each year would drop by about 12.5 percent.

22. These percentages have been calculated by multiplying the high projected average percentage of first-time buyers among all homebuyers (35 percent) by the approximate percentage of all capital flows formed by single-family capital requirements (70 percent) to get one answer (24.5 percent), and by multiplying the low projected percentage (20 percent) by 70 percent of all capital flows to get the other answer (14 percent).

Table 8-5. *Annual Number of First-Time Homebuyers within Age Distribution*
Thousands unless otherwise specified

| | Total number of households by age group | | | | | | Homebuyers by type and age group | | | | |
Age of household head	Number of households (1980)	Increase in number (1980–90)[a]	Percent rise (1980–90)	Number of households (1990)	Average number households (1980–90)	Percentage of average number (1980–90)	Percentage of home-buyers by age	Average annual number of homebuyers (1980–90)	Percentage of first-time buyers by age	Average annual number of first-time buyers	First-time buyers as percentage of all buyers
14–24	6,379	148	2.32	6,527	6,453	7.31	11.50	458	23.80	261	56.98
25–34	18,681	3,695	19.78	22,376	20,529	23.25	46.80	1,863	58.10	636	34.14
35–44	14,523	5,810	40.00	20,333	17,428	19.73	22.00	876	11.40	125	14.27
45–54	12,611	1,418	11.24	14,029	13,320	15.08	12.70	506	4.40	48	9.48
55–64	12,744	–178	–1.40	12,566	12,655	14.33	5.50	219	1.70	19	8.70
65 and over	16,359	3,142	19.21	19,501	17,930	20.30	1.50	60	0.60	7	11.70
Total	81,297	14,035	15.19	95,332	88,315	100.00	100.00	3,982[b]	100.00	1,095[c]	27.50

Sources: Nina Gruen, Claude Gruen, and Wallace F. Smith, *Demographic Changes and Their Effects on Real Estate Markets in the 1980s* (Washington, D.C.: Urban Land Institute, 1982), p. 13; and U.S. League of Savings Associations, *Homeownership*, pp. 13, 57, 65.
a. The factor used to reduce Gruen and Gruen's estimate was 0.80205714.
b. Average annual total home sales as a percentage of total households was 4.5 (number = 3,982).
c. First-time homebuyers as a percentage of all homebuyers was 27.5 (number = 1,095).

9

Managing the Problem
of Housing Affordability

A COMBINATION of federal policies raising interest rates and local policies raising housing prices has made homeownership much less affordable in the 1980s than in previous decades. Higher interest rates are rooted in much greater federal spending for defense and transfer payments, federal tax-rate cuts contributing to record peacetime deficits, and a federal monetary policy focused on reducing inflation. The nation's highest housing prices, found in areas such as California, have their origin in both rapid population growth and stringent local government restrictions on new housing production. These restrictions stem from strong local desires to protect the environments and the financial equities of existing homeowners. Both sets of policies reflect high social priority for goals other than making homeownership affordable. What public policies—if any—should be adopted in response to diminished housing affordability?

Possible Policy Responses to the Problem of Housing Affordability

There are three basic ways to deal with the consequent problem of housing affordability. One is to accept the conclusion that homeownership has been, and should continue to be, awarded lower social priority than in the past compared with that awarded other social objectives. This view regards the new lower priority of homeownership as a legitimate outcome of our political and economic decisionmaking processes. It confirms the wisdom of judging the social priority of different activities by their ability to bid for resources in relatively deregulated financial markets. Hence it calls for no additional policies to improve housing affordability.

Two other approaches reject the view that homeownership merits lower social priority than other goals. Both try to raise the priority of homeownership *relative* to these other goals, albeit by different tactics.

One would reduce the relative priority awarded to other now high-priority goals, without any new policies specifically favoring homeownership. This approach involves much smaller federal deficits to reduce interest rates, and far less restrictive local regulations to permit building many more lower-cost housing units. Implementing these broad policies, however, is probably beyond the capabilities of the groups most interested in housing, such as homebuilders, realtors, and building-trades unions.

The other approach seeks "priority parity" through new policies that would directly aid potential homeowners, thereby raising the social priority of homeownership relative to all other goals. This approach denies the desirability of judging the social priority of activities by their ability to compete unaided for capital in deregulated financial markets.

The wisdom of trying this third approach depends on whether any policies could accomplish its goal feasibly, effectively, and without undue costs. That possibility is the subject of this chapter.

Tactics for Improving Affordability

Seven possible ways to improve housing affordability are briefly stated below, along with the reasons that three of the approaches are not feasible. Subsequent sections discuss the other four in more detail.

1. *Keep the general interest rate structure quite low.* Then most potential homebuyers can qualify for mortgage loans large enough to buy appropriate homes. This tactic would certainly be desirable if low interest rates could be achieved by means other than slow real economic growth. But keeping interest rates low during general

prosperity requires keeping federal deficits low too, or intense competition for credit between public and private borrowers would raise rates. Hence this tactic will not work when large federal deficits occur during economic expansions. Yet such deficits seem quite likely in the mid-1980s.

2. *Return to extensive regulation of financial markets that would favor those institutions that invest in housing.* Then such institutions could attract funds at below-market interest rates and use them for mortgage loans at below-market rates. This could only be done without subsidies if savers in those institutions received below-market rates on their deposits. But deregulation has taught savers that they can get market interest rates on their funds and has generated alternative institutions willing to pay such rates. Thus savers will not voluntarily leave their money in institutions paying below-market rates. Only a massive federal subsidy would make this tactic possible; an example would be to reduce income taxes on interest earned on savings deposits. But Congress is not likely to adopt any such subsidy, especially because most of it would reward people for savings they would have made anyway. Hence this tactic is neither economically desirable nor politically feasible.

3. *Increase the tax advantages of homeownership compared with those of other uses of capital.* If such added advantages were large enough, they might enable first-time buyers to afford to buy appropriate homes despite high prices and high interest rates. But this tactic would benefit many more homeowners than just the relatively small percentage facing problems of affordability. Hence the losses in tax revenue sustained by the U.S. Treasury would be vastly greater then the benefits received by potential first-time buyers who truly needed help. Therefore, this tactic is unacceptable.

4. *Subsidize first-time buyers.* Focusing government housing aid only on first-time homebuyers would be much more efficient than aiding all homeowners. Several proposed forms of such subsidies are discussed further below.

5. *Use mortgage forms with low initial payments so that more households would qualify on the basis of the first-year relation of payments to income.* These could be adjustable rate mortgages (ARMs), graduated-payment mortgages, or mortgages with initial interest rates brought down by builders.

6. *Build smaller housing units at higher densities so home prices*

will be lower. This tactic does not involve any subsidies but would require many local governments to reduce the restrictions they now place on new housing construction.

7. *Shift the costs of creating new housing infrastructure from individual units to the entire local community.* Many city and state governments have recently ceased paying for construction of roads, streets, water and sewer systems, schools, and parks out of general community funds. Instead, they charge the developers of specific subdivisions for these improvements through various fees and exactions. This practice raises the prices of new homes, thereby making them less affordable. Returning to earlier practices would reduce those prices.

Matching Prototypical Households with Housing Units

Those most injured by recent declines in home affordability are potential first-time homebuyers. To determine how well various tactics would work in aiding such households, it is first necessary to describe their economic situation.

For this analysis, I have assumed that pretax, pretransfer median household income in 1983 was $21,750, and that the income of households at the top of the first quartile of the distribution was $11,400. A household with the latter income can be considered a potential low-income, first-time homebuyer. I will use households in these two financial situations to estimate the likely effectiveness of various tactics to aid first-time homebuyers. In addition, I will analyze the situation of a California household having the median income for households in that state and confronted by housing prices typical of that state. This household illustrates the situation of possible first-time buyers in high-priced markets.[1]

1. Data on the distribution of household incomes for 1981 are from U.S. Bureau of the Census, *Statistical Abstract of the United States, 1982–83* (Government Printing Office, 1982), p. 430. The median household income in 1981 was $19,074; the household income at the top of the first quartile was about $10,000, and that at the top of the third quartile was about $31,700. The consumer price index for all items rose by 9.8 percent from 1981 through June 1983, and real per capita personal income rose by 3.7 percent from 1981 through the second quarter of 1983, according to data from Council of Economic Advisers, *Economic Indicators*, August 1983, pp. 6 and 23. Therefore, it is reasonable to assume that nominal median household

One way to determine how much first-time buyers must pay for homes is to match the household income distribution with the distribution of home values across the existing inventory. In September 1983 the median price of existing single-family homes sold was $70,400, and the price of the homes at the top of the first quartile of all sold was about $50,000. The median price of such homes sold in California in August 1983 was about $114,000.[2] Under this approach, the problem facing first-time buyers can be posed as: what would help a household with an income of $11,400 buy a $50,000 home, or a household with an income of $21,750 buy a $70,400 home, or a California household with an income of $23,466 buy a $114,000 home? Because household incomes and home prices have not changed much in relation to each other since late 1983, the answers to this problem presented here are still basically valid.

This process of matching prototypical households with housing units is admittedly quite arbitrary. Moreover, I have matched the income distribution for all households against the housing price distribution for only 57 percent of all housing units, since the available sale-price data cover only single-family, owner-occupied units. These units undoubtedly have higher prices, on the average, than the ones left out. A more comparable match would exclude all renter households. That would raise both the median and first-quartile household incomes used for matching well above those cited above.

Nevertheless, I will stick with those households for three reasons. Most prior discussions of housing affordability have dealt with the median-income household in the entire distribution, so using that household makes this analysis comparable with earlier ones. In addition, many first-time buyers are former renters, so excluding all renters from the analysis would not be realistic. Finally, including

---

income rose by about 14 percent during 1981–83, and that the incomes at the top of the first and third quartiles rose by similar percentages. That assumption would make median household income in 1983 about $21,750, and that at the top of the first quartile about $11,400. The median-income household in California was assigned a 1983 income 7.89 percent above that of the U.S. median-income household because that was the spread in median incomes between California and the rest of the nation in 1979, according to the *Statistical Abstract, 1982–83*, p. 437.

2. National Association of Realtors, *Monthly Report: Existing Homes Sales*, October 1983, p. 11; and California Association of Realtors, *California Real Estate Trends Newsletter*, August 1983, p. 1.

the first-quartile household from the overall income distribution extends the range of incomes covered quite low—providing a point of comparison from which extrapolations can easily be made in considering incomes between the first-quartile figure and the median and thus increasing the potential scope of the analysis.

My analyzing the situation of this low-income household does not, however, imply that I believe it *should* be able to own its own home. Millions of U.S. households cannot realistically afford to be homeowners, and public policy has no inherent obligation to help them do so. Extending the range of the analysis down to relatively low levels should help make the situation of low-income households clearer, thereby helping policymakers decide under what conditions those households should or should not be assisted in seeking homeownership.

The Situation of Low-Income Households

Consider first the lowest-income household mentioned above. If it could devote 35 percent of its income to housing, or $3,990 a year, that amount would cover mortgage principal and interest, property taxes, and property insurance (referred to as PITI). I assume that property taxes equal 1.5 percent of market value, or $750 a year, and that insurance would equal one-third of that, or $250 a year. That leaves $2,990 for mortgage payments, or 26.2 percent of the household's income. At 13 percent interest, $2,990 a year would support a mortgage of only $22,332.[3] To carry ownership of a home costing $50,000 with such payments, the household would have to make a downpayment of $27,668, or 55 percent of the purchase price.[4] Unless this household has amassed savings equal to more than 25 percent of the home price, it cannot immediately afford this house.

---

3. These and all subsequent calculations concerning mortgage payments assume that each borrowing household makes its payments at the beginning of each month.

4. If it were in a 20 percent marginal bracket, the low-income household could save $150 a year by deducting its property taxes and $483 by deducting its first year's mortgage interest payments. This would reduce its *net* housing costs (principal, interest, taxes, and insurance, PITI, minus tax savings) to 29.4 percent of its income. But mortgage lenders do not take such savings into account in determining how large a loan they will make to each household. Therefore I have also ignored these tax savings in my calculations.

One way to assess proposed forms of assistance to a first-time homebuyer is to determine how much each aid would reduce the time needed to save a downpayment large enough to buy a home. Such a downpayment should decrease the size of the required mortgage enough so that the household could cover its monthly payments with no more than 35 percent of its income. Many low-income households would have to accumulate downpayments much larger than the traditional 20 percent to 25 percent of purchase price. As noted above, to buy a $50,000 home, a household with an income of $11,400 would need a 55 percent downpayment. This would reduce its mortgage to the $22,332 it could afford to carry, using 35 percent of its income for PITI.

The first step in this approach is to determine how long saving such a downpayment would require *without* any public assistance. I assume that each household starts with no prior savings and receives no funds from anyone else. How much can a household save each year out of an income of only $11,400? If it could devote 35 percent of its income to housing, but could rent quarters for less, it could presumably save the difference. I estimate that such a household could have rented relatively economical quarters in 1983 for $250 a month.[5] It could then save about $82.50 a month, or 8.7 percent of its income. If this household deposited $82.50 monthly at 10 percent compound interest subject to 20 percent income tax (a net 8 percent interest), it could save the $27,668 downpayment in 14.66 years. If the household lived rent-free with relatives and saved all 35 percent of its income at 10 percent interest (taxable), however, it could accumulate that downpayment in 5.50 years.

These estimates assume, however, that the price of this home would not rise while the household was saving to buy it, nor would the income or rent of the household increase. In the U.S. economy, such complete price stability is unrealistic. Hence I have also calculated how long it would take this household to save enough to buy this home if the price of the home, the household's income, and the household's rent were all rising at 5 percent a year. Annual increases

---

5. Median monthly gross rent in 1981 was $270 for all rental units except single-family units on 10 acres or more, and $284 for all such units not subsidized. About 43 percent of all such units and 38 percent of all such units not subsidized had rents of under $250. Data are from U.S. Bureau of the Census, *Annual Housing Survey: 1981*, pt. A: *General Housing Characteristics* (GPO, 1983), p. 12.

in the home price would raise the absolute amount of any given percentage downpayment. This increase in the household's savings target would be partly offset by the household's ability to carry a larger mortgage out of its higher income. The larger the mortgage it can carry, the lower the downpayment it needs to buy a house of any given price. Moreover, with a higher income the household could save more during the period for accumulating the downpayment. If the household were renting during that period, however, this benefit would be partly offset by a rise in its rent.

With all of these relations taken into account, a household with an income of $11,400 in the first year, paying $250 a month in rent during that year, could save enough to buy a home costing $50,000 in the first year in 20.68 years, assuming 5 percent annual increases in those three variables. By that time the price of this home would be $130,640, the household's income would be $29,800, and its monthly rent would be $653. If the household were living rent-free while saving, it could purchase this home in 6.52 years under the same conditions. These calculations assume that the household deposits its monthly savings in an account paying 8 percent interest net of taxes.

Under both sets of assumptions, this household must wait quite a long time to buy this home if it must rent while saving for the downpayment. By the definition of affordability "within a reasonable period" set forth earlier, it certainly cannot afford this house if it rents, and it just misses being able to afford it reasonably soon if it lives rent-free. If it can gain outside assistance in the form of rent-free quarters or equivalent aid, however, this household can buy this home within 6.5 years of starting to save for the downpayment. Although this time exceeds the one used to delimit "a reasonable period" earlier, it still does not seem an unduly long savings period in light of the past experience of millions of American households. Hence even a household with an income this low probably does not have a serious problem of housing affordability if it can gain such private assistance from relatives or other sources.

Yet this conclusion assumes that the household will receive a great deal of private assistance. After all, permitting another household to live with one for 6.5 years without receiving any rent in return would represent a great sacrifice for almost any household except a wealthy one with substantial extra space in its home.

Similar calculations can be made for the other two households described above. The situations of all three households, and the time required for them to save downpayments large enough to buy the homes with which they have been matched, without outside assistance, are set forth in table 9-1. Column A shows the situation of the household with a 1983 income of $11,400; column B shows the situation of the median-income household; and column C shows the situation of the median-income California household. The outcomes for the last two households are discussed later.

Table 9-2 shows the results for households A, B, and C under the assumptions of no annual increase in housing prices, household incomes, and rents, and of a 5 percent annual increase in these variables. To simplify the presentation below, however, I will only discuss the results when these variables rise 5 percent a year because that is more realistic.

Effectiveness of Specific Aids to Potential Low-Income First-Time Buyers

How effectively would such a low-income household be aided by various subsidies? In answering that question, I will not judge effectiveness by the benefits of each subsidy versus its costs to taxpayers. Rather, I will determine to what extent a moderate size of each tested subsidy would reduce the time these three households need to be able to afford the homes with which they were matched above. This approach is clearly incomplete because it ignores program costs. As will be shown, however, it yields important conclusions despite that drawback. Details of the analysis of each of these subsidies are presented in appendix B.

The specific subsidies analyzed are as follows:

—a tax-free downpayment savings account (no federal income taxes on interest earned by funds in the account);

—a 100-percent tax credit for deposits in a downpayment savings account;

—direct downpayment assistance grants of $2,000 to first-time buyers;

—state or local mortgage revenue bonds free from federal taxation that reduce mortgage interest rates to homebuyers from 13 to 10 percent;

Table 9-1. *Financial Situation of Three First-Time Homebuyers*
Dollars unless otherwise specified

	Position of home and buyers		
Item	*Top of first quartile*	*Median income and home price*	*California median income and price*
Home price	50,000.00	70,400.00	114,000.00
Household income	11,400.00	21,750.00	23,466.00
Home price/income	4.39	3.24	4.86
35% of income	3,990.00	7,612.50	8,213.10
Property tax (1.5% of home price)	750.00	1,056.00	1,710.00
Insurance (0.5% of home price)	250.00	352.00	570.00
Total for debt service (35% of income − taxes − insurance)	2,990.00	6,204.50	5,933.10
Monthly payment possible	249.17	517.04	494.43
Marginal income tax bracket (percent)	20	33	35
Total income tax after deductions			
As percent of gross income	5	10	10
In dollars per year	570.00	2,175.00	2,346.60
Mortgage multiplier (times monthly payment) at 13% interest, 25 years	89.63	89.63	89.63
Mortgage amount supportable	22,331.80	46,340.36	44,313.32
Downpayment required (home price − mortgage)	27,668.20	24,059.64	69,686.68
As percent of home price	55.34	34.18	61.13
Monthly rent while saving downpayment	250.00	310.00	450.00
Savings to accumulate downpayment			
Paying rent (annual)	990.00	3,892.50	2,813.10
Paying rent (monthly)	82.50	324.38	234.43
Living rent-free (annual)	3,990.00	7,612.50	8,213.10
Living rent-free (monthly)	332.50	634.38	684.43

Addendum
Years required to accumulate downpayment via monthly savings deposits in account with 10% interest gross (but taxable at marginal rate)

If home prices, incomes, and rents do not rise annually			
Paying rent	14.66	5.16	14.74
Living rent-free	5.50	2.86	6.74
If home prices, incomes, and rents rise 5% a year			
Paying rent	20.68	5.98	21.59
Living rent-free	6.52	3.24	8.35

Source: Author's calculations.

Table 9-2. *Effectiveness of Different Subsidies for Three First-Time Homebuyers*

Number of years needed to save required downpayment

Policy	If home prices, incomes, and rents do not rise			If home prices, incomes, and rents rise 5 percent a year		
	A1	B1	C1	A2	B2	C2
No public assistance[a]						
If paying rent	14.66	5.16	14.74	20.68	5.98	21.59
If living rent-free	5.50	2.86	6.74	6.52	3.24	8.35
Tax-free savings account[b]						
If paying rent	13.32	4.79	12.44	17.75	5.56	16.50
If living rent-free	5.25	2.73	6.13	6.23	2.99	7.35
Tax credit for amounts saved[c]						
If paying rent	11.03	3.50	9.67	14.59	3.92	12.65
If living rent-free	4.93	2.26	5.47	5.72	2.50	6.53
Direct downpayment assistance grant[d]						
If paying rent	14.03	4.79	14.47	20.44	5.69	21.49
If living rent-free	5.17	2.63	6.58	6.28	2.93	7.98
Tax-exempt mortgage revenue bond[e]						
If paying rent	12.88	3.12	13.23	17.63	3.40	18.67
If living rent-free	4.61	1.61	5.89	5.39	1.73	6.98
Tax credit substituted for mortgage deductibility[f]						
If paying rent	13.25	1.87	12.25	18.41	2.10	16.73
If living rent-free	4.79	1.00	5.30	5.58	1.08	6.35

Source: Author's calculations. Positions of homes and buyers A1–C2 are as defined for positions A–C in table 8-1.

a. Original situation; monthly deposits in 10 percent savings account (taxable).

b. Ends tax on housing savings account interest.

c. One hundred percent tax credit reduces year's income taxes by total amount saved that year up to maximum of initial total liability.

d. Provides one-time, tax-free grant of $2,000 to reduce downpayment required.

e. Reduces mortgage interest rate from 13 percent to 10 percent; also allows mortgage coverage over 75 percent.

f. Replaces 50 percent of mortgage interest deduction with tax credit; credit amount subtracted from remaining mortgage interest deduction. These figures assume repeated application of tax credit to remaining tax until total eligible tax credit is exhausted.

—a tax credit substituted for 50 percent of mortgage interest deductibility.

The results of these subsidies for the low-income, first-time home-buyer described above are summarized in column A2 of table 9-2. It shows the effects of each subsidy on the time this household needs to save a downpayment large enough to enable it to purchase and carry a home costing $50,000. Column A2 assumes a 5 percent annual rise in home prices, household incomes, and rents during the savings period; column A1 shows the same effects under no annual increases in these variables.

Each effect is shown for two cases in which the household devotes 35 percent of its income to housing. In one case, it rents its own quarters and saves the rest of the 35 percent; in the other case, it lives rent-free and saves the entire 35 percent. The second case can be considered a proxy for receiving direct financial contributions to the downpayment from relatives. The first double row of time periods shows how long such accumulation would take without any public aid. Each other double row depicts how long such accumulation would take if the household benefited from the indicated subsidy. Each subsidy is considered separately; hence interest from the downpayment account is taxed at the applicable marginal rate except under the first subsidy.

The effects of a subsidy are enormously affected by whether each household must rent or can live rent-free while trying to save the downpayment. Thus, if the household at the top of the lowest quartile of the income distribution must rent, none of the subsidies analyzed would enable it to afford the existing single-family home at the top of the lowest quartile of the price distribution if home prices, incomes, and rents rise 5 percent a year. But if the household can live rent-free, three of these subsidies would make that home affordable within six years or less.

The most effective subsidy shown is a 100 percent tax credit for amounts put into a downpayment savings account. This subsidy would reduce the time for saving the required downpayment by 29 percent (6.09 years) if the household were renting, or by 12 percent if it were living rent-free. But even with such a subsidy, this household would take 14.59 years to save enough to buy a $50,000 home if it were renting, or 5.72 years if it were living rent-free. Postponing homeownership for 5.72 years is not an excessive hardship. But postponing it for 14.59 years clearly means that the household cannot afford this home. Yet this result could be avoided only by expanding the subsidies used to much greater size than analyzed here, as long as interest rates are anywhere near as high as they were in 1983.

Even if home prices, incomes, and rents did not rise at all after 1983, this household's housing affordability problem would not be much smaller. Then it would need 14.66 years to save a sufficient downpayment with no assistance if it rented, or 5.50 years if it lived rent-free. The most effective subsidy—a 100 percent tax credit for deposits in a downpayment savings account—would cut this period by 25 percent to 11.03 years if the household rented, or from 5.50 years to 4.93 years if it lived rent-free. For renting households, a waiting period of 11.03 years is still a severe hardship. Moreover, it is not likely that home prices, incomes, and rents will remain stable, so this result is probably overly optimistic.

Subsidizing Other First-Time Buyers

How effectively would these subsidies improve affordability for the other households mentioned earlier? They have higher incomes than the first household. In addition, the home that the household with the U.S. median income has been matched with in this analysis has a lower price in relation to household income because the distribution of housing prices is flatter than the distribution of incomes. Thus the 1983 price of the first-quartile home was 4.4 times the 1983 income of the first-quartile household, whereas the median home price was only 3.4 times the median household income. Therefore, the higher is a household's income, the more likely will specific subsidies enable it to buy a housing unit in the "matched" position among existing homes, unless it resides in a high-priced housing market like those in most of California. (The median-priced home sold in California in August 1983 was 4.86 times the median California household income.) This implies that *problems of housing affordability are most acute for lower-income groups*.

The home-buying situations of these other two households are also shown in table 9-1 (columns B and C). The analysis is the same for all three households, except that their marginal income tax rates rise with their incomes, and the rents they pay while accumulating downpayments, if they live apart from their relatives, also rise with their incomes.

The effectiveness of various policies aiding first-time buyers is shown in table 9-2. This table is set up the same way for households B and C as explained earlier for household A.

According to table 9-2, the 1983 median-income household (household B) would not need any public subsidy to afford buying the median-priced home within a reasonable period after starting to save for the required downpayment. This household would have to devote 35 percent of its income to rent and savings for just under 6 years to accumulate the downpayment required if no outside financial aid is received. It would have to save for only 3.24 years if it could live rent-free with relatives. Both these estimates assume that home prices, incomes, and rents would be rising at 5 percent a year; shorter periods would be required if these variables rose more slowly.

These savings periods are not serious barriers to homeownership; millions of American households have saved much longer to buy their first homes. *Hence the median-income household does not need public assistance to buy the median-priced, existing single-family home within a reasonable period, even if that household is a first-time buyer.*

Moreover, first-time buyers typically have incomes well above the national household median. This can be seen in figure 9-1, which charts the percentages of three different sets of households in four income groups on the basis of 1979 data gathered in surveys by the U.S. League of Savings Associations. The household sets are all first-time homebuyers, all homebuyers who have purchased homes before, and all households. Clearly, most first-time buyers have even less need for public subsidies than does the median-income household.

All the subsidies analyzed here at least slightly improve household B's ability to attain homeownership. Three reduce duration of the downpayment accumulation process by more than one-third: a tax credit substituted for 50 percent of mortgage deductibility, a tax-exempt mortgage revenue bond that cuts the interest rate from 13 percent to 10 percent, and a 100 percent tax credit for deposits in a downpayment savings account. The period for saving the downpayment, however, is relatively short for this household even without

Figure 9-1. *Income Distribution among Homebuyers and All Households, 1979*

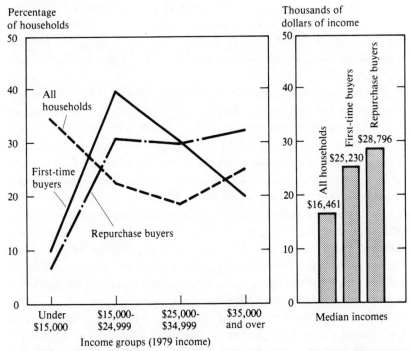

Source: U.S. League of Savings Associations, *Homeownership: Coping with Inflation* (Chicago: USLSA, 1980), pp. 15-21.

subsidies. Hence none of these aids reduces the time needed by more than 3.9 years.

The other two households face much longer savings periods before they can afford the housing units to which they have been "matched" in this analysis. The situation of the low-income household without public assistance was analyzed earlier. The third household analyzed here (household C) illustrates the severity of housing affordability problems in California. The median housing price there is about 60 percent higher than the U.S. median, whereas the median income is only about 8 percent higher. Without public aid, the median-income household in California would have to save for 21.59 years to buy the median-priced home there if it paid rent, or 8.35 years even if it lived rent-free. The California median-income household is not greatly aided by four of the five subsidies analyzed here. Its biggest benefit comes from a 100 percent tax credit on savings, which reduces household C's savings time by 41 percent if it rents, or 22 percent if it lives rent-free. Yet the household would still have to save for 12.7 years in the first case, and for 6.5 years in the second. In neither case can it afford to buy the median-priced California home by the definitions of affordability set forth earlier.

The plight of this household shows how difficult it is to design any one remedy for problems of housing affordability that is well-suited to market conditions across the nation. States with unusually severe affordability problems should probably develop their own remedies if they want to ameliorate those problems. Such initiatives are especially appropriate if affordability problems have been greatly aggravated by local regulatory behavior. In California stringent local and state government restrictions on building new homes are one of the principal causes of higher housing prices.[6] Because Californians adopted these restrictions voluntarily, they presumably did so for their own benefit. Hence much of the cost of any public policies to aid first-time buyers there should be borne by California residents, not by federal taxpayers in general.

Moreover, as pointed out earlier, past first-time homebuyers have had incomes much higher than average. Hence most of today's potential first-time buyers are probably at least as well off as the median-income household analyzed here (household B). But that household did not really need any subsidies to purchase the median-priced existing single-family home. Therefore most potential first-time buyers do not need subsidies to buy appropriate existing homes, even under recent adverse home-buying conditions.[7]

Thus the case for adopting nationwide federal subsidies to aid first-time homebuyers is extremely weak. If such subsidies were strictly confined to first-time buyers with low incomes, they might

6. Other causes are also important. They include strong demand for housing because of heavy in-migration from abroad and from the rest of the United States and national monetary and fiscal policies. Hence California's severe affordability problems are not solely due to decisions made by current California residents.

7. When mortgage interest rates rise well above the 13 percent used in this analysis, problems of housing affordability become much more severe. Such an increase in rates happened intermittently in 1980–82, and could happen again for short periods, but such super-high rates are not likely to persist for long.

at least seem equitable. But most first-time homebuyers in the past have not had low incomes. Moreover, subsidies enabling low-income households to buy homes would be very large per household because they need so much help. Finally, if the federal government is going to subsidize housing for a selected group of households, millions of very poor renters need such aid far more than do any households able to consider buying their first homes.

Why the Plight of First-Time Buyers Receives Public Attention

If the preceding analysis is correct, why is there such an outcry about how difficult it is for first-time buyers to purchase homes? For one thing, it is certainly *more difficult* for first-time buyers to purchase homes today than it was during 1950–75. Both young people and their parents are therefore struck by the apparently worsened position of the former.

Moreover, in a few regions such as California and Hawaii, where home prices are much higher than the national average, first-time buyers are genuinely strapped. California contains about 10 percent of the nation's population but a higher fraction of its opinion leaders, so conditions there tend to be perceived as more widespread than they really are. In addition, many first-time buyers want to live in or near the high-priced neighborhoods where they grew up, even though they cannot afford the housing there. These high-standard buyers generally come from upper-income or upper-middle-income households whose members wield disproportionate weight in forming national views on housing. They consider large portions of the lower-priced housing inventory as "inappropriate" or "inconvenient." This assessment is especially likely if the lower-priced areas are older, mainly occupied by minorities, or distant from high-income neighborhoods.

This situation is made worse because many lower-priced new housing subdivisions are much farther from downtown areas today than in the past. Many first-time buyers can afford new homes only in fringe areas such as San Bernardino, California, or South Elgin, Illinois. They live much farther away from main activity centers than their parents did at similar life-cycle stages, even though many activities have decentralized to the suburbs. Moreover, prevailing housing quality standards have enormously improved during the past thirty years. Consequently, what many first-time buyers today consider "minimally acceptable dwellings" are much larger, better-built, and more fully equipped than the homes their parents purchased at comparable ages.

Finally, the home-building industry has ardently campaigned on behalf of first-time buyers to stimulate new housing demand. Faced by a home-building depression in 1980–82, the industry looked for any plausible justification for federal subsidies to increase demands slashed by high interest rates. Yet the federal government was cutting its spending on many domestic programs for the poor, so advocating more subsidies to homeownership on top of existing tax benefits seemed inequitable. Helping first-time buyers attain the politically sacred goal of homeownership appeared much more defensible. In addition, it appealed to middle-class legislators whose own children were having difficulty buying homes near where they grew up.

Nevertheless, *the above analysis argues against providing any sizable public subsidies to first-time homebuyers unless such subsidies go only to households with low incomes.* Even then, such subsidies can be justified only if federal monetary and fiscal policies keep the general interest rate structure much higher than in the past for long periods.

Using Mortgage Forms with Low Initial Payments

Payments that are smaller than traditional on a mortgage of given size during its first few years would ease affordability in two ways. If lenders compared only first-year payments with the borrowers' incomes in judging loan eligibility, borrowers with incomes of a given size could qualify for larger loans. This practice would reduce required downpayments and shorten the time it takes borrowers to save them. Because most borrowers' incomes will rise over time, future increases in mortgage payments would not necessarily raise the percentage of borrowers' incomes absorbed by such payments. So use of graduated-payment mortgages that have this feature is one way to manage the affordability problem.

The amount by which initial monthly payments can be reduced is limited by the need to provide lenders with competitive yields. If total monthly payments fall below payments of only interest on the outstanding balance, lenders are temporarily obtaining noncompetitive yields. This situation might be acceptable to them if it did not last long, and if it were later accompanied by payments that were higher than usual. Alternatively, lenders could add such interest deficiencies to principal, thereby extending loan durations.

Another problem is that the unpaid balance on the loan can rise above the market value of the home if much negative amortization has been necessary in the early years. Such a rise increases the risk of default. The problem is one of the main reasons that most lenders do not like such loans and therefore have not used them much.

Some graduated-payment mortgages reduce the first year's total payment by as much as 30 percent below what it would have been under a traditional mortgage. The annual payment then rises each year for five to ten years, leveling off at an amount slightly larger than under a traditional mortgage. How much would such a mortgage reduce the problems of affordability described earlier?

The low-income household shown in table 9-1 (household A) could afford to pay $249.17 per month for a mortgage. If the household were using a graduated-payment scheme with a first-year payment 30 percent below that of a standard mortgage, its payment would have the same principal-carrying power as a standard payment of $355.96. Hence it could carry a mortgage of $31,903, or one 43 percent larger than the standard mortgage its payments would support. I assume that the household's income would rise fast enough so that it could carry the higher future payments without undue difficulty. This larger mortgage would reduce its downpayment requirement from $27,668 to $18,097, or by 36 percent. The time needed to save that downpayment would decrease from 20.68 years to 14.81 years (down 28 percent) if it were paying rent, or from 6.52 years to 4.42 years if it were living rent-free. In the latter case, this period would make the home affordable as defined earlier.

If the median-income household shown in table 9-1 (household B) used a similar mortgage, it could carry a total loan of $66,267, or 94 percent of the price of the home it is buying. Thus, to take advantage of a graduated-payment mortgage *before* purchasing a home, the household would have to borrow more than 75 percent of the home price when it made the purchase. It could then make a smaller downpayment that would take less time to save.

To measure the possible effect of graduated-payment mortgages, I assumed that households using them could borrow up to 95 percent of the home purchase prices concerned. This would allow household B to reduce its first-year downpayment requirement to $4,133. Hence the time required to save the downpayment would be reduced from 5.98 to 1.12 years (down 81 percent) if the household were paying rent, or from 3.24 to 0.57 years if it were living rent-free.

A graduated-payment mortgage would enable the California median-income household (household C) to support a mortgage of $63,368 in the first year. The first-year downpayment requirement would be $50,632, 27 percent below that shown in table 9-1. Using a graduated-payment scheme would reduce the time needed to save the downpayment from 21.59 to 16.47 years (down 24 percent) for a rent-paying household, or from 8.35 to 6.21 years for one living rent-free.

Graduated-payment mortgages, however, are not popular with lenders. Such loans are riskier and offer lower yields than other types, partly because the security underlying them is weakened unless home prices rise rapidly. That has not been happening recently. The compound annual rate of increase in the average price of existing single-family homes sold in the United States was 15.0 percent during 1977–80, but only 4.8 percent during 1980–84.[8] Such loans will therefore probably not be used enough to reduce affordability problems very much.

Building Smaller and Higher-Density Housing Units

One way to make housing more affordable is to reduce the average price of new units. Prices of most new housing components, however, are rising along with or faster than prices in general. Therefore the most practical way to reduce housing prices is to make new units smaller, with fewer amenities, and at higher densities. To what extent would this remedy the affordability problem?

The median size of new single-family units built in the United

8. National Association of Realtors, *Monthly Report: Existing Home Sales*, September 1984, p. 9.

States was 1,385 square feet in 1970, and it rose steadily to 1,645 square feet in 1979. Median size then declined by 6 percent, to 1,550 square feet, in 1981. Yet this size is quite large compared with that of many new single-family homes built right after World War II—or with many current designs. Recent issues of both *Professional Builder* and *Builder* magazines have featured many new designs of both attached and detached single-family homes containing lesss than 1,000 square feet. These units are often priced well below the 1981 median price of $68,900 for a 1,550-square-foot unit.

Increased densities could reduce housing costs still further. Higher density typically decreases costs of land per unit, land development, heating and cooling, and interim financing. Densities can be raised far above the levels of single-family detached homes without requiring more than three-story contruction and without sacrificing aesthetics, as hundreds of projects around the nation have demonstrated.

Smaller units at higher densities could probably reduce housing prices below the median price by about one-half the proportion by which their size fell below the median unit's size. For example, a 1981 unit containing 800 square feet would have been 48.4 percent below the 1981 median size of 1,550 square feet, so its price would have been 24.2 percent below the median price of $68,900—or $52,226. Similarly, a unit containing only 500 square feet would have sold for $45,563.

A mortgage on 75 percent of the price of a 500-square-foot home selling for $45,563 could be carried by a household with an annual income of $15,251 if it spent 30 percent of its income on mortgage payments.[9] In 1981 about 60 percent of all households had higher incomes than that; hence they could have afforded at least such a home.[10] In contrast, only about 48 percent of all households could have similarly afforded the median-priced new home built in 1981.

---

9. This assumes a 13 percent, twenty-five year mortgage. The household would also have to pay property taxes equal to 1.5 percent of the home's price, and insurance equal to 0.5 percent of that price. So its total housing cost payments (for PITI) would equal 36 percent of its income. Thus, assuming that it spends 30 percent of its income for mortgage payments alone is almost equivalent to assuming that it spends 35 percent of its income for PITI—the basis for the earlier analysis of households A, B, and C.

10. Data on income distribution are from *Statistical Abstract, 1982–83*, p. 430.

If the low-income household (household A) were able to buy a housing unit just one-half the size of the $50,000 unit shown in table 9-1, the initial price of that smaller unit might have been one-fourth lower, or $37,500. Household A would need a first-year downpayment of only 55 percent of the one it needed to buy a $50,000 home. It could save the smaller required amount in 11.60 versus 20.68 years (down 44 percent) if it rented its own dwelling, or in 3.32 versus 6.52 years if it lived rent-free. These calculations assume 5 percent annual increases in home prices, household incomes, and rents during the savings period. Thus the maximum potential saving from building much smaller, higher-density units would greatly reduce the affordability problem faced by low-income households. Even so, that problem would remain formidable.

The relative effect of cutting housing prices by 25 percent would be even greater for the median-income household (household B).[11] The time required for it to save its downpayment would fall from 5.98 to 0.99 years (down 83 percent) if it paid rent, or from 3.24 to 0.5 years if it lived rent-free.

For the California median-income household (household C), a price decline of 25 percent would reduce the time it needed to save its downpayment from 21.59 to 12.44 years (down 42 percent) if it rented, or from 8.35 to 4.52 years if it lived rent-free. Thus the lower prices possible through smaller sizes and higher density would help median-income, first-time buyers much more in California than in most other regions.

Difficulties of Reducing Size and Raising Density of New Housing

These calculations show that lowering unit sizes and raising densities could greatly improve housing affordability for most first-time buyers. Yet median housing size declined only slightly since the affordability problem became acute in 1980. Why?

One reason is strong homebuyer preference for detached single-family housing, as clearly revealed by repeated surveys of nearly all

11. Because the home price would be lower, both property taxes and insurance payments would also be lower, leaving a larger residual from 35 percent of the household's income to support mortgage payments. Hence the household could support a larger mortgage than when buying a home costing $70,400.

ages and income groups.[12] Acceptable single-family detached units can be made much smaller than 1,500 square feet, but they cannot be made as small or as low-priced as attached units, including those in multifamily structures. But many households who *prefer* single-family detached units will nevertheless *actually buy* other types of housing if that is all they can afford.

The main obstacle is the fear of existing homeowners that permitting smaller units near them will reduce the market values of their homes. This fear frequently combines with the desire to exclude households of lower socioeconomic status from the neighborhood and to avoid the congestion and traffic that are produced by higher-density settlements. The resultant hostility to smaller or higher-density housing is most prevalent in suburban communities with a high proportion of homeowners. Elected officials there are quite sensitive to their constituents' views, so they often adopt zoning ordinances, building codes, and subdivision rules that essentially ban new small or high-density units. Such stringent rules are the most important cause of high housing prices in many areas.

Several factors make changing this situation difficult. For many homeowners, the financial equity in their homes is their single most important asset, vital to their retirement years. Hence they fear any policies that might cause their homes either to lose value or just to appreciate more slowly.

In many homeowner-dominated communities, few residents have anything to gain from permitting new smaller, higher-density housing. The only direct beneficiaries would be homebuilders, owners of parcels on which such housing would be built, and the potential residents. Such landowners form only a small part of the local populace, and the potential residents do not yet either live or vote within these communities. Hence it is difficult to create local political support for low-priced housing within individual suburbs, no matter how critical the need for it in the metropolitan area as a whole. This is a crucial social drawback of dividing each metropolitan area into so many small, separate political jurisdictions.

Unfortunately, little persuasive evidence has been compiled that

12. See *Professional Builder*, November 1981, p. 132. Fewer than half the single-person households interviewed in another survey, however, listed such homes as their first choice. See Urban Land Institute, *Land Use Digest*, vol. 16 (October 15, 1983), p. 1.

shows that lower-priced housing can be built without hurting nearby home values. Such construction has occurred in relatively few places, so compiling *any* evidence on its influences is difficult. In addition, it is difficult to change local land-use policies through pressures from higher levels of government. Only at state or federal levels do elected officials have jurisdictions broad enough to encompass both large numbers of potential first-time buyers and many homeowner-dominated communities. But these officials have little political leverage against local governments. They also have little desire to expend their limited political capital in challenging local land-use controls.

Such controls are particularly sacred to conservatives. In many housing markets, however, local land-use controls directly conflict with another basic conservative principle: relying on relatively free markets to allocate resources. The main political goal of many suburban governments is to block the operation of free markets so as to prevent entry of any lower-cost, higher-density housing. Faced with this conflict between two of its central principles, the Reagan administration has almost always endorsed local control. The Reagan administration has verbally espoused reducing local obstacles to lower-cost housing, but it has assiduously avoided seeking forceful sanctions against local governments that would create real pressure on them to decrease these obstacles. An example of such a sanction would be denial of federal Community Development Block Grant funds to any cities that did not zone certain minimal percentages of their residential land for smaller, high-density housing.

Effective sanctions on land use have never been imposed on local governments by any federal administration.[13] One reason is the immense variability of local housing-related conditions across the nation. This diversity makes it almost impossible to define a uniform set of land-use standards appropriate in all communities. Hence national or state governments cannot force local communities to

---

13. The federal government has successfully influenced local governments to change the *forms* of their land-use controls, especially by adopting zoning regulations. This was done by offering planning funds to communities that drafted such regulations and by withholding some federal aid from those that did not. But no such success has accompanied any past federal efforts to influence the *substance* of land-use decisions in ways opposed by local voters.

accept small, high-density housing by imposing uniform rules everywhere, as they have for civil rights or even highway and sewage-system construction standards.

Prospects for Smaller Size and Greater Density of New Housing

Under these conditions, local communities will continue to resist creation of small, higher-density housing within their boundaries until they become convinced that it will benefit them. Only a concerted effort to persuade them by homebuilders, realtors, developers, real estate lenders, and groups of moderate-income households has any chance of changing their minds. Even then, the odds are favorable that most suburban communities will not lower current barriers to such housing.

One argument useful in that effort is that both the children and the parents of many people now living in high-priced communities cannot afford to remain there unless lower-cost housing units are permitted. Even present residents may have to leave when their life-cycle positions make them want to move from large, expensive homes into smaller ones.

Another argument is that maintaining a strong market for the sale of costly homes requires admitting as many households as possible into lower-cost forms of homeownership. If only a few households can afford to get on the lowest rung of the homeownership ladder, not many will be able to climb to where they can afford the expensive homes of existing residents when those homes are eventually put up for sale. That will reduce the ability of those residents to sell their homes for the high prices they are expecting.

In addition, the economic base of many exclusive communities will be undermined if few moderate-income workers can live near enough to work there. Contemporary society still needs many low-wage workers to operate efficiently. If the only housing such workers can afford lies more than an hour's commuting distance from a community, that community may have difficulty in providing a full range of services for local residents and firms. Such widespread separation between the homes and workplaces of low- and moderate-income households is becoming more prevalent in some parts of the nation, especially in California.

Shifting Infrastructure Costs of New Housing
off Homebuyers

Many communities have recently stopped paying for the infrastructure costs of new housing developments through general obligation bonds. Three factors have caused this change in traditional
practice: the rising cost of building new sewer systems, water systems, roads, highways, schools, and parks; limitations on local government taxes and spending that arose from the "taxpayers' revolt"
of the 1970s; and reduction of former federal aid for such improvements.

As a result, many local governments are now charging each development firm for the infrastructure required by its projects. These
charges comprise high building permit fees, required donations of
land and cash for schools, household charges for education and rec-
reation facilities, special assessments for utilities, development fees,
and other exactions. Developers in turn pass on these costs to the
buyers of homes in each project, thereby adding to housing costs.
The amounts these charges add to housing costs vary greatly from
place to place; no nationwide average data are available. I estimate,
however, that shifting costs of new infrastructure back onto the
entire community could reduce housing prices by as much as 10
percent in areas now bearing such costs directly. What effect would
such a shift have on the affordability problem described earlier?

For the household with a 1983 income of $11,400 (household A),
a drop in home price of 10 percent would cut the time it needed to
accumulate its downpayment (without government aid) from 20.68
years to 17.47 years (down 16 percent) if it were paying rent, or
from 6.52 years to 5.32 years if it were not. Thus household A still
faces a long downpayment-saving period unless it can live rent-free.

For the median-income household (household B), a 10 percent cut
in home price would reduce the time needed to save its downpayment from 5.98 years to 4.19 years (down 30 percent) if it were
renting its own quarters, or from 3.24 years to 2.18 years if it were
living rent-free.

For the California median-income household (household C), a 10
percent fall in home price would reduce the time needed to save its
downpayment from 21.59 years to 17.86 years (down 17 percent) if

it were renting, or from 8.35 years to 6.74 years if it were not. It would still have an acute affordability problem.

Table 9-3 compares the effectiveness of the approaches (other than direct subsidies) discussed above in reducing the time each household would need to save enough to buy the home matched with its position in the income distribution.

Which First-Time Buyers Most Need Public Assistance?

Except in high-priced housing markets, first-time buyers with incomes at least equal to the national median would not have much difficulty saving to buy the median-priced existing single-family home under two conditions. One is that they be willing to spend up to 35 percent of their current incomes in saving for downpayments or in making mortgage payments. The other is that mortgage interest rates not exceed 13 percent. These conditions are likely to prevail most of the time in the mid- and late 1980s. Without any public aids or major changes in existing policies, such households could accumulate downpayments large enough to buy the median-priced home by waiting less than six years, even if they rented housing in the meantime.

Therefore, except in high-priced housing markets, if any public policies are adopted to aid first-time homebuyers, they should focus only on households with incomes below the median, preferably not much higher than the first quartile of the distribution.

In high-priced housing markets such as much of California, first-time buyers with incomes higher than the median also face serious problems of housing affordability. A key cause of those problems, however, consists in restrictive local and state government controls on land-use. Therefore any special remedies designed to aid households with incomes above the median in these areas should be adopted and financed by state or local governments there, not by the federal government.

Effectiveness of Particular Remedies

The specific tactics most effective in improving housing affordability for low-income households are (1) occupancy of smaller and

Table 9-3. *Effectiveness of Other Aid Policies for Three First-Time Homebuyers*
Years needed to save required downpayment

	If home prices, incomes, and rents do not rise			If home prices, incomes, and rents rise 5 percent a year		
Policy	A1	B1	C1	A2	B2	C2
No public assistance[a]						
If paying rent	14.66	5.16	14.74	20.68	5.98	21.59
If living rent-free	5.50	2.86	6.74	6.52	3.24	8.35
Graduated-payment mortgage[b]						
If paying rent	11.23	1.02	11.9	14.81	1.12	16.47
If living rent-free	3.85	0.54	5.17	4.42	0.57	6.21
Smaller and higher-density housing units[c]						
If paying rent	9.11	0.99	9.47	11.6	0.99	12.44
If living rent-free	2.95	0.50	3.93	3.32	0.50	4.52
Shift of infrastructure cost off homebuyers[d]						
If paying rent	12.72	3.61	12.85	17.47	4.19	17.86
If living rent-free	4.53	1.97	5.68	5.32	2.18	6.74

Source: Author's calculations. Positions of homes and buyers A1–C2 are as defined for positions A–C in table 8-1.
   a. Original situation; monthly deposits in 10 percent savings account (taxable).
   b. Increases mortgage supportable from given payment by 43 percent.
   c. Reduces price of housing unit by one-half percentage reduction in physical unit area; in this case size declines 50 percent, price drops 25 percent.
   d. Reduces home prices to buyer by 10 percent.

higher-density housing units, reduced by as much as 50 percent below the size of the median-priced units; (2) use of graduated-payment mortgages; and (3) a 100 percent federal income tax credit for current income deposited in a special savings account for down-payment accumulation. Each of these tactics makes it possible for low-income households to afford ownership of homes at the lowest quartile of the housing price distribution within a reasonable period—but only if they can live rent-free while saving their down-payments or if they receive other, outside aid. Those favorable conditions are not available to many such households. For low-income households that must rent their own quarters, none of these tactics makes such homes affordable within a reasonable period. Combinations of several tactics, however, would be more effective in helping such households.

Most other tactics often recommended as helpful to first-time homebuyers would effectively help those with incomes at or above the median but would be quite ineffective for those with relatively low incomes. These tactics include tax-free savings accounts, use of mortgage revenue bonds free from federal taxes, federal income tax credits substituted for mortgage deductibility, and shifting infrastructure costs from homebuyers to their communities in general. Combining several of these tactics, however, might effectively aid low-income, first-time homebuyers as well.

In sum, the immense variability of conditions in the U.S. housing market makes it difficult to help first-time homebuyers effectively through uniform national policies without causing substantial inequities in many areas. Moreover, in the past most first-time homebuyers have had incomes well above the national median. Their general economic situation is far superior to that of many poorer households, including most renters. It does not seem fair to propose added federal aids to first-time buyers in general while cutting back other forms of aid (such as food stamps) to much poorer households and failing to extend the rental housing voucher program to any sizable fraction of poor renters.[14]

Therefore, *the federal government should not provide any subsidies designed to help first-time buyers purchase homes in addition to the tax benefits for homeownership already embodied in existing laws.* If further housing-oriented assistance is to be furnished by the federal government, poor households in general, and poor renters in particular, deserve it far more than do first-time homebuyers as a group.

Some state governments in areas of high housing costs may wish to aid first-time buyers within their boundaries. The best way to do

---

14. See the President's Housing Commission, *The Report of the President's Housing Commission* (Washington, D.C.: The Commission, 1982), p. xxiii: "Housing payments are not meant to be an entitlement program: the nation cannot afford yet another system of entitlements expanding endlessly out of effective control." Yet on page xxv the report states that "The Commission recommends the continuation of these aids for homeownership [tax benefits from mortgage interest and property tax deductibility]," even though such aids constitute an entitlement program far costlier than housing payments would be if made into such a program. This blatant inconsistency is discussed more fully in Anthony Downs, "The President's Housing Commission and Two Tests of Realistic Recommendations," *Journal of the American Real Estate and Urban Economics Association*, vol. 11 (Summer 1983), pp. 182–91.

so would be to compel local governments to reduce the zoning and other restrictions that have raised housing costs there. Another fruitful state tactic would be restricting the ability of local governments to make developers bear all the infrastructure costs associated with new housing. But direct subsidies to first-time buyers are just as unwise at the state level as at the federal level, and for the same reasons.

10

Imbalances in the Rewards and Costs of Risk Taking

PARTIAL DEREGULATION has removed many barriers that prevented financial institutions from conducting activities outside their areas of specialization. But it has not eliminated the favorable connections of a few types of institutions with the federal government. These connections reduce the potential costs to the managers and owners of such institutions of making risky investments, thereby producing serious imbalances in financial markets. How those imbalances arose, and how they threaten the stability of real estate and other financial markets, are the subjects of this chapter.

Balancing Rewards, Costs, and Underlying Resources in Private Risk Taking

When making investments, managers of each fully private financial institution strive to achieve an appropriate balance among three elements: the rewards from taking risks, the costs of taking those risks, and the institution's underlying ability to absorb possible losses from those risks.

The riskier any potential investment is, the higher is its expected cost, other things being equal, because the probability that such an investment will generate losses is greater than in less risky ventures. To offset these higher expected costs, investors normally demand higher returns from risky investments.

But whether institutional investors will undertake ventures of any particular riskiness also depends on the underlying financial strength of their institutions. The greater an institution's net worth, or equity, is in relation to the size of its possible losses from a proposed venture, the lower is the likelihood that failure of the venture would cause serious financial trouble for the institution, up to and including its dissolution. Hence stronger equity positions—relative to the size of individual investments—increase the ability of institutions to take risks prudently.

What is the appropriate balance among these elements? The answer varies with the nature of each institution's activities, current economic conditions, and expectations about future conditions. Financial markets, however, constantly make judgments about the appropriateness of the balance of risks attained by individual, fully private institutions. These judgments are expressed in the willingness of investors to buy stock in such institutions if the institutions are publicly held, of lenders to make loans to them, and of risk raters to assign desirable ratings to their securities. These outside evaluators use several criteria for judging how prudently each institution handles risks. Examples include debt-equity ratios on balance sheets, rates of profit against both gross revenues and net worth, rates of default or other losses against both gross revenues and net worth, and ratios of equity capital to total assets. In general each individual institution is evaluated by measuring these criteria against the ratings of other institutions like it that are considered to be prudent and successful.

In fully private institutions the rewards and costs of taking risks ultimately fall on the stockholders. The consequences can, however, also affect the managers who make risk-taking decisions. Those managers usually share in any profits achieved and can be fired or can lose compensation as a result of serious losses. It is true that managers of large, publicly held corporations are rarely dismissed by stockholders in the course of normal operations. But their positions are often jeopardized by outside takeovers led by disgruntled stockholders or speculative investors. The public sector, however, is not directly affected by either the rewards or costs of private risk taking, except in the collection of income tax revenues.

In depository institutions risk taking can affect an institution's ability to attract funds—hence, usable resources—as well as the welfare of its managers and stockholders. If an uninsured institution has a reputation for sound and prudent management, it will be able to attract and retain resources from others much more easily, and at lower costs, than if it has a reputation for reckless and imprudent management.

Evaluating the Financial Prudence of Public or Quasi-Public Institutions

It is much harder to evaluate the appropriateness of risk-taking behavior in public or quasi-public financial institutions, such as the Government National Mortgage Association (GNMA, "Ginnie Mae"), the Federal Home Loan Mortgage Association (FHLMC, "Freddie Mac"), and the Federal National Mortgage Association (FNMA, "Fannie Mae").

FNMA has private stockholders and a certain financial net worth on its books. But it also has special connections with the federal government. These include the government's power to appoint some FNMA directors, and FNMA's legal ability to ask the U.S. Treasury to advance up to $2.25 billion if it gets into financial difficulties. Although the Treasury is not *required* to provide any funds to FNMA, most expert observers believe it would not allow FNMA to fail; that belief in itself significantly influences financial market behavior. The Treasury thus ultimately bears some of the risk of whatever investments FNMA makes. Because such risk bearing is usually an attribute of equity ownership, the federal government can reasonably be considered to own an *implicit equity position* in FNMA. Yet no value for the federal government's equity appears on FNMA's balance sheet.

The concept of *implicit equity* could have many different definitions. The federal government does not directly share in the profits of FNMA, as might explicit equity owners, although it taxes FNMA's net income (when that income is not sheltered by loss carry-forwards from previous losses). But such taxation occurs for all businesses, including those with no special ties to the federal government. Thus the power to tax cannot be considered implicit equity unless one defines the government as having such equity in all businesses. That definition deprives the concept of virtually any meaning. When FNMA suffers operating losses, explicit equity owners do not have to pay out cash. The federal government would also not have to pay out cash unless FNMA was in danger of insolvency. Then it would probably advance funds (although it is not legally required to do so). Explicit equity owners would not have to pay out cash even then, although they would suffer the loss of their equity values if FNMA actually became insolvent.

If the federal government is seen as an implicit equity owner in FNMA, then, in theory, the balance sheet of FNMA ought to be adjusted. FNMA's ability to draw on the U.S. Treasury for funds could be treated as an asset, evaluated, and placed on FNMA's balance sheet. It would be offset by an addition to net worth representing the value of the Treasury's implicit equity. This adjustment would raise FNMA's capital base, changing the amount against which its debt-equity ratio and earnings ratio are computed. But how should the Treasury's equity share be evaluated? The method is uncertain, but this approach would reduce current estimates of FNMA's profitability against invested capital and of its debt-equity ratio.

FHLMC is entirely owned by the Federal Home Loan Bank system, and GNMA is a federal agency within the Department of Housing and Urban Development. Both FHLMC and GNMA have nominal equity positions on their books, but those positions are not really *economically based* on either the earning power or the riskiness of their behavior.

For all three institutions, reasonable judgments about the prudence of their risk taking cannot be made on the basis of comparing their financial results with their stated net worth positions. Equally relevant are the unstated but implicit equity positions of those public or quasi-public institutions that actually bear some of the risks of whatever behavior these three agencies undertake.

Effects of Risk-shifting Arrangements on Institutional Behavior

Many arrangements in business (and in other aspects of life) are designed to shift risks from those whose behavior incurs them to someone else. The latter is usually compensated by the initial risk bearer in proportion to the severity of the risk shifted. Such risk shifting is the basis of all insurance activities. It also underlies such other activities as private security forces and commodity and financial futures markets.

By shifting risk away from itself, an investing institution decreases its expected losses from undertaking some activity. Because the expected rewards of that activity presumably remain unchanged, it has achieved a larger net expected gain from undertaking that activity. But it has also incurred the added costs of paying the party to whom it has shifted these risks. If those additional costs are much smaller than the expected losses it has avoided, the institution has a greater net incentive to undertake that activity than it did before. Almost all insurance schemes seek to increase the rewards from undertaking risky activity by shifting expected losses to someone else at a cost lower than the decline in those losses to the initial actor.

Without such insurance the initial actor would often be unwilling to undertake the activity at all. The expected losses from the activity might be larger than the expected rewards. Even if that were not true, the actor's underlying equity position might be so small, compared with those expected losses, that the organization's survival would be placed in too much jeopardy if it undertook the activity and failed.

Many types of risk-shifting arrangements exist in U.S. financial markets today, but three are especially important for this analysis: private insurance, government insurance, and statutory requirements or permission for the federal government to back the liabilities of specific institutions.

In all fully private insurance arrangements (such as private mortgage guarantee insurance), the insured party pays the full expected costs that the insurer incurs in providing the insurance. Those costs of course are always lower than the drop in expected losses to the insured party, or that party would not buy the insurance. But the insuring party in turn does not expose itself to expected losses any larger than the revenues it collects from those it insures, less an allowance for return on capital. Hence no one is exposed to more risk than is prudent, so no incentives for risk taking can be said to be distorted or biased by this arrangement.

A strong argument can be made, however, that the federal deposit insurance used by almost all banks and thrift institutions now results in the insuring agencies' bearing imprudently large risks. Those agencies are the Federal Deposit Insurance Corporation (FDIC) and the Federal Savings and Loan Insurance Corporation (FSLIC). Changes in conditions caused by the revolution in real estate finance have increased the expected losses these agencies now bear to a much larger total size than all the combined premiums they collect from the insured institutions. This effect had created the undesirable likelihood that federal taxpayers may have to pay large costs to help these agencies cover their liabilities. The costs to FSLIC of handling distressed savings and loans from 1982 through 1984 were so large that in 1985 the agency had to raise additional funds through a special assessment against all the associations it insured.

Moreover, federal deposit insurance has notably increased the incentives for managers of banks and thrifts to make risky loans. Those incentives are now much larger than either the incentives that managers faced before the real estate revolution or the incentives that they would face if they had to pay premiums that covered the full costs of the expected losses they have shifted to the federal agencies. Thus, *within* each of these large financial institutions, there is a serious imbalance between the rewards and costs of risk taking faced by the officials responsible for investing. As a result at least some of these managers have been making—and will probably continue to make—large numbers of imprudent investments.

This situation was recognized by an outgoing chairman of the Federal Home Loan Bank Board (FHLBB) in a report he authorized and approved entitled *Agenda for Reform*. Published in 1983, the report stated:

> Under the system in place today, the federal government shares in any losses while gains accrue entirely to those who have interests in depository institutions. A rational course of action in these circumstances is for the firm to engage in activities that may be excessively risky.[1]

The special connections with the U.S. Treasury enjoyed by certain public or quasi-public financial institutions have produced—at least potentially—a similar imbalance in them between the rewards and costs of risky investing. Their managers can gamble on making large

1. Federal Home Loan Bank Board, *Agenda for Reform* (Washington, D.C.: FHLBB, March 1983), p. 16.

gains from taking certain risks without having to pay either the full expected losses associated with those risks or the full costs of insuring against such losses. It is not clear whether these managers have yet actually taken such gambles. But they or their successors could certainly do so in the future under the present rules of the game.

Recent Developments in the Riskiness of Investments Made by Fully Private Institutions

How did these imbalances in financial institutions arise? Perhaps the potential for imbalances has always existed. But such distortions were recently rendered much more likely to occur by partial deregulation, improvements in electronic communications, and changes in federal monetary and fiscal policy that raised interest rates. The managers of banks and thrifts with publicly traded stock have always been under strong competitive pressure to obtain yields as high as possible from their loans and other investments so as to maximize the earnings of their stocks. One way to increase those earnings was to grow larger, since a broader asset base built on any given amount of capital could produce more earnings per share.

Until relatively recently private financial institutions grew mainly by attracting more business from their immediate vicinities. Distant potential depositors were either not aware of these institutions or did not have enough confidence in them to entrust them with their funds. In addition, making loans or other investments involving more distant potential borrowers was not practical because of the detailed knowledge of the borrower's business required for prudent investment. These limitations did not bind some of the nation's largest banks, which have built up worldwide networks of branches over many years. Hence they achieved large shares of their operations and profits through transactions with distant clients. But most of the nation's banks and thrifts still focused on doing business with customers relatively nearby.

This situation was radically changed by a combination of effective worldwide electronic communications and federal deposit insurance readily available even to large depositors. Insurable limits were extended to $100,000 per account in 1980. Specialized deposit brokers appeared who used electronic means to contact potential depositors all over the world and to transfer these funds to client institutions. It therefore became possible to attract large amounts of additional savings deposits within a short time by offering a slight interest rate premium *as long as the depositors were protected by federal insurance.* With such protection, depositors did not worry about how risky the institution's investments were. On the investment side it became possible to place huge amounts of money quickly either by making giant loans to foreign governments (as many banks did) or by purchasing mortgages or mortgage-backed securities (MBSs) on the secondary market (as many thrifts did).

Using these methods, a bank or thrift could quickly grow from modest to enormous size, thereby rapidly expanding its earnings potential. For example, the Financial Corporation of America—a California savings and loan association—shot up in total assets from less than $2 billion in 1980 to over $30 billion in 1984. (This expansion was accelerated by a large merger along the way, one approved by regulatory authorities.) Its basic strategy was to accumulate short-term deposits through brokers and its own staff by using electronic collection and to invest these funds in long-term, fixed-rate mortgages. This strategy would produce huge profits if short-term interest rates fell well below the rates at which the long-term mortgages were being made, but it would mean financial disaster if short-term rates rose close to or above the latter. The managers of this association were willing to gamble on this strategy because (1) they had relatively small personal investments at risk in the form of stockownership; (2) they were not jeopardizing the interests of their depositors, since most risks of loss were shifted to the insuring agency; and (3) the potential gains to both owners and managers if the strategy succeeded were tremendous.

This particular institution was the most extreme practitioner of a strategy that hundreds of other savings and loans were also following, albeit less dramatically. The total assets of all savings and loan associations increased by $64.1 billion in 1983, compared with an annual average of $58.5 billion in the last half of the 1970s and much lower averages in preceding periods. Savings and loans made $135.3 billion in mortgage loans in 1983—23 percent more than in the highest previous year (1978).[2] They then made over $165 billion

2. *Federal Home Loan Bank Board Journal*, vol. 17 (March 1984), p. 50.

in such loans in 1984. These record levels of activity were caused by the revolutionary factors described in chapter 2, but they also reflected a risky management strategy of making as many loans as possible at prevailing, relatively high nominal rates.

Managers hoped that the short-term rates they were paying for their funds would soon fall. Then they would make enormous profits from the rising rate spread between their fixed-rate assets and their liabilities at variable rates. Even though many of those loans were adjustable rate mortgages, or ARMs, limits on the way the rate adjustments worked would not permit the mortgage holders to cover the rising current costs of the funds underlying the ARMs if short-term rates rose quickly. Hence managers were gambling on favorable changes in interest rates, partly because they were able to shift onto the FSLIC most of the risk of losses from unfavorable changes. When short-term rates rose in 1984, the riskiness of this strategy became even more apparent.

Equally risky was the strategy of many large commercial banks concerning loans to foreign governments. They were not gambling on increasing rate spreads because their loans were at floating rates above the costs (also floating) of the funds involved. Rather, the banks were gambling on favorable international economic conditions prevailing almost continuously over the relatively long terms of these loans. Without such constant international prosperity, the chances that some of the economically weak nations borrowing these large amounts might at least partially default were considerable. Most depositors would never have left their funds in banks engaging in such risky behavior if their accounts had not been federally insured.

Moreover, both large-scale depositors in, and the managers of, the largest U.S. banks were gambling on their belief that the Federal Reserve Board and the U.S. government would never let any of them default because of the potentially disastrous consequences for the entire U.S. banking system. This belief was correct, as the behavior of these regulators during the 1984 rescue of the Continental Illinois Bank and Trust Company proved. The Comptroller of the Currency stated unequivocally that the government would not let any of the ten largest U.S. commercial banks fail, even if the government had to absorb all of their losses itself.

Thus managers of institutions that enjoy federal deposit insurance know that they are not bearing even the full insurance costs of shifting potential losses from any risky investments they make to the insuring agencies—hence ultimately to U.S. taxpayers. This knowledge increases the net incentives for managers to make risky investments. They have responded by doing so on a larger scale than at any time since the 1930s. Although judging the overall riskiness of institutional investments is difficult, rates of failure among financial institutions provide some relevant evidence. The number and size of failing institutions, both commercial banks and savings and loan associations, have been at record levels during the past few years. The failures reflect both adverse general conditions, as discussed earlier, and the increased incentives for managers to undertake risky investments. To what extent each of these factors is causally responsible cannot be reliably determined.

Even so, it would almost certainly be wrong to infer that the availability of federal deposit insurance to banks and thrifts was the single most important cause of their recent greater risk taking. A multitude of other factors also contributed, including the continued weakness of both agriculture and the petroleum industry long after the 1982 recession. They also included an unusually clear statement of risk assumption by the federal government (made by the Comptroller of the Currency during the Continental Illinois affair), a huge flood of savings into banks and thrifts caused by deregulation that pressured lending officers to seek more and more investments, and expanded electronic capabilities for both increasing deposits and placing investable funds. The net result was an unprecedented combination of forces providing both motives and opportunities for banks and thrifts to engage in greater risk taking than had previously been considered prudent.

Recent Developments in the Riskiness of Investments Made by Public and Quasi-Public Institutions

The effects of especially favorable connections with the U.S. Treasury on the riskiness of management decisions made by GNMA, FHLMC, and FNMA are harder to detect. GNMA's current behavior involves few risks for the federal government because all the mortgages backing GNMA's pools have previously been insured by the Federal Housing Administration (FHA). Hence FHA, not GNMA, bears all the risk of defaults. Since FHA is neither a depository nor a directly lending institution, the riskiness of its behavior will not be analyzed further here.

FHLMC uses conventional mortgages to back its securities; hence FHA insurance is not involved. FHLMC, however, requires private insurance for mortgages included in its pools and other arrangements. Moreover, since FHLMC does not hold any portfolio of mortgages backed by shorter-term liabilities, it is not exposed to the type of interest rate risk that has proved so dangerous to both FNMA and the entire thrift industry. The default rates on mortgages in FHLMC pools have been well below the average for the mortgage industry because of more stringent underwriting standards. Hence there is no evidence yet that FHLMC has taken advantage of its special risk-shifting connections with the federal government to undertake investments that would be considered imprudent if those connections did not exist.

FNMA has been continuing to buy long-term, fixed-rate mortgages and to add them to its portfolio during the past few years, even though these mortgages are funded with liabilities carrying much shorter maturities. These new portfolio additions are to a great extent replacing older fixed-rate mortgages that are being paid off. Most of those older mortgages, like the new ones being purchased by FNMA, have interest rates above FNMA's current average cost of funds. Such mortgages thus are profitable assets, even when FNMA is losing money overall. In addition, FNMA has been putting many of these new mortgages into pools behind MBSs, which do not add to its interest rate risk. Moreover, it has been buying as many ARMs as it can to reduce such risk. But to the extent that FNMA has added long-term, fixed-rate mortgages to its portfolio, its management has been gambling on favorable movements in interest rates.

This gamble has been encouraged by the management's belief that nominal interest rates were at or near the peaks they would attain during the next decade or so. Hence long-term loans made at these high rates would provide a reasonable basis for high profits against shorter-term liabilities over that future period. Yet if short-term interest rates were to rise significantly—as they did in 1984— this behavior would increase FNMA's likelihood of suffering current operating losses.

Whether this gamble constitutes imprudence encouraged by FNMA's connection with the Treasury, or merely a prudent assessment of market risks, is very difficult to judge objectively. In my opinion it is a prudent gamble because it adds to FNMA's current earning power and reduces potential losses from higher rates, unless rates go extremely high. But there is certainly a *potential* for FNMA's existing or future management to react to that risk-shifting and cost-reducing connection by undertaking excessively risky investments.

This conclusion is borne out by the net loss embodied in FNMA's existing mortgage portfolio if that portfolio were evaluated at current market value. It is true that many other financial institutions would similarly suffer large losses if their portfolios of bonds and other fixed-rate instruments were on their books at current market values instead of at original costs. Moreover, this situation to a great extent is the result of unforeseeable developments not within the control of the managers of these institutions. But in FNMA's case a reasonable argument can be made that freedom from having to pay the full costs of possible defaults encouraged FNMA's past managers to amass a larger portfolio of long-term, fixed-rate loans backed by shorter-term maturities than they would have amassed without such freedom.

How the Imbalance among Financial Institutions Could Affect Competition

These special federal connections create a second imbalance *among* financial institutions by giving competitive advantages to some that would be unfair to others if both were permitted by deregulation to conduct the same activities. For example, because of federal deposit insurance, banks and thrifts can attract funds at net costs to themselves lower than FNMA must pay to sell its securities, or lower than fully private investment bankers and insurance companies must pay to raise capital. If banks and thrifts were permitted to engage in the same activities as these other organizations, the former could offer lower prices than the latter and still make reasonable profits. The resultant handicap would severely restrict the ability of FNMA or fully private investment bankers and insurance companies to remain in business.

A similar problem would arise if FHLMC were converted into a fully private organization. Such a conversion has been urged by those who believe that FHLMC could perform its current functions equally well if it were in the private sector. I believe that is the case. But if the market truly thought FHLMC had lost all its ability to call upon federal government backing, FHLMC would have to pay higher costs to raise money than FNMA if the latter retained its present federal connections. In that case FNMA could underprice FHLMC in providing services, as could thrifts or banks if they engaged in the same activities as FHLMC. Even a price difference of a few basis points would shift an enormous amount of business from one agency to another in this highly price-sensitive market.

Another competitive imbalance caused by uneven connections with the federal government has already had enormous effects in real estate markets in the past few years. Syndicators gain tax benefits as well as income and value appreciation from owning real estate. They therefore can pay higher prices to buy real estate than can pension funds and insurance companies. When syndicators were attracting large inflows of capital in 1983 and 1984, their high bidding raised the prices, and lowered the yields, on income properties in many markets, as noted earlier.

Unrestricted competition in financial markets is thus inconsistent with preserving the advantages certain institutions receive from their special connections with the federal government. If complete deregulation allows every type of financial institution to engage in every type of activity, those that retain special federal connections will have unfair advantages over those that do not. This imbalance will benefit the favored institutions at the expense of the nonfavored ones. It will also benefit customers of those favored institutions at the expense of federal taxpayers in general. These customers will receive services at prices lower than their "true" cost, whereas taxpayers will have to bear any extraordinary losses caused by managers of favored institutions who engage in excessively risky investments.

By early 1985 financial deregulation had not yet permitted completely unrestricted competition. Banks, thrifts, investment bankers, stockbrokerage firms, insurance companies, and most other financial institutions were still prevented from conducting various activities outside their traditional specialties. But strong political pressure existed for these remaining barriers to be abolished or at least reduced drastically.

Those seeking to deregulate commercial banks further did receive a setback because of the near failure of the huge Continental Illinois Bank and Trust Company in 1984. The massive and costly federal efforts to rescue that bank revealed the basic inconsistency mentioned above. Nevertheless, the proponents of nearly complete financial deregulation still urged changing the rules so that everyone could go into everyone else's business.

There was much less political pressure to eliminate or modify the principal connections with the federal government described above. In particular, the possibility of abolishing federal deposit insurance was not given serious consideration by influential congressional or industry leaders. Yet as long as such insurance remained in force, and remained limited to banks and thrifts, it would be impossible to create a truly "level playing field" that allowed fair competition among all types of financial institutions.

Policy Alternatives for Federal Deposit Insurance

How might an appropriate balance between financial deregulation and special federal connections be achieved? Possible answers are summarized below. The first and last alternatives are clearly unacceptable; the remaining three viable options are examined further in the subsections that follow.

—*Extend federal deposit insurance of some kind to every type of financial institution, thereby providing the same advantage to all.* This policy is clearly unacceptable because it would encourage excessively risky behavior by *all* types of financial institutions at the potential cost of U.S. taxpayers. It would eliminate inequality among institutions by making the behavior of all of them equally undesirable. This policy is not considered further.

—*Eliminate federal deposit insurance altogether.* It would presumably be replaced by insurance purchased by depository institutions from fully private insurance companies. The costs of shifting risks away from the depositors would then be fully borne by each individual financial institution, not partially by the U.S taxpayers. This policy is analyzed below.

—*Retain federal deposit insurance as it is now, but strictly limit the activities that insured institutions are allowed to undertake.* Then insured institutions could not use this advantage to compete unfairly with institutions that did not have federal insurance. This would limit or even reverse recent partial financial deregulation of banks and thrifts. Federally insured institutions would not be allowed to undertake activities usually performed by insurance companies, investment bankers, mortgage brokers, stockbrokers, secondary mortgage marketing companies or agencies, and the like. This policy is also discussed below.

—*Retain federal deposit insurance for banks and thrift institutions, but change the way it is administered to make the managers of those institutions much more sensitive to the riskiness of their investing behavior.* This option would require setting insurance premiums for each institution in relation to the riskiness of its behavior and perhaps would require each to have much higher ratios of equity capital to total assets. This policy is also analyzed below.

—*Retain federal deposit insurance exactly as it exists now, without changing either its nature or the way it is administered.* This policy seems unacceptable for the many reasons described earlier. Yet there is a good chance that it will prevail because of the great difficulty of getting any other policy accepted by all the financial institutions and other interests concerned.

Abolishing Federal Deposit Insurance

If present arrangements should be changed, why not get rid of federal deposit insurance altogether? Few other nations have anything like federal deposit insurance protecting their financial systems. Yet they manage without undue disruptions or any general loss of confidence in those systems.

It is true that individual depositors cannot be expected to judge how prudently the managers of each depository institution are behaving. But that vigilance would not be necessary if banks and thrifts used private deposit insurance. Then the private insurers would carefully scrutinize the behavior of each financial institution to set appropriate deposit insurance premiums. Those premiums would vary from institution to institution, depending on the risk-taking behavior of each, unlike current uniform premiums for all institutions of the same size. If managers of any institution were taking excessive risks, they would have to pay much higher premiums than their competitors, and that would soon be widely known. Or perhaps no insurer would accept their business, and they would have to inform their depositors of that fact. This would cause most depositors to withdraw their funds if they could still get fully insured accounts elsewhere. Managers would therefore have to check their risk-taking behavior to be sure they could get insurance coverage. Thus use of private insurance would eliminate present incentives for excessive risk taking made possible by federal deposit insurance. It would also end all exposure of U.S. taxpayers to potential losses. Yet individual depositors would still be protected up to some limited account size, as they are now.

This policy, however, also has some important disadvantages. Private insurance would cost depositors vastly more than federal insurance does now. If necessary, the federal government can levy taxes or print money to cover any losses for which it becomes liable. Private insurers can do neither, so they would have to build up enormous reserves by charging much higher premiums than the FDIC or FSLIC now require. Even then, the federal government should probably retain responsibility for covering the costs of economic catastrophes such as the Great Depression of the 1930s. It is doubtful if any private insurance system could protect consumers from such disasters without charging impractically large premiums. Even if private insurance were designed to cover only noncatastrophic circumstances, its premiums would still be much larger than present federal deposit insurance premiums.

More important, private insurance would be less effective than federal insurance in sustaining the public's confidence in the solvency of financial institutions. That failing would be especially likely during periods of financial strain—precisely when maintaining such confidence is vital. The public might be skeptical that private insurance firms could support all covered deposits in case of a financial emergency. Precisely such skepticism toward a private insurer of state savings and loans in Ohio started a run on their deposits in 1985. The run on savings and loans led the governor of Ohio to close seventy-one thrifts, as described in chapter 11. The state government also forced most of those thrifts to adopt federal deposit insurance to bolster public confidence in them.

This skepticism would be increased if some private insurers began canceling their coverage of banking institutions because they believed a general financial crisis was coming or because they regarded those particular institutions as too risky. Yet private insurers would have to be able to cancel under normal contracts in order to bring market discipline to bear on the financial institutions they were insuring.

Increasing public confidence in the banking system beyond what private firms could do themselves was the main reason that federal deposit insurance was created in the 1930s, and it remains a vital function. Financial strains that might shake depositor confidence have certainly not become extinct. Thrift institutions went through one during 1980–82. Large commercial banks with major international loans experienced another in 1983. So there is still an important role for federal deposit insurance.

Using federal insurance to maintain public confidence in our banking and monetary systems should not be viewed as merely providing an unnecessary subsidy to private financial institutions. Rather, it is vital to the nation's economic and social welfare. If people start losing their trust in even just a few large banks or thrifts, their fears are likely to become contagious and spread to the entire system. This would be particularly probable if they had any doubts about the private insurance underlying the whole system. Such a financial panic would paralyze the economy and might undermine support for the larger political system. Public loss of confidence in any sizable part of the banking and monetary systems would thus cause enormously adverse external effects.

Free markets are often unable to adjust effectively to external effects because those effects do not act solely or even primarily through market prices. Hence non-market-oriented policies, usually operated by a government, are often needed to deal with such "externalities." In this case, leaving all deposit insurance to purely market forces might unduly expose the nation to huge negative external effects as well as impose much higher insurance costs on all depositors.

Stringently Regulating Federally Insured Institutions

Another way to restrain federally insured institutions from unduly risky behavior would be to impose more stringent federal regulations on their investments. For example, to reduce interest rate risks, thrift institutions could be required to make only five-year, variable rate loans. To reduce default risks, thrifts could be forbidden to invest more than a small percentage of their assets in real estate equities or any other nonmortgage instruments, or could be limited to making mortgages that would cover not more than 70 percent of appraised property value.

In addition, both banks and thrifts could be prohibited from expanding into activities formerly restricted to entirely different institutions. Thus they would not be allowed to sell insurance, act as stockbrokers, carry out investment banking, issue MBSs, and so forth. They would not be prevented from doing so because these activities are terribly risky in themselves; rather, limiting competition in each such field would reduce the risks of operating in that field for those permitted to do so. In addition, possible conflicts of interest among these activities would be avoided. Furthermore, the risks of operating in any specialized field are typically higher for newcomers to that field, and such heightened risk would be avoided.

This policy would reverse the strategy of deregulating financial institutions begun during the past decade. It would substitute the judgments of federal regulators concerning prudent risks for the judgments of freely operating markets. The FHLBB rejected this approach because of its conviction that "unless there is a clear and compelling reason to believe that the market cannot operate effectively, market-oriented pricing and management are inherently superior to government regulation."[3] I agree with that assumption. Therefore, I believe that this policy is inferior to arrangements that are more market oriented.

Making Federal Deposit Insurance More Risk-Sensitive

To be effective, however, such arrangements must produce a much more even balance between market forces on both sides of depository institutions' balance sheets than now exists. As of early 1985, deposits themselves were almost completely insured by the federal government, and investments were only partially regulated. But if further deregulation leaves investing almost entirely to market forces, while deposits remain fully insured, managers of depository

3. FHLBB, *Agenda*, p. 22.

institutions will undertake even riskier investments than at present. Hence much stronger market forces must be introduced on the deposit side if deregulation is to proceed farther on the investment side or even to remain at its present level without serious adverse consequences.

But is a more market-oriented approach to federal deposit insurance possible? If so, what would it involve? The FHLBB set forth several possible components of such an approach, including the following recommendations.

—*Reduce insurance coverage of depositors to make them more sensitive to the riskiness of institutions in which they place their funds.* This could be done by eliminating de facto coverage of uninsured depositors, requiring coinsurance (by repaying only a share of possible losses), or reducing the maximum amount insured per account. The last tactic might seem ineffective because of the ability of brokers to spread large amounts of funds among many small accounts, each within whatever insurance limits were set by the regulators. But if the maximum insured amount were reduced to $50,000 per account or even lower, and if no person were allowed to have or participate in having more than one account per institution, the transaction costs of spreading large amounts of money among many institutions might become formidable.

—*Make brokered deposits in banks and savings and loans ineligible for federal deposit insurance.* This policy was proposed by FSLIC in early 1984. It would make it more difficult for thrift institutions to attract large amounts of savings through brokers from depositors totally unacquainted with the institutions in which they were depositing funds.

—*Improve the capital adequacy of insured institutions.* Because the capital of insured institutions stands between possible losses and collecting on federal deposit insurance, the larger that capital is, then the less is the risk for the federal insurance agency, other things being equal. Moreover, the greater is the capital that investors in these institutions stand to lose, the more cautious they are likely to be in making investments. Capital adequacy could be improved by making it easier for mutual thrift institutions to convert to stock institutions. The FHLBB recently changed some regulations for that purpose. Capital adequacy could also be improved by requiring higher reserves for all types of institutions.

—*Improve the quality and extent of information available to depositors and to FSLIC about the economic status and riskiness of each insured institution.* The more depositors know, the more easily they can make judgments about the security of different institutions. The more FSLIC knows, the more easily it can anticipate financial difficulties and formulate effective tactics in advance for coping with them.

—*Vary deposit insurance premiums in relation to the degree of risk exhibited by each insured institution.* This variation would require measuring risk in some objective manner. Of the three basic types of risk applicable to financial institutions, two—interest rate risk and default risk—can probably be measured in reasonably practical ways. The third—management risk—cannot. Interest rate risk could be measured by comparing the duration and maturities of each institution's liabilities with those of its assets.[4] Default risk is the type traditionally evaluated by financial examiners; hence measurements of it could be devised using the techniques examiners have used in the past, such as financial ratios. Using capital adequacy as a factor to influence insurance premiums would help reflect both these risks. Neither type could be measured precisely or unequivocally. Yet varying deposit insurance premiums with riskiness in even a rough way would create at least some incentive for managers to restrain the tendency to undertake excessively risky ventures that is encouraged by current flat-rate premiums. Classifying individual institutions as "high-risk" and publicizing that classification would also alert depositors and investors to be wary of those institutions. Nevertheless, there is considerable skepticism in this industry about regulators' ability to assess accurately the riskiness of different financial institutions, or to charge differential premiums in a manner free from political influence.[5]

Just how large should combined reserves and capital be as a per-

4. The concept of *duration* is discussed at length in the FHLBB report. Ibid., pp. 91–95.

5. The FHLBB report also describes several tactics that would make the Federal Savings and Loan Insurance Corporation itself more sensitive to the risks it faces in the market. These include increasing insurance premium rates, whether they are flat-rate or variable; hedging in futures markets; and changing the nature of FSLIC asset holdings. These tactics are not included, however, as part of the market-oriented strategy in the text because they do not change the sensitivity to risk of the insured institutions themselves. Ibid., p. 19.

centage of total assets? In December 1983 all savings and loan associations combined had total assets of $771.7 billion and a total net worth of $30.8 billion, or 4.0 percent of assets.[6] A large but unmeasured part of these assets, however, consisted of good will rather than marketable securities or real estate. How that unmarketable portion would affect the balance is not clear. On the same day, all commercial banking institutions combined had total assets of $2,113.1 billion and a total net worth of $154.1 billion, or 7.3 percent of assets.[7] *It seems reasonable to expect both types of institutions—especially thrifts—to raise their total capital gradually to equal between 6 percent and 9 percent of their total assets.* (Setting the exact capital target to be level requires an in-depth analysis beyond the scope of this study; hence I have used a rather wide range for purposes of illustration.) Each thrift should be required to move toward this target along some definite schedule based on its initial reserve position and its earning capacity. Continued eligibility for federal deposit insurance, the premiums charged for that insurance, or both should be contingent on the institution's meeting that schedule. But I think that much more extensive analysis of the optimal target and of the appropriate processes for reaching it should be undertaken than is possible in this book before any final decisions about it can be made.

The Future of Federal Deposit Insurance

Changing the administration of federal deposit insurance so as to make managers of insured institutions more sensitive to the costs of taking risks appears to be the policy most congruent with a fundamental strategy of deregulating the U.S. economy both as much and as soon as feasible. I believe that deregulation is a desirable long-run strategy if it can be pursued effectively without creating unfortunate side effects—such as excessive risk taking by federally insured financial institutions. Therefore I agree with the FHLBB's recommendation in *Agenda for Reform* that such a policy should be tried in the

6. *Federal Home Loan Bank Board Journal*, vol. 17 (March 1984), p. 50.
7. Board of Governors of the Federal Reserve System, *Federal Reserve Bulletin*, vol. 70 (August 1984), p. A17.

near future. It should include increasing the capital requirements for all federally insured institutions.

Unfortunately, no one can determine in advance whether this policy will be effective enough to prevent the potential abuses of the existing system described earlier. Therefore, even though this policy should be the first one tried, federal regulators should also suspend further deregulation of banks and thrifts for a long enough time to observe whether such abuses are actually stopped. They should also try to limit further expansion of nonbanking firms (such as Sears, Roebuck and Merrill Lynch) into operating banks and thrifts while this observation period is under way. If these policies succeed in limiting excessive risk taking, then further deregulation of financial activities could be cautiously resumed. If such potential abuses are not prevented, however, then further deregulation should be halted, and consideration should be given to going back to more intensive regulation.

Other Obstacles to a Proper Balance in Risk Taking

Another important obstacle to achieving a proper balance in risk taking *among* financial institutions is the existence of special federal connections other than federal deposit insurance. Among these are the relations of key institutions in the secondary mortgage market—GNMA, FNMA, FHLMC, and the Farmers' Home Administration—to the U.S. Treasury. These obstacles will be analyzed in chapters 12 and 13, which examine secondary mortgage markets.

Unfortunately, it is not possible to analyze all the other special connections of financial institutions to the federal government in a book concentrating on real estate. Nor is it possible to deal with all the complex questions raised by financial deregulation of banks and other institutions. Hence fully resolving all the issues relevant to achieving a proper balance in risk taking among all financial institutions is beyond the scope of this study. Nevertheless, I have included herein those recommendations concerning institutions oriented toward real estate that I believe are desirable on the basis of all the considerations set forth.

The Possibility of No Satisfactory Balance

It is quite possible that no satisfactory balance between the costs and rewards of risk taking in U.S. financial institutions can be achieved through public policy, or perhaps at all. Political and regulatory authorities might decide that federal deposit insurance cannot be abolished without jeopardizing the long-run stability of the U.S. financial system. Yet such insurance should clearly not be extended to institutions other than banks and thrifts. Its continuance would therefore leave these institutions with a competitive advantage over all other financial institutions in raising capital.

I have recommended changing the way in which such insurance is administered to make managers of insured institutions more sensitive to the costs of making risky investments. But the suggested means of doing that may not have effects strong enough to create a true balance between the rewards and costs of risky investment in the eyes of the managers and owners of all banks and thrifts. The managers and owners of at least some banks and thrifts make quite risky investments because they believe that the costs of doing so have been shifted in the most part to federal agencies. If this occurs among even a relatively small fraction of all such institutions, it could cause substantial costs that would have to be borne by federal taxpayers and could upset the efficient operation of the entire financial system.

In that case it might be necessary to "reregulate" banks and thrifts to a degree that does not initially appear desirable at all. A return to such intensive regulation would represent a second-best or even third-best alternative to complete financial deregulation, which appears much more appealing in the abstract. But such reregulation might nevertheless be the most effective arrangement actually achievable, given the situation described in this and other chapters. That conclusion, however, should certainly not be accepted as valid until after changes in the way federal deposit insurance is administered, along the lines described above, have been tried.

11

Turmoil among Financial Institutions

THE REVOLUTION in real estate finance upset long-established ways of functioning among all financial institutions. The resulting disarray created both uncertainty and confusion in many real estate financial markets.

Turmoil Rampant in the Mid-1980s

In the early and mid-1980s more existing banks and thrifts suffered bankruptcy, or were perilously threatened by it, than at any time since the Great Depression of the 1930s. One of the nation's ten largest banks—the Continental Illinois Bank and Trust Company of Chicago—had to be rescued from imminent failure in the spring of 1984 through massive intervention by federal regulators. Most of the nine other largest banks had outstanding loans to foreign countries in amounts much larger than the banks' entire net worths. Yet many of these debtor countries were struggling to meet accelerating interest costs. An indication of the turbulence sweeping through the nation's financial institutions was that the cover story in *Business Week* for October 29, 1984, was entitled "Behind the Banking Turmoil?"[1]

The entire thrift industry was still precariously close to insolvency in early 1985. It could easily enter that condition if interest rates

1. *Business Week*, October 29, 1984, pp. 100–10.

were to rise close to their levels of 1981–82. Some of the industry's problems led to a minor financial panic in Ohio in March 1985. A small government securities firm in Florida became insolvent, jeopardizing major investments in it by Home State Savings Bank, a medium-sized Cincinnati thrift. That institution was insured by the privately owned but state-regulated Ohio Deposit Guarantee Fund—not by the Federal Savings and Loan Insurance Corporation (FSLIC). When depositors rushed to withdraw their funds from the affected thrift, it appeared that *all* the Ohio Deposit Guarantee Fund's resources would be absorbed in propping up this one institution. Hence worried depositors in other state-insured institutions began withdrawing their funds too. This run on state-insured deposits prompted the governor of Ohio to close all 71 state-insured thrifts for several days, thereby declaring the first widespread "bank holiday" since the Great Depression.

Resolution of the resultant crisis took only about a week, but it required the intervention of the Federal Reserve Board and the FSLIC. Moreover, both the international value of the U.S. dollar and the U.S. stock market dropped sharply—although only temporarily—as a result of these events, indicating general sensitivity to events affecting the U.S. banking and thrift industries. A similar situation occurred in Maryland a few weeks later, requiring the governor to limit individual withdrawals to non-FSLIC-insured associations to $1,000 per depositor. It is true that the security of federally insured thrifts, which overwhelmingly dominate the industry, was never endangered. But these episodes entrenched federal deposit insurance more firmly than ever, as calls were heard to extend it to more and more thrifts. That in turn guaranteed more future conflicts between financial deregulation and minimizing undue risk taking by financial institutions (as discussed in chapter 10).

Fiscal insecurity, however dramatic its manifestation, was not the only problem facing the financial industry in the early and mid-1980s. Enormous ambiguity surrounded the functions that should be performed by each type of financial institution. This uncertainty permitted many to "invade" the long-established territories of operations of other types, creating general confusion. Banks were engaging in discount brokerage and seeking to sell insurance; insurance companies were buying Wall Street brokerage firms; the largest brokerage firm was operating a huge money market fund that functioned like a bank; other brokerage firms were trying to buy banks and thrifts; and commerical banks legally prohibited from interstate banking were founding "nonbank banks" in many states at once.

Equally confusing was the behavior of federal regulatory agencies. Almost immediately after threatening not to protect depositors of more than $100,000 in case of financial difficulties, the Federal Deposit Insurance Corporation (FDIC) and Federal Reserve Bank suddenly guaranteed not only all large depositors, but all creditors, of the huge Continental Illinois Bank when it almost failed in 1984. The Comptroller of the Currency declared that the nation's ten largest banks would all be similarly protected if they encountered serious problems. Leading congressmen then excoriated that policy as unfairly discriminatory against smaller banks. One possible implication was that *all* banks might be fully backed by the federal government if they got into trouble. Yet the two major federal deposit insurance funds had nowhere nearly enough capital to support such a universal guarantee if bankruptcy became much more widespread.

What implications do these seemingly chaotic events and trends have for the future of real estate finance? The answers for secondary mortgage markets will be analyzed in chapters 12 and 13. This chapter discusses the effects of the revolution on five other key real estate financial institutions: thrifts, pension funds, life insurance companies, investment banking firms, and independent real estate developers.

The Future of Thrift Institutions

The environment of thrift institutions has been radically altered by the revolutionary developments described in chapter 2. Even the basic function for which thrifts were founded—making long-term mortgage loans based on short-term savings deposits—probably is no longer economically viable over the long run. Great volatility of economic conditions has increased the probability that short-term interest rates will exceed long-term rates for periods long enough to make that function untenable—or at least extremely risky. Therefore thrifts must greatly change their past behavior if they want to survive. How will they do so, and what effects will these changes have on real estate markets?

The answer can be divided into two parts: the first concerning the immediate jeopardy faced by thrifts, and the second concerning their behavior over the longer run. That behavior will in turn reflect seven important tendencies that thrifts will exhibit in the future. Some of these tendencies may appear rather inconsistent because they apply to different time periods. For example, most thrifts will continue to concentrate on real estate in the near future but will increasingly diversify their activities over the long run. The immediate jeopardy faced by thrifts and the seven longer-run tendencies they are likely to exhibit are discussed in the following subsections.

The Solvency Crisis of the 1980s

In early 1985, *the entire thrift industry was quite close to insolvency in the balance-sheet sense, although not in the cash-flow sense.* Federal financial backing will undoubtedly prevent actual bankruptcy of any large part of the industry under any probable future economic conditions. Nevertheless, the thrift industry *is likely to remain in a weak capital position until interest rates in general stabilize for some time.* High and volatile interest rates from 1979 onward drastically eroded the thrift industry's net worth. In 1970 the net worth of all savings associations equaled about 7.0 percent of their total assets. By 1980 that ratio had slipped to 5.3 percent.[2] During 1979–82 thrifts were often forced to pay higher average rates to their depositors, who mainly used short-term accounts, than they received from their borrowers, who mainly used long-term mortgages. Consequently thrifts lost money. By 1984 their net worth, computed by generally accepted accounting principles, equaled only 2.9 percent of their total assets—0.4 percent if "good will" and other intangible assets were excluded.[3] By early 1985 hundreds of

2. U.S. League of Savings Associations, *1982 Savings and Loan Source Book* (Chicago: USLSA, 1982), p. 43.

3. The Working Group of the Cabinet Council on Economic Affairs, *Recommendations for Change in the Federal Deposit Insurance System* (Washington, D.C.: The Group, January 1985), p. 14; and James R. Barth and others, *Thrift Institution Failures: Causes and Policy Issues* (Washington, D.C.: Federal Home Loan Bank

the 3,200 savings and loan associations still in existence were either economically unviable or actually insolvent.[4]

The seriousness of the situation was partially concealed by ingenious—and sometimes fictitious—accounting methods adopted with the approval of federal regulatory agencies. For example, thrifts using the mutual form of ownership (instead of the stockholder form of ownership) could elect to use regulatory accounting principles instead of generally accepted accounting procedures. Under regulatory accounting procedures such thrifts could sell old low-yielding mortgages at prices below book value, immediately show all the cash they received as an asset, but spread the resultant book losses over long periods of time. This procedure magically converted what actually were large losses into insignificant ones. It also enabled the thrifts to reinvest the funds thus received at higher interest rates than those obtained on the old mortgages sold—but only if the thrifts shifted to investing in higher-risk instruments. Hence this conversion process encouraged association managers to incur greater default risks. By 1985 the FSLIC considered that about two-thirds of the thrifts under its supervision that were in economic difficulty were endangered mainly because of poor-quality loans rather than adverse interest rate spreads.[5]

In addition, the Federal Home Loan Bank Board (FHLBB) distributed stock in the Federal Home Loan Mortage Corporation (FHLMC) to its member thrifts and permitted them to show that stock as an added asset. Yet all such stock had previously been held by the FHLBB itself, which in turn was owned *by the same thrift associations*. Hence that stock had already been carried indirectly as an asset on the books of those associations. When this apparent ownership transfer occurred, FHLMC stock was revalued upward by several hundred million dollars, thereby adding that amount to

---

Board, March 20, 1985). It is necessary to specify the use of generally accepted accounting principles for 1983–84 data because the FHLBB allowed savings and loans to use modified accounting principles (regulatory accounting principles), which counted as asset items not allowed under the generally accepted principles. This discrepancy between accounting procedures was not relevant to the earlier net worth ratios because regulatory accounting was introduced after these were computed.

4. G. Christian Hill, "Ohio S&L Crisis May Spur Industry Changes," *Wall Street Journal*, April 8, 1985.

5. Barth and others, *Thrift Institution Failures*, p. 8.

thrifts' net worth. (This addition was largely offset, however, by a special assessment made on all associations by FSLIC in 1985 to augment its depleted reserves, as noted below.)

Such accounting sleight of hand was designed to make the net worth of thrifts appear stronger than it actually was, thereby leading depositors to believe that nearly all thrifts were healthy. This strategy was based on the assumption that the industry could keep on operating effectively as long as individual depositors and institutional investors had enough confidence in virtually all individual thrifts to keep putting money into them and to leave it there, even if many of those institutions were in reality insolvent.

Nevertheless, by 1985 so many thrifts had liabilities well below their assets that FSLIC would have been hard pressed to bail them all out if it had to. The *Wall Street Journal* reported in April 1985 that at least two thrifts had negative net worths exceeding $1.1 billion each.[6] The cost to FSLIC of merging both of them with healthy financial institutions would probably exceed $3 billion. But the FSLIC's total insurance reserve at the end of fiscal 1984 was just over $6 billion. Veribanc, a bank consulting firm, estimated in April 1985 that 300 associations had a combined *tangible* net worth of almost *negative* $28 billion. Yet the reported balance sheets of these thrifts showed a combined *positive* net worth of almost $12 billion, in part because of accounting maneuvers such as those mentioned above.[7] Faced by such conditions in early 1985, FSLIC levied a special assessment against all savings and loan associations that it covered to bolster its reserves.

FSLIC's position was undermined by the risky behavior of a few large thrifts already close to insolvency. Their managers chose a strategy of rapid deposit growth that was based on offering high savings rates and on large-scale investing in fixed-rate mortgages with relatively high rates. Such mortgages usually carry a greater chance of default than those with lower rates, other things being equal. If interest rates in general were to fall, this strategy would provide large capital gains on such mortgages. That profit would help these thrifts overcome the economic drag of their older mortgage portfolios. But if interest rates were to rise again, these thrifts

6. Hill, "Ohio S&L Crisis," p. 6.
7. Ibid.

would rapidly go broke: they would not be able to raise rates on their assets (the fixed-rate mortgages) as fast as rates on their liabilities (savings accounts) would go up. These managers realized how risky their strategy was, but followed it anyway. They reasoned that they were already close to insolvency and at the mercy of national economic policies; therefore they had nothing more to lose by gambling on falling rates, since rising rates would cause them to become bankrupt in any case. One of the reasons for their choice was that FSLIC had the obligation of making their depositors whole if the thrifts became insolvent, as discussed in chapter 10.

As a result of all these factors, if interest rates were to rise to levels higher than those of early 1985 and were to stay there for any prolonged period, FSLIC could easily be confronted with far more demands on its reserves than it could meet. There is little doubt, however, that Congress would not allow FSLIC to become bankrupt, no matter how large the liabilities it had to assume. If charges against FSLIC exceeded its resources, Congress either would merge FSLIC with the larger and economically healthier FDIC that insures banks or would made direct appropriations to cover FSLIC's liabilities. In no case would Congress be likely to allow depositors to lose any of their federally insured funds. Hence the thrift industry in early 1985 was not in any real danger of imminent collapse or disappearance, despite its thin equity in relation to its total liabilities.

Attracting More Capital into Thrifts

Nevertheless, *the industry's financially fragile situation in early 1985 raised the fundamental question of how it would be able to build a larger and more stable capital base in the future.*[8] The most important step toward such an outcome would be a national economic strategy that would reduce the interest rate volatility that prevailed from 1979 through the mid-1980s. That possibility is discussed in chapter 14. If interest rates became relatively stable over a prolonged period, and if short-term rates remained lower than long-term rates for most of that time, the process of borrowing short and lending long would no longer drive thrifts toward insolvency. Hence

8. I am greatly indebted to Leon Kendall of the Mortgage Guarantee Insurance Corporation and to Jay Janis of the Gibralter Savings and Loan Association for insights into the future of the thrift industry used in this subsection.

they could slowly regain some of their net worth by earning profits during most of that time.

Competent thrift managers would use a period of relative rate stability to restructure their balance sheets so as to make the maturities of their assets and liabilities match more closely. They would seek to shorten the maturities of their assets by acquiring more adjustable rate mortgages (ARMs), making short-term consumer loans, and making floating rate commercial loans. At the same time they would try to lengthen the maturities of their liabilities by deemphasizing demand deposits and "hot money" while emphasizing certificates of deposit and longer-term borrowing from the FHLBB.

Unfortunately, such maturity changes would tend to reduce the average interest rate spread between assets and liabilities. Rates on assets would fall as average maturities were shortened, and those on liabilities would rise as average maturities were lengthened. That relation is inescapable with a positive yield curve (short-term rates lower than long-term rates). Hence such restructuring would require earning extra profits from other activities. That necessity would imply that only exceptionally well-managed associations could achieve such results. Even so, there are enough well-managed thrifts so that the industry as a whole might greatly reduce its long-term interest rate risk through such balance-sheet restructuring if given two to three years under stable interest rates.

Moreover, under such stable economic conditions some private investors would probably be willing to inject additional financial capital into the healthier segments of the thrift industry. This infusion of capital would require conversion of more mutual savings and loans into the stockholder form of ownership. Such conversion was prohibited for federally chartered associations until the early 1980s, but it has been both legalized and encouraged by the FHLBB since then.

Stronger capital bases for stock association could be created through several kinds of transactions. One would be the merger of large associations that had relatively high net-worth-to-asset ratios with smaller associations that had lower such ratios but were still clearly solvent. This transaction would strengthen the smaller thrift without grievously weakening the larger one. A second capital infusion might come from banks' buying savings and loan associations, if deregulation made that permissible. (It was already being allowed during the early 1980s in a few cases in which banks were the only institutions willing to rescue ailing thrifts, as Citicorp rescued First Federal Savings and Loan in Chicago.) Banks in general have larger net-worth-to-asset ratios than do thrifts, so such purchases could markedly strengthen the capital base of the thrift industry. Some large nonfinancial corporations might also be willing to buy thrifts to enter the financial services business, especially because they would thereby benefit from federal deposit insurance. Moreover, if the economic climate appeared stable enough, many individual investors might be persuaded to buy stock in thrifts. Finally, the industry's capital base would be strengthened by the gradual disappearance of the weakest firms—through merger with stronger ones and abetted by infusions of FSLIC insurance reserves.

Thus the future capital strength of the thrift industry and the source of that strength will depend mainly on how federal monetary and fiscal policies will affect interest rate volatility. If these policies keep volatility high, as they did from 1979 through 1982, the federal government may have to supply much of the capital needed to keep the thrift industry solvent. This federal support may be partially concealed by misleading accounting practices, but it will nevertheless remain as long as such volatility persists.

But if federal monetary and fiscal policies restore stability to interest rates—even at relatively high levels—then competent thrift managers can increase capital from earnings and reduce interest rate risk through balance-sheet restructuring. In addition, private investors will then gradually put more capital into the industry. Such developments would eventually restore a large enough capital base to remove most of the thrift industry from its currently perilous position.

Long-run Tendencies

Beyond engaging in near-term maneuvers to avert insolvency, the thrift industry will likely exhibit several tendencies over the longer run. These tendencies are discussed in the following subsections.

SHORT-TERM EMPHASIS ON REAL ESTATE.   Nearly all thrift institutions will continue to focus most of their activities on real estate in the near future, although many will undertake development as well as mortgage lending. Many will continue to concentrate on real estate in the long run, too. This conclusion follows partly from sheer institutional inertia. It takes a long time for a large number of well-established institutions to develop new expertise and to enter entirely new fields of activity. Thrifts have focused for decades on real estate finance, and their managers and other staff members understand real estate markets much better than other markets. Hence, as these institutions struggle to survive in their new environment, they will be compelled for a time to keep on seeking profits in those areas they know best. This continuity is particularly likely because so many other institutions are already well established in the other activities that thrifts might undertake. Examples are consumer lending, commercial lending, and stockbrokerage.

Thrifts will not entirely withdraw from real estate in the long run, either; most of those that survive will still concentrate more on real estate than on any other field of operations. The main reason is the sheer size of real estate investment compared with alternative activities—there is no other industry large enough to absorb the money flows or the activities of the thrift industry. It is true that, as noted below, the number of thrift institutions will decline considerably, so that absorbing their capital flows elsewhere would not require as large a set of alternative investments as it would today.

Even so, real estate finance will remain the single largest absorber of all capital flows in the economy, with the possible exception of federal deficits. During 1970–82 all mortgage flows combined absorbed 30 percent of all credit flows as measured by the Federal Reserve Board's flow of funds accounts.[9] This share was almost double that absorbed by the next largest user—the federal government. Hence, even if mortgages absorb a far smaller share in the future and the federal government absorbs more, real estate will still account for a vastly larger portion of total capital flows than any other nonfederal financial activity.

But the mixture of real estate activities that thrifts will undertake will change somewhat, and probably quite rapidly.

—Many more thrifts will undertake real estate development as equity investors rather than as lenders. In most cases this investment will be done through joint ventures with homebuilders and other de-

9. Board of Governors of the Federal Reserve System, *Federal Reserve Bulletin*, tables on overall flows for various years, 1920–82.

velopers. Joint ventures with thrift institutions will become an important means by which homebuilders finance their future activities.

—Thrifts will devote a larger share of their activities than in the past to nonresidential projects, both through loans and joint development ventures. Most thrifts concentrated almost exclusively on housing in the past, but they will branch out into other kinds of properties for two reasons. First, housing will offer more limited opportunities under certain possible economic conditions. If interest rates remain high in real and nominal terms, there will be fewer new homes built and fewer existing ones sold than in the past. Second, nonresidential projects offer prospects for retaining properties as earning assets for longer periods than do most home-building projects. Having such assets will be very important if inflation rates are high because real estate assets are better hedges against inflation than are most financial assets. This trend has already begun. The share of all mortgage loans originated by savings and loan associations that involved nonresidential properties rose from 3.6 percent in 1979 to 12.9 percent in 1983.[10]

—Thrifts will sell a higher proportion of the mortgages they originate into the secondary market. Some thrifts will not want to hold assets with long terms and fixed rates. Even those holding such assets will prefer doing so with mortgage-backed securities (MBSs) rather than with mortgages because such securities have greater liquidity.

—The most viable thrifts will try to minimize the share of long-term, fixed-rate mortgages in their portfolios (either as mortgages or as the basis for MBSs). Some thrifts already have policies of not retaining any such mortgages they originate in order to minimize their additional interest rate risk. These thrifts will only originate traditional mortgages if they can immediately sell them in the secondary market, and they will not buy any MBSs based on such mortgages. This practice will be discussed further in chapters 12 and 13.

DECLINING NUMBERS OF THRIFT INSTITUTIONS. The number of institutions clearly distinguishable as thrifts will decline sharply because of mergers, failures disguised as mergers, and the movement of existing thrifts into other fields. Such shrinkage was already well under way during 1982–84, mainly because of the financial difficul-

---

10. *Federal Home Loan Bank Board Journal*, vol. 17 (February 1984), p. 36.

ties experienced by a majority of thrifts during 1981 and 1982. There were about 4,000 federally insured savings and loan associations in the United States in 1980. That number has already fallen and will drop much further, even though many new thrifts are also being formed. Andrew Carron's studies of the thrift industry indicate that "mergers of weak firms will continue at a high rate beyond 1983, leading to an industry of 2,500 firms or less. . . . There are more than 20,000 banks and thrifts in the United States (not including another 21,000 credit unions). This total could easily be reduced by half within the decade."[11]

DIVERSIFIED FUNCTIONS.   As individual thrifts move into different activities, the typical mix of functions they perform will become more diversified, unless prevented by regulatory authorities. Within two decades it may even be difficult to clearly distinguish a "thrift industry." Many thrifts will seek to move away from concentrating on making mortgage loans for their own portfolios. Most will still originate mortgages, but many will sell almost all such mortgages in the secondary market, becoming essentially mortgage bankers. Others may shift more into real estate development.

Still others will move into consumer banking (including consumer lending), where their widespread branches may provide an advantage in competition with institutions that do not have such branches. Many commercial banks are moving away from consumer banking because of its high real estate and transaction costs. This shift will present an opportunity for thrifts, whose managers are skilled in retail contacts with consumers. Some thrifts will also begin commercial lending, although it will take them some time to become established. Many are starting by buying participations in commercial loans originated by other institutions, including private placements made by investment banking and brokerage firms. Other functions being considered by thrifts include selling insurance, stockbrokerage, and originating and selling municipal bonds.

This multiplicity of possibilities means that many different combinations and mixtures of functions will arise. The largest thrifts will probably move into all or most of the above functions eventually. Smaller ones will become specialized in just one or two of those

11. Andrew S. Carron, *The Rescue of the Thrift Industry* (Brookings, 1983), p. 27.

functions. Hence it will soon be difficult to tell which financial institutions are still "thrifts" in some meaningful sense, which have become "banks," and which are in other categories—including broadly based financial institutions performing diverse services.

A higher percentage of all types of surviving thrift institutions, however, will be based on the stockholder form of ownership rather than on the mutual form. Thrifts need larger capital reserves to handle future risks effectively. They can raise additional capital more easily through stock issues than through the mutual format. In addition, the mutual form of ownership encourages less efficient management, in part because it provides no true stockholders looking over management's shoulder. For both these reasons, stock companies should be more efficient than mutuals, and a higher percentage of them should survive.

INCREASED SERVICE FEES. Most thrifts will seek to increase the shares of their gross incomes and profits arising from fees for service. In the past thrifts earned most of their incomes on the spread between the interest rates they received from mortgage borrowers and the interest rates they paid to savings depositors. But when this spread became very small or even negative, thrifts had to find other sources of income. One source was the fees they earned for performing various services, such as originating or servicing mortgages, providing insurance, making appraisals, and so forth. This shift away from dependence on interest rate spreads will be greatly accelerated in the future as thrifts continue to move away from borrowing short and lending long.

One unintended result of the desire to earn more fees has been a pressure to increase the number of loans and other transactions carried out, regardless of their quality. Even if a loan is marginally desirable purely from an underwriting perspective, it may generate a sizable fee that improves the association's earnings. Hence thrift officials have a strong incentive to make such loans if funds are available. This pressure to make deals has led many thrifts to reduce their underwriting standards, thereby increasing the average riskiness of their loans and contributing to the financial shakiness of the entire industry.

DIVERSIFIED SOURCES OF FUNDS. More thrifts will obtain funds from sources other than household savings deposits, including the purchase of funds from money brokers and large nationwide brokerage and investment firms. It is easier to obtain money with longer maturities from such sources than by dealing directly with households. The latter course has two important disadvantages. One is the high capital and operating cost of establishing branches convenient to consumers, or of maintaining those already in existence. This cost may be reduced if most "branches" are automated teller stations. Such limited outlets reduce real estate and transaction costs but also reduce the opportunity for institutions to sell multiple services to their customers (and to collect other fees).

The second drawback is that households are now able to use new demand deposit accounts that have no interest rate ceilings. Those accounts are "spoiling" consumers who formerly received lower rates or no interest on passbook or demand deposit accounts. It is true that savings institutions will probably make available higher-rate accounts with longer maturities to try to reduce the maturity mismatch between their liabilities and their assets. But it may be more efficient to market such accounts through means other than face-to-face contact with individual households by thrift staff members.

One means of such marketing would be to establish outlets, whether automated or not, in large retail establishments run by other firms. Sears is contemplating doing this for savings, as it has for insurance and real estate brokerage. At least one other large department store chain is also negotiating to locate savings outlets in its stores. Under these arrangements some face-to-face contact by thrift staff would continue, but in facilities created, owned, and operated by others.

Another means of such marketing is to obtain funds from investment brokerage firms with nationwide sales staffs of brokers dealing with wealthy individuals, insurance companies, and pension funds. These firms have already made large investments in developing such broker networks and the contacts they enjoy. Equally important, the brokers involved can positively sell savings to persons and institutions with money, rather than leaving the savings initiative to such clients.

TAILORING INVESTMENT INSTRUMENTS TO SAVERS.   Recent experience shows that savings funds can be more effectively obtained through positively selling specific investment vehicles to specific savers than through mass advertising or passively waiting for savers to act on their own. Firms with nationwide sales forces—such as brokerage houses or life insurance companies—are better able to conduct such positive selling to individuals and institutions than are thrifts. If the individual accounts they bring in are large enough, brokers can earn front-end commissions large enough to motivate more intensive sales efforts than thrifts can display, and thrifts can afford to pay those big commissions.

Thrifts are handicapped not only by being geographically rooted in only one or a few areas, but also by not having staffs skilled in selling investments and already in touch with and known to large numbers of affluent potential buyers. It may be possible for some large thrifts to develop such sales staffs, especially if the thrifts are already operating in many regions. But few can do so with as comprehensive a geographic coverage as that already possessed by Merrill Lynch, Prudential-Bache, or other national brokerage firms.

Therefore, such nationwide investment-selling firms are likely to raise funds for thrifts by selling specific investment vehicles developed by thrifts. The ability to offer federally insured investments can make such vehicles especially attractive to investors. This has already been done on a modest scale. For example, Merrill Lynch and Company marketed insured certificates of deposit for California Federal Savings and Loan Association in 1982, raising millions of dollars outside the normal channels tapped by thrifts.

CONTINUED PORTFOLIO DOMINANCE OF MORTGAGES.   Future thrifts as a group will continue to hold large amounts in mortgages in their portfolios—either directly or in the form of securities backed by such mortgages. This will be true despite the great interest rate and inflation risks associated with holding such investments, even ARMs. One reason is that thrifts already hold an immense portfolio of mortgages (over $675.6 billion in the middle of 1984); more than 76 percent of the dollar value of these mortgages consisted of loans on dwellings containing one to four units.[12] Thrifts cannot get rid of these mortgages with a wave of some magic wand, especially because many of their older, low-yielding fixed-rate mortgages have a market value far below book value. Hence thrifts could not sell

12. Federal Reserve Board, *Federal Reserve Bulletin*, vol. 70 (September 1984), p. A37.

those assets without sustaining a huge loss that would more than bankrupt them.[13]

In addition, thrifts are likely to continue receiving significant inflows of savings deposits from households that will, on average, leave large shares of those deposits in these institutions "permanently." Of course, some individual households will make frequent withdrawals, but those losses will be offset by the deposits of others. A certain share of total household deposits can also be considered "hot money." It is likely to be withdrawn quickly if alternative investments with even just slightly higher yields become available. But another significant share of household deposits can be considered "stable money" or permanent savings. This money will be left in thrift institutions as long as their savings rates are even roughly competitive with yields on conveniently available alternative investments. Such low-mobility deposits can serve as the backing for long-term mortgages without causing any unfavorable results from mismatched maturities. If thrifts continue to capture a significant share of future household savings, this residue of permanent savings will become larger too. Hence thrifts can keep adding to the portfolios of mortgages they hold over the long run without necessarily suffering adverse consequences.

Therefore, a key question is: what share of future household savings will thrifts be able to capture? Increases in total savings deposits at thrifts averaged about 41 percent of personal savings flows during 1971–82. In 1983 total savings deposits at savings and loan associations rose by $66.1 billion, whereas personal savings were $118.1 billion. Thus savings and loan associations captured about 56 per-

13. The thrift industry as a whole would be totally bankrupt if its assets were valued at their current market value. At the end of 1982 the interest return on all mortgages held by insured savings and loan associations was 10.68 percent. The effective interest rate being charged at that time was 13.93 percent. If the total mortgage loans outstanding of insured savings and loans, in the amount of $482.234 billion, were revalued so that the 10.68 percent yield was equal to 13.93 percent of the new value, the new total would be $369.724 billion. Hence their assets would be worth $112.5 billion less than indicated on their combined balance sheet. But that balance sheet showed a combined net worth of $86.35 billion if its mortgage loans outstanding were shown at their current market value. Data are from *Federal Home Loan Bank Board Journal*, vol. 16 (September 1983), p. 34; and vol. 17 (February 1984), p. 37.

cent of total personal savings.[14] This is undoubtedly a distortion caused by the initial attraction of funds from other sources into the new no-ceiling accounts at savings and loan associations.

Some insight into the future ability of thrifts to capture savings can be gained by comparing their recent performance with that of their main rivals, commercial banks. In 1983 the savings deposits of commercial banks rose by $144.0 billion, but their demand and time deposits fell by $43.6 billion, for a net gain of $100.4 billion. Thus savings and loan associations captured 40.0 percent of the combined deposit increases in both such associations and commercial banks.[15]

During 1970–81 total over-the-counter deposits in savings and loan associations increased by $378 billion compared with a rise of $594 billion in time and savings deposits at commercial banks. Thus, in that longer period, savings and loan associations captured 39 percent of their combined savings gains.[16]

During 1972–81 total household financial assets rose an average of $211 billion annually; those in savings and loan associations rose an average of $35.3 billion, and those in commercial banks an average of $38.7 billion.[17] In this longer period, therefore, savings and loans captured about 48 percent of the combined share of these two types of institutions in greater household financial assets. But all thrifts, including mutual savings banks, captured about 53 percent of the combined share. Gains by savings and loans in the financial holdings of households averaged about 42 percent of average personal savings in that period compared with 46 percent for commercial banks.

Thus all thrifts combined will probably capture as much as 50 percent of all the added savings deposits gleaned by both thrifts and commercial banks in the future. Moreover, the share of thrifts should equal at least 45 percent of personal savings (although not all of the savings captured by thrifts will be directly invested in real

14. U.S. League of Savings Associations, *1984 Savings Institutions Source Book* (Chicago: USLSA, 1984), pp. 21, 24.

15. Ibid., p. 23.

16. U.S. League of Savings Associations, *1982 Savings and Loan Source Book*, p. 19.

17. Data are from chapter 4 and USLSA, *1982 Savings and Loan Source Book*, p. 18.

estate). Therefore the amount of long-term mortgages that thrifts will be able to add to their portfolios in the future should be quite large.

Changes in the Behavior of Domestic Pension Funds toward Real Estate

Domestic pension funds are almost certain to possess the fastest-growing institutional pool of assets in the nation during the next decade or two. Total assets of all U.S. pension funds, including federal old-age, survivor, and disability insurance funds, equaled about $794.2 billion in 1981. During 1970–75 such assets grew at a compound annual rate of 9.19 percent. During 1975–79 they grew at a rate of 11.18 percent a year, and during 1979–81 at a rate of 12.90 percent.[18]

If the future growth of pension fund assets is projected at 10 percent a year compounded, these assets would reach a total of $1,872.7 billion in 1990. Hence the assets of pension funds would rise by annual averages of $92.1 billion during 1981–85, and by $142.0 billion during 1985–90 (all in current dollars). If pension assets grow at the very high rate of 15 percent a year compounded, pension funds would have total assets of $2,794.0 billion in 1990. Those assets would rise by annual averages of $148 billion during 1981–85 and $260.1 billion during 1985–89 (also in current dollars). These calculations include pension fund assets held and managed by insurance companies and other intermediaries.[19]

Almost every large group of potential capital users is hoping to capture a significant share of these added assets, usually a much larger share than in the past. Real estate borrowers have been prominent among those gazing wistfully at this expanding pool of money.

18. American Council of Life Insurance, *1982 Pension Facts, 1983 Update* (Washington, D.C.: ACLI, 1983).

19. Average annual growth of pension fund assets includes both reinvestments of income on current assets and additions to assets through further worker contributions, net of payments to retired workers collecting pensions. Thus no separate computation needs to be made to allow for the reinvestment of capital already accumulated.

Yet pension funds as a group have up to now invested only a tiny fraction of their assets in real estate, probably less than 5 percent altogether as of 1980. Is this behavior likely to change in the future, and could it change enough to make a great difference in real estate markets?

Reasons for Increased Real Estate Involvement

There are five reasons for pension fund managers' considering raising the share of their assets devoted to real estate. Most important is *comparative yield*. If real estate investments offer "risk-corrected yields" notably higher than those of alternative uses, and if this fact becomes widely recognized, pension funds would be under great pressure as fiduciaries to take advantage of those higher yields. I refer to risk-corrected yields because two securities can offer quite different nominal yields if one is immensely riskier than the other and therefore carries a much higher risk premium. In that case the investment with the higher nominal yield may have a much lower risk-corrected yield—that is, the yield after discounting for its greater probability of default or loss.

A second cause of greater pension fund investment in real estate would be *marked acceleration of inflation*. Rapidly increasing inflation would motivate pension fund managers to acquire more real estate equities as hedges against that inflation. But it would also motivate them to reduce their investments in fixed-rate, long-term mortgages, other things being equal. If they bought many mortgages at all, those mortgages would have to have variable rates or some other means of protecting investors against both inflation and interest rate risk. Whether pension funds' net placement of funds in real estate would rise would therefore depend on the severity of inflation and on its expected duration.

Another possible motive for pension fund managers' putting more money into real estate would be *skepticism about the future profitability or security of alternative investments*. In mid-1983 some pension fund managers were skeptical that the stock market, which had soared from August 1982 to the spring of 1983, would be able to advance further or even to maintain its level at that time. Hence they increased the share of their current funds flowing into real estate. Such skepticism about stocks and bonds will be greatest when fears of greater inflation are high; hence this motive is intertwined with the preceding one.

Political pressure to support both homeownership and the housing industry could create another motive for some pension funds to put more funds into real estate. This motive is most likely to affect public employee pension funds and union pension funds because both are more susceptible to political pressure than are private corporate pension funds. Some state employee funds have already indicated a willingness to put money into supporting their local housing markets by buying mortgages originated there, perhaps even at below-market interest rates. Union funds have also argued that their members would gain from such investments because they might stimulate more jobs in their industries, and therefore more long-run contributions to their pension funds. If such pressures arose, they would almost certainly focus on greater investment in housing rather than in nonresidential real estate, and they would also be most likely to appear when economic conditions involved high nominal interest rates, slow overall economic growth, and low housing starts.

A final reason for raising the share of real estate in pension fund assets would be the desire to achieve *greater diversification for its own sake*. Pension fund managers are legally required by the Employees' Retirement Income Security Act to act as prudent fiduciaries when investing the assets they control. A reasonable argument could be made that they have failed to diversify those assets as much as a prudent person would in this uncertain world. In particular, they have kept excessively high percentages of stocks and bonds and have acquired inadequately low percentages of real assets. They did so despite an average inflation rate in the 1970s higher than in the past and the superior performance of real estate investments compared with stocks and bonds during that decade.

There has been, however, no explicit pressure on pension fund managers from regulatory authorities to increase the share of assets held in real estate. Nor is such pressure likely to develop, especially if a market-oriented administration remains in power. Hence this motive will not by itself change the investment behavior of pension funds very much. It could, however, reinforce one or more of the previously stated motives if that motive gained strength as circumstances unfold.

The analysis above implies that pension funds will greatly raise the share of assets they invest in real estate only if future economic conditions involve (1) accelerated inflation; (2) such high interest rates in general that housing transactions become sharply depressed, as in 1980–82; or (3) much higher yields on real estate investments than on alternatives. All three conditions would appear if inflation soared.

Yet even if pension funds greatly increased the fraction of their current income and reinvestment flows going into real estate, they would almost certainly provide only a small share of the total funding requirements of the nation's real estate markets. In addition, most past investment in real estate by pension funds has focused on nonresidential real estate, not on housing. This concentration is likely to continue in the future. Most pension fund managers do not feel comfortable in owning rental housing. They fear rent controls and do not want to become even indirectly involved in the problems of managing such property. There is no efficient way for them to own single-family homes, so they can invest in them only by buying mortgages or MBSs. But such investments are exposed to high inflation and interest rate risk unless they are based on variable rate instruments, which will become more common in the future. The best real estate investments from the viewpoint of pension funds are equity ownership of, or participating mortgages on, nonresidential income properties. These equity investments offer good hedges against inflation, good yields, low management problems, and low political visibility.

Public employee and union pension funds may well be pressured to aid the housing industry if it is hurt by adverse economic conditions. Hence those funds might raise their shares of real estate investments allocated to housing. Other pension funds are likely to do so only if yields from MBSs in housing are noticeably higher than those from alternative investments or if the housing industry is in such dire straits that Congress requires all pension funds to allocate a certain share of funds to it. The latter course is quite unlikely in the conservative, market-oriented political atmosphere of the 1980s.

Continued Importance of Pension Fund Investment

As a result, pension fund investments in housing will still be a relatively small part of total housing fund requirements. The total amounts invested by pension funds in real estate, however, will be large enough to form an important share of total funding requirements for nonresidential real estate, especially if pension funds increase the overall percentage of added assets they put into real estate.

The importance of this share can be seen from calculating how much pension funds might invest in real estate during 1985–89 if their total assets grew at 15 percent a year compounded and if they put one-third of their added assets into real estate. These assumptions are likely to err on the side of overestimating pension funds' real estate investment. Even so, pension funds would then invest an average of $86.6 billion a year in real estate during 1985–89. If they put one-half of that amount into housing—again unlikely—that investment would amount to $43.3 billion a year in housing and another $43.3 billion in nonresidential properties. These would be very important shares of likely total requirements for nonresidential funding but much less important shares of likely total requirements for residential funding.[20]

Yet housing is the part of real estate most likely to suffer from inadequate funding in the future if economic circumstances are adverse to real estate in general. Such circumstances would include high nominal interest rates. High rates would inhibit individual households from purchasing homes before they would inhibit nonresidential developers or purchasers from engaging in their typical transactions. Thus housing finance would benefit more than nonresidential finance from greater allocation of pension fund money to real estate in general, since nonresidential finance will attract large amounts of pension fund money in any case. But housing is the type of real estate least likely to get added pension fund money without major political interference in market-oriented allocation decisions.

In sum, the following conclusions about future pension fund investment in real estate emerge from the analysis above.

—Pension funds will probably allocate at least slightly higher fractions of their future added assets to real estate than they have in

20. On the basis of separate analyses of future requirements for real estate funding not incorporated in this book, I estimate that pension funds could supply a *maximum* of 15 percent of total residential mortgage funding requirements during 1985–89 and would be more likely to supply no more than 6.5 percent. In contrast, they could supply from 25 percent to 35 percent of nonresidential funding requirements in that period.

the past. They are especially likely to raise those fractions if inflation speeds up. But then their increased spending on real estate will go almost entirely to more equities, not to more mortgages or MBSs, unless the last two are structured to offer protection against inflation and interest rate risk.

—In the absence of high inflation, pension funds will devote more money to real estate mainly if it offers higher yields than those on alternative investments. This is particularly true of greater pension fund investment in housing.

—Even if pension funds greatly increase the fraction of their future added assets devoted to real estate, that share will remain far less than half their added asset flows.

—Pension fund investments in nonresidential real estate will be a primary source of financing such real estate, even if pension funds do not increase the share of their total investment going into real estate. That is true because total nonresidential requirements form only about 20 percent of total real estate capital requirements, and because pension fund real estate investments will be primarily non-residential. Pension funds could very well provide over 25 percent of all nonresidential real estate capital requirements in the future.[21]

—Pension fund investments in housing will certainly not be a primary source of total residential financing—probably less than 10 percent of residential mortgage requirements alone.

—Pension fund investment in real estate will be at its likely maximum only if certain legal and managerial obstacles to such investment are removed in the near future. These barriers include tax laws that now prohibit management of cash flows in trusts that issue MBSs (see chapter 13).

Institutional Changes in Insurance Companies That Affect Real Estate Finance

Insurance companies have traditionally financed a large share of all nonresidential real estate projects and transactions, and they have financed many residential projects as well. Hence the future

21. This conclusion draws in part on a quantitative analysis of future requirements for real estate funding that is not included in this book, as mentioned in the preceding note.

behavior of insurance companies is important for real estate finance. Especially relevant aspects of that behavior are (1) the extent to which insurance companies will act as money managers for pension funds, (2) direct relations between insurance companies and real estate developers, and (3) possible diversification of insurance companies into financial services that they have not traditionally performed.

Management of Pension Fund Assets

In recent years traditional sources of insurance company growth have slowed sharply, whereas services provided for pension funds have expanded rapidly. Growth of pension fund assets entrusted to life insurance companies accounted for 37.8 percent of the total increase in the assets of life insurance companies during 1970–75, 49.3 percent in 1975–80, and 57.7 percent in 1980–81.[22] This growth is relevant to real estate because pension fund assets managed by life insurance companies are often invested in real properties. Two forms have been especially important in recent years.

EQUITY POSITIONS. Several large life insurance companies have established pools of funds used to buy equity positions in real estate. Pension funds and other investors can purchase shares in these "separate accounts." The properties involved are managed by the life insurance companies and will presumably be sold after appreciating in value. The life insurance companies themselves usually do not own any shares in their own pools. Rather, they profit from management fees they charge shareholders.

This arrangement allows pension funds to participate in equity ownership of a diversified set of real properties without actually having to buy or manage any properties directly. In theory it also provides the shareholders with more liquid investments than direct ownership of the real estate would. In practice, however, shareholders have not always been able to "cash in" on their shares immediately, especially when many seek to do so simultaneously.

The Prudential Life Insurance Company began the first such pool in the early 1970s. It is still by far the largest, now containing over

22. American Council of Life Insurance, *1982 Life Insurance Fact Book*, p. 69, and *1982 Pension Facts*, p. 9.

$2 billion in assets. Many other pools, however, have been established since then. Moreover, specialized pools of various types have been set up to permit more "rifle-shot" investments. Some focus on certain types of property, such as shopping centers. Others, designed to attract union-run pension funds, purchase only properties constructed with union labor. Some newer pools are "closed-end" funds that buy only a fixed number of properties and then liquidate after those properties are sold—in contrast to most "open-ended" funds established earlier, which continue selling shares and both buying and selling properties without any preestablished limits on size or duration.

One disadvantage of open-ended funds is the difficulty of estimating the current value of a share whenever an investor wants to withdraw funds. Many properties held in the fund are presumed to have appreciated in value but have not yet been sold; hence the precise amount of appreciation must be estimated by appraisers. In contrast, most closed-end funds are established on the assumption that no withdrawals will be permitted until the entire fund is liquidated. Then actual market sales of property will unequivocally establish share values of the fund.

These life insurance special accounts have become a major source of equity capital for nonresidential property transactions, including both new development and sales of existing properties. By 1983 all such pools contained over $20 billion in combined assets. They became especially popular with pension funds during the period of accelerating inflation in the late 1970s. At that time, many pension funds wanted to obtain real estate equities but did not have sufficient staff expertise to do so directly. Many large life insurance companies already had such staffs, so they went into investment management in this fashion. When inflation began decelerating in the early 1980s, however, some pension funds tried to withdraw their assets from these pools, and the growth of such pools slowed markedly. Nevertheless, these vehicles are likely to remain key sources of equity capital for nonresidential real estate.

BULLET LOANS. A second important form of real estate investment made by life insurance companies that is ultimately dependent on pension fund money is the "bullet loan," which became prominent in the early 1980s. Pension funds seeking high yields on their assets, but for limited duration, have invested funds in guaranteed income contracts provided by life insurance companies. These contracts in essence are bonds with terms of five to ten years and guaranteed yields. They involve little or no amortization; the entire principal is due at the end of the initial period. Insurance companies have turned around and have lent the same funds to real estate developers on "bullet" mortgages, so-called probably because they have involved only one shot of money (and that for a relatively short period).[23] These mortgages also have little or no amortization within their duration of five to ten years. Hence developers who have used them to finance real estate transactions have had to find equivalent funds from other sources when these loans expired.

Such financing abandons the safety of self-liquidation built into the amortized long-term mortgages that have financed most real estate transactions since the 1930s (but not before then). There is a much higher risk of default at the end of the bullet mortgage unless the lender is willing to "roll over" the entire amount at that time. But pension funds have presumably made such limited-term loans partly because they have future pay-out obligations due when those loans expire. So neither the insurance companies nor the developers can count on rolling over their funds without any infusion of new capital.

In theory most of this higher risk would fall on the developers or other ultimate borrowers. They would be responsible for finding new funds when the bullet loans expired. But in reality much of that risk is borne by the insurance companies. Most real estate developers have minimal initial equity in new construction projects anyway, and very limited corporate reserves. When pressed to pay off their bullet loans, many might be unable to refinance or even to sell at sufficient prices to cover the amounts due. The insurance companies would then have to come up with their own sources of funds to pay off the pension funds when their guaranteed income contracts expired. Because large life insurance companies have vastly more reserves than do real estate developers, the former are especially likely to bear the ultimate risk if adverse economic conditions make it hard for developers to refinance.

23. Perhaps such mortgages were called "bullet" loans because using them to pay for real properties was like playing Russian roulette, since it assumed that the borrower would somehow be able to replace these funds when the loan expired.

This analysis shows that *merely matching loan maturities does not eliminate risk; it may actually increase risk if those maturities are not appropriately tied to the economics of the specific properties serving as collateral.* Bullet loans impose no *interest rate risk* on those who make them, but they greatly increase *default risk* because their maturities are so short compared with the economic life of the collateral involved. In view of the greater risk of such loans, insurance companies are likely to stop making them whenever they can be replaced by other types of mortgages. Hence it would be unwise to count on insurance companies' continuing to perform this form of intermediation for pension funds at recent high-volume levels.

Direct Investment in Real Estate

To what extent will insurance companies continue performing other forms of intermediation for pension funds in the future? Some observers believe that large pension funds will start investing money directly in real estate without going through insurance companies as agents. Why should pension funds pay sizable management fees to insurance companies when the former can do for themselves what the latter have been doing for them?

Some large pension funds have already started directly investing in real estate rather than having insurance companies or mortgage bankers do it for them. But such pension funds will continue to be exceptional for three reasons. First, most pension fund managers want someone else included in the real estate investment process with whom they can share the blame in case anything goes wrong. Shared responsibility is particularly important because the Employees' Retirement Income Security Act imposes heavy penalties on institutions and individuals that fail to exercise their fiduciary responsibilities in a prudent manner. But determining whether investing in a specific real property was prudent is always a matter of opinion. Most pension fund executives want someone else to be involved in decisions about what investments to make so that they can cite the opinions of those others as confirmation of their own prudence.

In addition, most pension funds have relatively small investment management staffs. They cannot support the large number of skilled professionals necessary to achieve a well-diversified real estate portfolio. If risk is to be minimized, such a portfolio should contain properties that not only are of diverse type but also are located throughout the nation. Creating the required "balanced blend" of individual properties takes expert knowledge of many different markets because real estate is such a geographically particular commodity. Aetna Life and Casualty, for example, has about 200 people in its real estate investment department alone, not counting the personnel in any of its mortgage banking correspondents across the nation (which Aetna uses instead of maintaining its own regional offices). To avoid the huge costs of such staffs, most pension funds must rely on outsiders to do their real estate investing. Large life insurance companies that already possess such staffs are logical candidates for undertaking direct investment in real estate. Thus only a few of the very largest pension funds can even consider conducting their own direct investment programs.

Life insurance companies are logical candidates to work with pension funds in making real estate investments because these two financial organizations are also linked by many other ties. Life insurance companies sell annuities, do actuarial analyses, and perform many other services that are useful to pension fund managers. Hence the latter usually have built up trusting relations with particular life insurance firms. They are predisposed to use those same firms to handle their real estate investments as well.

For all these reasons, *life insurance companies are likely to continue to act as intermediaries in real estate investment for pension funds.*

Diversified Activities

In addition, some life insurance companies will undoubtedly seek more funds to invest from sources other than their traditional lines of business. For example, the Prudential Life Insurance Company purchased Bache, a large stockbrokerage firm. It also initiated many real estate development projects with its own staff (discussed further below). There is a high probability that one or more life insurance companies will set up pooled real estate equity funds or pooled mortgage funds in which owners of individual retirement accounts (IRAs) can invest. Insurance companies may even undertake real estate syndication directly, since many have large staffs experienced in real estate investment and underwriting. Moreover, large insurance companies will be strongly motivated to purchase and expand either banks or thrift institutions to gain access to deposits at the low cost permitted by the use of federal deposit insurance, as discussed in the preceding chapter. Whether they will actually do so depends on the extent of further financial deregulation in the future.

If such deregulation continues to remove past barriers governing the type of activity that different kinds of firms can undertake, greater diversification by large insurance companies seems almost certain. One reason is that more and more firms from other industries will start selling insurance; hence insurance companies may be forced to invade the traditional activities of others if they are to continue to grow. Yet it is not likely that all large insurance companies will transform themselves into identical "financial supermarkets" offering the same menu of diverse services. Rather, the insurance industry is likely to evolve in such a way to make possible a much greater diversity in the mixture of activities that each firm may offer. It will also contain many firms of different overall size, ranging from supergiants such as Prudential to much smaller, specialized firms. Yet most of these firms will continue to regard real estate investment as an important means by which to invest their funds.

The Rise of Wall Street Firms in Primary and Secondary Mortgage Markets

One result of the revolution in real estate finance has been a notable expansion of activity in both primary and secondary mortgage markets by Wall Street investment banking firms. Salomon Brothers and Goldman Sachs have been among the leaders in this "invasion" of the territory traditionally dominated by thrifts and the "Big Three": the Government National Mortgage Association (GNMA), the Federal National Mortgage Association (FNMA), and the Federal Home Loan Mortgage Corporation (FHLMC). The investment bankers have packaged groups of mortgages originated by others, have issued MBSs based on those packages, and have sold those securities to pension funds and other long-term portfolio holders. Such *creation* of MBSs, however, is still hugely dominated by the Big Three.

Investment banking firms have a more important role in *trading* new and existing MBSs. There is now a large ongoing market for such securities. Accurate data on the magnitude of its activities are difficult to obtain. FHLMC has estimated, however, that the value of mortgage-related securities traded for *new issues alone* totaled $75.8 billion in 1982 and $58.5 billion in the first half of 1983.[24] It also estimated that broker-dealers—including investment banking firms—accounted for about 29 percent of all secondary market purchases of mortgage loans in 1982.[25]

Investment bankers and accounting firms have also worked with homebuilders to permit the latter to raise mortgage funds directly from pension funds and other long-term portfolio investors without going through thrift institutions. Use of this "builder-bond" approach was encouraged by a wrinkle in the federal income tax laws that permitted builders to postpone paying most of their income taxes on current home sales. Builders lent money to home-buying households in the form of first mortgages, which they then packaged into large pools. Using these mortgage pools as collateral, the builders issued debt, or builder bonds, and sold the bonds to pension funds and other portfolio investors.

Thus the builders were still holding the mortgages, although they passed the payments from them through to the bond purchasers. The builders were therefore being paid for their homes in installments (including the mortgage payments). Consequently their income tax liabilities accrued only as they received the installment payments over time. But because they sold bonds for almost the full value of the mortgages, and had already collected the downpayments, builders were receiving most of the sale prices of their homes almost immediately. This ingenious arrangement provided them with large cash flows on which most income taxes were deferred for many years.

Homebuilders profiting from this legal tax evasion claimed that they were passing the benefits on to homebuyers in the form of lower sale prices. This was probably true to some extent, but the principal beneficiaries were clearly the homebuilders themselves. Investment bankers collected fees for helping builders set up the mortgage pack-

24. Federal Home Loan Mortgage Corporation, *Secondary Mortgage Markets*, vol. 1 (February 1984), p. 37.
25. Ibid., p. 41.

ages and bond issues and for selling the latter, so they were profiting too. At first only large builders used builder bonds. But in 1984 consortiums of smaller builders—encouraged by accounting firms and investment bankers—joined in this practice.

Thrift institutions objected to this arrangement because it bypassed their function of originating mortgages, permitting builders to raise money directly from pension funds and other long-term mortgage holders. The U.S. Treasury objected because the practice reduced builders' income tax liabilities. It also seemed grossly unfair because it favored builders in ways not available to most taxpayers. As a result, the Treasury sought to end builder bonds as part of its tax reform package initially proposed in late 1984. But builders were still using such bonds at the time this book was completed in early 1985.

These developments raise important questions. Will Wall Street firms gradually take over more and more of the financial intermediary functions in housing markets that were performed in the past by thrift institutions? Will such changes greatly reduce the long-run importance of thrift institutions in real estate finance? My predictions about the future of thrift institutions have been set forth earlier in this chapter. Those institutions will certainly have to adjust to operating in a more deregulated environment than in the past. Part of that adjustment will be to face more competition from Wall Street investment bankers and other relatively new players in real estate financial markets. I believe that the relative market share of such players will probably be much larger than it was before financial deregulation began. But I do not believe that Wall Street firms will come anywhere near replacing thrift institutions as the most important financial intermediaries oriented toward real estate.

The main traditional source of capital supporting real estate investment has been household savings, and that will remain its chief support. In recent years households have put a larger share of their savings directly into pension funds in comparison with traditional savings accounts because employment contracts and income tax laws made contributions to pension funds more advantageous. That tendency will continue in the near future unless savings accounts receive added tax benefits.

Tax-deferred IRAs and Keogh accounts (retirement accounts for self-employed persons), however, have been expanded and will grow rapidly too. Thrifts can handle such accounts, so the growth of IRAs and Keoghs will give thrifts an opportunity to recapture some of the retirement-oriented savings they had lost to pension funds.

Moreover, deregulation may permit thrifts also to undertake some of the activities traditionally undertaken by investment bankers. Hence the real question is whether the managers of thrifts can compete with the managers of Wall Street firms in a largely deregulated financial environment. I believe that the long-run answer will be yes. For one thing, thrifts will undoubtedly retain one key advantage in trying to attract household savings: federal deposit insurance. Moreover, those thrifts with managers who cannot compete will shrink, merge, or disappear. In contrast, those with managers who compete successfully will grow, diversify, and take over the market shares of their less successful competitors.

In the end, the overall share of all real estate financial markets held by thrifts will probably be somewhat smaller than it is now, and that held by Wall Street firms will be a bit larger. But the huge financial base of the thrift industry, plus its continuing benefits from federal deposit insurance, almost ensure that it will remain the single most important source of real estate finance over the long run.

The Future of Independent Real Estate Developers

Recent trends in real estate finance have raised fundamental questions about the future functions of independent developers. In some nations, notably Great Britain, capital suppliers often use developers as paid agents to manage the creation of new properties for a fee. Most British developers do not obtain any equity ownership at all. In other cases the large financial institutions supplying the capital also do their own development, eschewing the services of independent entrepreneurs. Neither of these arrangements has been very common in U.S. real estate markets. Will they both become more widespread in the future?

For decades, most new real estate projects in the United States have been initiated by independent entrepreneurs rather than by large financial institutions. Developers typically carry out the following steps in producing a new project:

—inventing a basic concept;

—acquiring or optioning a site;

—developing a project design;

—obtaining government permission to carry out that design on that site;

—getting a commitment for a long-term loan based on that design and that government permission (although the loan will not actually be funded until after the project is built and perhaps occupied);

—borrowing short-term construction funds with which to build the project;

—supervising and carrying out the project's construction;

—renting space in the project to tenants, both before and after it is built;

—managing the project after it has been completed and initially occupied;

—eventually selling, refinancing, expanding, or renovating the project.

Developers may also syndicate some or all of their equity interest in the project or share in the ownership with a specialized syndicator. In most cases the developer retains all or at least some of the equity ownership, even though most of the capital is put up by others.

When in the 1970s inflation undermined the willingness of capital suppliers to accept long-term, fixed-rate debt as an investment, it raised serious questions about the future of independent developers. If the capital supplier is putting up nearly all the money needed to create a project, and retaining an equity interest that involves assuming much of the risk, what function is the developer performing that justifies his or her emerging as the majority owner? Why should the capital supplier not be the majority owner, or even the sole owner? And if the capital supplier is merely hiring the developer to create the project for a fee, could not the capital supplier use its own personnel for that task? Why should an independent developer participate in the project at all?

Some observers believe that this line of reasoning will eventually eliminate independent developers from U.S. real estate markets. That will not happen. Independent developers are here to stay in U.S. real estate markets. They perform certain functions that cannot easily be carried out by the large organizations that supply most of the capital used to finance sizable real estate projects, especially nonresidential ones.

The most important of these functions is *entrepreneurial risk assessment.* Large organizations run by paid staff members, rather than by owners, simply do not have the same perspective on taking risks as do individual entrepreneurs who put their own assets on the line. On the one hand, salaried staff members are less willing to take risks by gambling on untried ventures. Persons in most large organizations are usually penalized more for conspicuous failure than they are rewarded for conspicuous success, so their incentives are overweighted on the side of caution. Entrepreneurs, in contrast, are motivated by the possibility of reaping enormous profits from their own success.

On the other hand, salaried staff members do not feel the same jeopardy of failure as do entrepreneurs who stand to lose their own capital. I once told a highly placed executive in a large insurance company that a certain project was worth $26 million less than his firm had paid for it. Instead of expressing dismay, the executive said, "We have so many investments across the country, they'll never even notice it on our balance sheet." He certainly would have noticed if the money had been his own.

These two differences in perspective produce altogether different attitudes toward risk taking among entrepreneurial developers and executives of large corporations. The former are better able to assess the realities of the different risks typical in creating new real estate projects. Moreover, individual developers are not constrained by the clumsy decisionmaking processes found in large financial institutions. Hence independent developers can act much faster, more decisively, and with great innovation than their institutional counterparts. Speedy decisionmaking is critical in taking maximum advantage of the opportunities that arise in a typical large-scale real estate development project. Yet large financial institutions make decisions through committees that cannot respond to rapidly unfolding events nearly as swiftly as independent developers. A sign in a Jesuit residence house in Cleveland speaks to this aspect of corporate structure: "God so loved the world that He didn't send a committee to save it!" Committees are not only slow but are also less willing to take chances by trying new methods or ideas. Yet precisely such imaginative innovation is one of the most important characteristics of good real estate development.

The developer's key function is to overcome the basic inertia of society that resists creation of anything new. A good developer is therefore both a creative initiator of some new idea and an imaginative and persistent overcomer of the obstacles to bringing that idea into reality. Thus a developer should combine innovative genius with tireless persistence. This combination of traits is far less likely to exist within a large corporation than in an independent entrepreneurial firm.

The last comparative advantage of independent developers is that they can offer equity-based compensation to attract top-quality entrepreneurial talent. Those persons most able to carry out the functions of development described above will be strongly attracted by compensation schemes that promise a share of future ownership and future profits from capital gains, as well as current salaries and bonuses. Independent development firms can use such schemes. They do not have to defend their compensation arrangements to either public shareholders or large personnel departments.

In contrast, large corporations must use relatively uniform means of compensating employees with about the same degree of responsibility, although these staff perform different functions. Therefore corporations cannot offer equity ownership as a reward only to people in their real estate departments. In some cases, such institutions have set up separate real estate subsidiaries precisely to adopt compensation arrangements in them that differ from their "normal" procedures. Yet corporations are almost always more constrained, even in such subsidiaries, than are independent development firms. As a result the latter can usually better attract and retain those people most talented in performing the development function.

These advantages mean that independent development firms will continue to be vital actors in U.S. real estate markets in the foreseeable future. Even so, their functions will not be exactly the same as in the past. In particular, now that capital suppliers have tasted the fruits of (at least partial) equity ownership, most will want to continue doing so. Therefore few developers will be able to borrow all the money necessary to finance their transactions from capital suppliers without yielding a significant share of the equity ownership to these suppliers.

In some cases joint ventures will be entered by both parties. In other cases developers will retain nominal ownership, so as to make use of the tax benefits thereof, but will give up certain benefits of ownership in other forms. For example, participating mortgages provide the capital suppliers with a share of both ongoing cash flows and final sales receipts as well as regular monthly or annual payments on their debt. Such mortgages thus offer a quasi-ownership position. Other similar quasi-ownership arrangements will become much more prevalent than in the past.

In addition, some developers will agree to act on a fee basis, turning over the entire equity position to the capital suppliers at the completion of the project. This arrangement will occur in a far larger percentage of cases than it did before the early 1980s. Yet developers' retention of at least some equity interest will remain the prevailing arrangement—partly because capital suppliers would prefer to have someone else manage their properties and partly because the best incentive for good project management is an ownership position.

The prevailing balance of terms in most real estate development or purchase transactions will depend in part on economic conditions. The more financial capital that is available for real estate investment, the more competition there will be among financial institutions to sponsor projects of good quality. That competition will reduce an institution's bargaining power in dealing with the best developers. Hence the latter will be able to retain more ownership, under better terms, than when there are shortages of investable funds. Then the capital suppliers will have a stronger bargaining position and will use it to capture a higher share of the equity, to negotiate better terms, and to increase the percentage of deals in which developers act solely for a fee. Thus independent developers will remain key actors in real estate markets.

12

The Nature of Secondary Mortgage Markets

THIS CHAPTER explores the structure of secondary mortgage markets, their increasing importance, and key aspects of their operation. The next chapter discusses deficiencies of these markets, goals they might serve, desirable changes in their structure, and possible future policies concerning them.

Activities Carried Out in Mortgage Markets

Both primary and secondary mortgage markets revolve around several different activities that can be carried out in various combinations by specific firms. These activities are

—*mortgage origination*, consisting in creating mortgages by lending money against real property, as explained in chapter 4;

—*mortgage servicing*, consisting in collecting monthly payments from borrowers and forwarding the funds to the mortgage holders (both savings and loans and mortgage bankers are in this business, usually in conjunction with mortgage origination);

—*mortgage brokerage*, involving earning of fees by bringing buyers and sellers of mortgages together, but not actual purchase of mortgages;

—acting as *mortgage dealer*, involving purchasing mortgages and holding them in inventory until an ultimate purchaser can be found (dealers thus take some risk that interest rates—hence mortgage prices—will change adversely while they have sizable inventories);

—the *mortgage-portfolio* business, consisting in raising money in capital markets through savings accounts, bonds, notes, or other instruments, then using that money *to buy and hold* mortgages in a portfolio;

—the *mortgage-conduit* business, consisting in buying mortgages, packaging them in some way, and selling them—or securities based on them—to someone else to hold (different from being a dealer because it involves changing the mortgages into some other type of security).

Individual firms embody many different combinations of these activities. Most firms that engage in servicing, brokerage, or dealership, however, usually also perform the other three functions. More details about how these activities work in practice are presented later in the chapter.

How Mortgages Enter Secondary Markets

Mortgages created when originators make loans backed by real estate in *primary markets* can enter *secondary markets* in the following ways.

—Institutions that originate mortgages but want to hold *fewer* than they are currently creating (for example, savings and loan associations and mortgage bankers) sell some of the mortgages they originate to other institutions.

—Institutions that originate mortgages but want to hold *more* than they are currently creating (for example, savings and loan associations) buy additional mortgages from other originators.

—The Government National Mortgage Association (GNMA) buys mortgages insured by the Federal Housing Administration (FHA) or the Veterans Administration (VA), packages the mortgages in groups, issues securities based on those packages, guarantees timely payment of interest and principal, and then sells those securities to investors.

—The Federal National Mortgage Association (FNMA) buys mortgages originated by mortgage bankers or savings and loans, either adds these mortgages to its portfolio or packages groups of them, issues securities based on those packages, and sells them to investors.

—The Federal Home Loan Mortgage Corporation (FHLMC)

buys mortgages, packages groups of them, issues securities based on those packages, and sells them to investors.

—Non-government-associated financial institutions—such as banks, mortgage companies, or even homebuilders—package mortgages that they have issued themselves or purchased, issue securities based on those packages, and sell them to investors; in most cases these securities are insured by private mortgage guarantee companies.

How Mortgage Market Activities Work in Practice

Thrift institutions are in the *mortgage-portfolio business* in primary mortgage markets when they originate the mortgages they hold. But they may also buy additional mortgages or mortgage-backed securities (MBSs) to hold through secondary markets; that is, from other mortgage originators or third parties. Most of the profits in this business come from the spread between interest rates on the mortgages purchased (the assets of the business) and those on the underlying savings accounts, bonds, or notes (the liabilities of the business). Fees for carrying out transactions also contribute to profits. FNMA has been (and still is) in this business, as are most savings and loan associations.

The mortgage-portfolio business is viable only as long as interest rates on the mortgage assets purchased are notably higher than those paid on the underlying liabilities. But mortgages usually have longer maturities than those liabilities. Even the interest rates on most adjustable rate mortgages (ARMs) cannot be altered as much or as often in response to current market conditions as the rates on the liabilities supporting them. Firms in this business therefore run the risk that the average interest rate on their shorter-term liabilities will rise above that on their longer-term assets during periods of economic volatility.

When that occurs, such firms start losing money, and their net capital value begins to erode. This happened to FNMA and to most of the thrift industry during 1981–82, when short-term interest rates were far above long-term rates for many months.[1] Because eco-

---

1. U.S. Bureau of the Census, *Statistical Abstract of the United States, 1983* (Government Printing Office, 1984), p. 515.

nomic conditions have been much more volatile since 1970 than during the previous thirty-five years, this *interest rate risk* has become much greater than in the past. It is the main hazard of the mortgage-portfolio business. *Default risk*—the possible loss of income, principal, or both owing to borrowers' failure to repay—is a second important risk in this business.

The primary sources of profits in the *mortgage-conduit business* are both fees and interest rate spreads. FHLMC is in this business, and most of GNMA's activities are too. FNMA has become much more active in it during the past few years.

The activity of secondary mortage markets originally consisted mainly in sales of mortgages by savings and loan associations and mortgage companies to each other. Associations in regions with high savings levels but low construction activity often had more savings than they could profitably invest locally. Conversely, those in fast-growth regions with high-level construction but low-level savings needed to import capital. Hence associations in capital-rich areas bought mortgages originated in capital-scarce areas and added them to their portfolios. In 1970, 36.7 percent of all original mortgages for one- to four-unit family housing were resold in the secondary market. That percentage has risen much higher since then. It was nearly 50 percent in 1980–81 and rose to over 75 percent in 1982, *excluding* "swaps" in which thrifts directly exchanged mortgages for the same amount of MBSs.[2]

A large part of the secondary mortgage market is given to the activities of FNMA, which has long purchased many mortgages for retention in its huge portfolio. Fannie Mae pays for such purchases by floating bonds and notes in the general credit market. Because FNMA's total mortgage portfolio exceeded $80 billion in early 1985, it has successfully shifted large amounts of credit from the bond market to real estate markets.

A second mechanism for accomplishing the same shift is the

2. David O. Maxwell, "Can the Secondary Mortgage Market Meet the Challenge of the 1980s?" speech delivered at the Federal National Mortgage Association, Washington, D.C., December 14, 1982. Data on the share of all mortgage originations for family housing containing one to four units flowing through secondary mortgage markets came from Timothy Howard, "The Outlook for Interest Rates, Housing, and the Mortgage Market," Conference for Investor Analysts, sponsored by FNMA, Washington, D.C., December 1, 1983.

"mortgage pools" created by GNMA. Ginnie Mae buys mortgages already insured by FHA against possible default on payment of interest and principal, packages groups of these mortgages, issues securities backed by those packages, guarantees timely payment of interest and principal, and sells them to pension funds and other financial investors. Such activity constitutes the *mortgage-conduit business*. These mortgage pools are considered low-risk securities by investors because of their guarantees from two federal agencies. Hence they have become popular as a means of investing in real estate without the usual risks. They have many of the traits of long-term bonds, including long maturities and fixed interest rates. The ways in which they differ from long-term bonds are discussed later in the chapter.

Who owns MBSs issued by GNMA? As of 1980 almost half of those securities outstanding (49.6 percent) were held by parties whose identity was unknown. The largest known holders were savings and loan associations (15.6 percent), mutual savings banks (9.7 percent), pension funds (9.5 percent), mortgage bankers (6.2 percent), and commercial banks (5.7 percent).[3] If the unnamed parties have the same composition as the known holders, the proportions held by each of these institutions would approximately double.

During 1977–83 the dollar value of total mortgages outstanding rose 78.4 percent, but that of total mortgages in pools rose 305.6 percent.[4] As a result, the percentage of all mortgages outstanding that were held in pools rose from 6.9 in 1977 to 15.6 at the end of 1983. Moreover, additional mortgages in pools accounted for only 12.3 percent of all additional mortgages outstanding in 1977–78, about 18 percent in 1978–81, but about 75 percent in 1981–82. This fraction fell to 40 percent during 1983, when thrifts and banks were flooded with additional deposits. Thus mortgage pools became much more important relative to all mortgage lending during a period when thrift institutions were greatly weakened, and less important when thrifts grew stronger again. It is true that thrift institutions themselves hold a large share of the securities based on

3. Cited in John Tuccillo, "Structural Change and Federally Related Secondary Market Agencies," speech prepared for a Federal National Mortgage Association conference, Washington, D.C., December 14, 1982.

4. Board of Governors of the Federal Reserve System, *Federal Reserve Bulletin*, vol. 68 (November 1982), p. A41, and vol. 66 (August 1980), p. A41.

these pools. Yet the pools have helped keep mortgage funds flowing when the thrifts have cut back on their lending.

These data cover mortgages in all pools originated by the "Big Three"—GNMA, FHLMC, FNMA—and by the Farmers Home Administration and other agencies. GNMA pools, however, accounted for 56 percent of total pooled mortgages outstanding in the second quarter of 1984.[5] FHLMC performs a similar function by packaging mortgages, issuing securities based on them, and selling those securities. But Freddie Mac usually deals in conventional mortgages not previously insured by FHA. FNMA has also recently begun creating MBSs.

The last important channel for moving mortgages from their originators into secondary markets consists in issuance of MBSs by banks, homebuilders, and others. This has been a relatively small source of funds compared with the other four channels, although it may grow in the future (especially because legislation encouraging it was passed in late 1984).

Social Functions and Objectives of Secondary Mortgage Markets

On the basis of the congressional acts that created the major institutions of the secondary markets and the actual operations of those markets, the fundamental *social functions* of these markets are to enable achievement of the following goals (compared with the degree to which those goals would be achieved without such markets):

—increasing the total size of capital flows into housing markets;

—reducing the cyclical instability of those capital flows;

—increasing the efficiency of capital allocation, both in the economy in general and within housing markets;

—decreasing the real cost of housing finance to the ultimate consumers occupying households;

—increasing the percentage of American households that own their own homes;

—helping the federal government finance certain subsidized

5. Federal Reserve Board, *Federal Reserve Bulletin*, vol. 70 (August 1984), p. A37.

housing units for which funding would otherwise be difficult to find.

These goals are stated rather abstractly. More concrete are particular tactics for achieving these broad goals. I will refer to them in the following subsections as the *specific objectives* of secondary mortgage markets.

Increasing the Liquidity of Mortgages and Mortgage Instruments

The institutions in secondary markets create greater liquidity by continually buying and selling mortgages originated by others. This ongoing market activity makes mortgage originators and holders confident that they can sell their mortgages for cash whenever they want to, without large losses of capital value. High liquidity reduces the risks of both being unable to convert assets from one form to another for convenience and being stuck with assets that are likely to decline in value. Hence improving the liquidity of mortgages increases the willingness of investors to originate, purchase, and hold them. This increased willingness helps accomplish several of the essential functions listed above—in particular, raising the size of capital flows into housing markets.

Increasing liquidity is especially important for mortgages compared with most other investments. Every mortgage is a highly particular financial instrument. In case of default, its underlying security depends on the potential market value of a specific real property. Hence determining the mortgage's true value requires knowledge of the real estate market where that property is located. But real estate markets are extremely place specific, so evaluating them demands detailed knowledge of a locality that is unavailable to most investors.

This situation makes most investors unwilling to purchase mortgages without some guarantee that the value of the *mortgages* can be more easily assessed than the value of the *underlying properties* themselves. For years, FHA or VA mortgage insurance provided such a guarantee. Investors unfamiliar with specific properties or even with real estate markets in general were willing to purchase mortgages on those properties if they were insured by FHA or VA. Investors had confidence that they would get their money back in case of default, regardless of the value of the underlying properties, because FHA and VA are agencies of the federal government.

But most residential mortgages do not carry FHA or VA insurance. Such "conventional" mortgages (a term meaning "not insured by FHA or VA") need some other arrangement to increase investors' confidence in their security. Private mortgage insurance is one such mechanism. Ability to sell these mortgages relatively quickly in an established, ongoing market is another. This ability has been institutionalized through the creation of large, well-financed organizations that are designed to buy and sell mortgages and are partially backed by the U.S. Treasury. FNMA was the first such institution, and GNMA and FHLMC were created later. Their capabilities and behavior created, and now maintain, the most important portions of the nation's secondary mortgage markets.

In addition, the standards initially established for underwriting and documenting mortgage transactions by FHA and VA, and later modified by FNMA and FHLMC, have produced much greater uniformity in the quality of investment instruments than previously existed. Equally important, the willingness of secondary market agencies to buy mortgages at any time during economic cycles maintained a continuity of liquidity formerly absent from mortgage markets, as discussed further below.

Strong secondary markets have therefore enormously enhanced the overall marketability of residential mortgages. This increased attractiveness has in turn greatly increased the willingness of investors to purchase such mortgages, thereby expanding the total flow of capital into housing markets and reducing its cost to homebuyers.

Transferring Money from Bond Markets to Mortgage Markets

Many persons and institutions with capital to invest are familiar with corporate and government bonds but not with real estate. They are willing to purchase bonds, notes, and other securities traded in bond markets, especially those whose issuers have been given high credit ratings by established rating organizations. But investors are not willing to buy real estate or mortgages, for the reasons discussed above.

A key function of FNMA is selling securities to these investors and transferring the funds thus raised into housing markets by buying mortgages there. This function was originally economically viable because corporate bond rates were lower than mortgage interest rates. Moreover, FNMA was originally a federal agency, so its bonds and notes were considered highly secure. Investors were willing to purchase them at lower interest rates than similar securities issued by private borrowers. Later on, FNMA was made a quasi-private organization that retained some ties to the federal government.

Two other institutions with closer federal ties—GNMA and FHLMC—were later created to perform similar functions, although in a somewhat different way. They package mortgages they purchase and sell securities based on those packages. Hence they do not build up separate portfolios of mortgages held as assets, on the one hand, and bonds and notes issued as liabilities, on the other (as does FMNA). Yet all three of these agencies are designed in part to shift capital from the nation's bond markets to its housing markets.

These agencies appear to have been remarkably successful, although statistically proving that conclusion is probably impossible. One relevant piece of evidence is a big drop in the interest rate spread between mortgages and corporate bonds. Two decades ago mortgage interest rates were typically 1.5 percentage points above corporate bond rates; today mortgage rates are slightly lower. Because many factors may affect this spread, however, the secondary mortgage markets cannot be proven to be primarily responsible.

Nevertheless, the secondary markets' shifting of capital has increased the total amount of funds flowing into housing markets, has reduced interest costs to housing consumers, and has made homeownership easier compared with what would have been the case without secondary mortgage markets. By moving capital from activities with lower returns to those with higher returns, the secondary markets have also increased the nation's overall economic efficiency.

Transferring Mortgage Capital Interregionally

Older, slowly growing regions of the United States often generate savings flows larger than current investment demands there. Conversely, newer, rapidly growing regions chronically need more capital, with which to build additional homes and other improvements, than their local residents save. The nation's economic efficiency is increased if savings surpluses from the older areas meet the investment needs of newer areas. Such geographic capital transfers are not easy to accomplish through real estate investments because of the highly localized nature of real property. Potential lenders in capital-surplus regions are not familiar with the real estate markets in capital-short regions; hence they are reluctant to invest their money there unless they buy mortgages guaranteed by FHA or VA.

Overcoming these geographic barriers required developing standardized procedures and instruments. If lenders in New England believe that conventional loans made in California are based on the same underwriting procedures they use themselves, they will be willing to buy such loans, even though they are unfamiliar with the specific properties involved. Many years ago FHA and VA developed standardized procedures and documents to make such interregional lending possible for mortgages they insured.

But most home mortgages do not have FHA or VA guarantees. Private mortgage insurance firms then created similar standards for conventional mortgages. But it was not until FNMA became a major force in the secondary market that a single set of uniform underwriting and documentation standards was firmly established. By the 1970s FNMA and FHLMC had become such a huge part of the marketplace that the standards they jointly demanded from mortgage originators became accepted almost everywhere.

Moreover, operations of the Big Three themselves allocate capital interregionally. FNMA, GNMA, and FHLMC sell securities in the nation's large money centers such as New York and Chicago, where investors' savings are funneled from all over the nation. Then these three institutions also buy mortgages from all across the country—but especially from areas with local capital shortages and rapid housing growth. Such high-growth areas originate many more mortgages than their local savings institutions can fund. When the originators there sell those mortgages to the Big Three, they are in effect shifting capital from surplus to shortage regions. That improves the nation's economic efficiency and lowers capital costs to borrowers in the capital-short regions. For example, among mortgages used as backing for FHLMC securities as of August 1982, 59 percent were purchased in the West, but only 10 percent in the

Midwest. In contrast, only 14 percent of FHLMC's outstanding standard participation certificates were held in the West, but 22 percent were held in the Midwest.[6]

Acting as Back-up Source of Mortgage Funds during High Interest Rates and Tight Credit

Before financial deregulation permitted thrift institutions to pay market interest rates on savings accounts, the thrift industry went through periodic "credit crunches." These credit shortages occurred whenever interest rates rose greatly in the boom phases of the general business cycle. With savings rates limited by federal ceilings, thrifts could not offer savers interest rates as high as those available from unregulated short-term investments. Hence many thrift depositors withdrew their funds to obtain higher rates elsewhere. This caused a shortage of loanable funds in the thrift industry, and many savings and loans had to restrict their mortgage lending sharply. Such credit crunches were especially notable in 1966, 1969–70, and 1973–74. Even after partial deregulation of thrifts, another severe credit crunch took place in 1981–82, when thrifts were again suffering large losses of deposits.[7]

Households and mortgage bankers who wanted to originate mortgages during these periods often had difficulty finding sources of funds. FNMA, however, usually continued buying mortgages to help ameliorate the prevailing credit shortage and to add to its profits. As a result, the share of total mortgage credit furnished by FNMA rose much higher during credit-crunch years than during other years. For example, during the last quarter of 1969 and the first quarter of 1970, FNMA accounted for almost half the increase in mortgage loans for one- to four-unit family housing. It also supplied about 26.0 percent of the total increase in such loans in all of 1982, compared with 8.5 percent in 1978. In 1982 GNMA mortgage pools expanded by an amount equal to 31.7 percent of the total rise

---

6. A. Thomas King and David Andrukonis, "Who Holds PCs?" *Secondary Mortgage Markets*, vol. 1 (February 1984), p. 13.

7. Bureau of the Census, *Statistical Abstract of the United States, 1981–1982* (GPO, 1982), p. 512.

in loans for one- to four-unit family houses, compared with 8.7 percent in 1978.[8]

Despite the efforts of secondary market institutions to offset cyclical instability in housing market funding, activities in those markets still exhibit large swings. Both new housing starts and sales of existing homes went through huge up-and-down movements during the 1970s and early 1980s. Hence, up to 1984, housing-oriented institutions and policies have failed to end the cyclical instability of housing markets. Yet the market fluctuations might have been much worse without them.

This stabilizing function may be less important in the future than in the past, however, since thrift institutions can now pay market interest rates on savings. Hence they will probably not lose deposits during future periods of high short-term rates, as they did in the past.

Absorbing Interest Rate Risk

Most financial intermediaries bear some "intertemporal risk" that arises when savers invest capital for different periods of time than those for which developers or other users borrow it. For example, as discussed earlier, thrift institutions traditionally borrowed funds for short periods from savers and lent those funds for long periods to mortgage borrowers. As long as short-term interest rates were below long-term rates, this practice was profitable. But using funds obtained at one duration to underwrite loans made for some other duration always involves intertemporal risk to the intermediaries doing it, unless the loans have adjustable interest rates (as in ARMs). That risk springs from the inherent possibility that interest rates will move in the future so as to cause losses for those intermediaries.

When short-term rates rose higher than long-term rates, thrifts were caught in a financial squeeze. The savers' accounts came up for reconsideration long before the mortgage loans did; many savers essentially had demand deposit accounts that were implicitly renewed every day. If thrifts did not raise the interest rates they were

8. Federal Reserve Board, *Federal Reserve Bulletin*, vol. 56 (October 1970), pp. A52, A53; vol. 66 (February 1980), p. A41; and vol. 70 (September 1984), p. A37.

paying savers when those accounts came up for renewal, they would lose the funds. Savers would simply move their money somewhere else to get higher rates. But if thrifts did raise rates to savers, they would sustain operating losses because they could not equally raise interest rates on the longer-duration mortgage loans they held as assets.

One of FNMA's key functions has been to bear this same intertemporal risk. FNMA had borrowed short to lend long from its inception. Hence it had built up a portfolio of over $40 billion in long-term, fixed-rate mortgages at relatively low rates before the revolution in monetary policy in 1979.[9] When short-term interest rates subsequently soared, FNMA was compelled to sustain large operating losses, especially in 1982.

Institutions willing to bear such intertemporal risks increase the efficiency of capital markets. Those intermediaries permit long-term investments to be financed with funds supplied only for short terms, or vice versa. Thus they redistribute resources over time to offset any mismatches between the maturities desired by capital suppliers and those desired by capital users. This is the equivalent in time of moving money in space from savings-surplus regions to savings-short regions. Without such institutions, maturity mismatches between capital suppliers and capital users would prevent a great deal of valuable economic activity.

Creating an Initial Market for Mortgages on Subsidized Housing Units

The original mortgages on certain subsidized housing projects for low-income households have risks of both default and administrative difficulties that are higher than usual. Hence private investors will not buy such mortgages unless they receive extremely high interest rates in return. FNMA's connection with the federal government allows FNMA to raise money in bond markets at much lower rates. The large size of its portfolio also allows it to dilute the risks

---

9. FNMA's total holdings of mortgages equaled $43.3 billion on December 31, 1978, according to the Federal Reserve Board, *Federal Reserve Bulletin*, vol. 66 (June 1980), p. A41.

from any small group of loans because its bonds and notes are backed by the entire portfolio. FNMA can then use some of the money it raises to purchase the mortgages on these subsidized projects, thereby reducing the financing costs involved. That purchase permits the housing authorities operating these projects to charge lower rents than would otherwise be possible. It is true that FNMA could readily sell these mortgages at a discount because they are redeemed at par value in case of default. But then FNMA would have to record a loss on its books because it would be selling the mortgages below its initial cost. Hence, once it acts as the initial financing source for such projects, FNMA is often saddled with these mortgages for a long time.

Diversifying and Expanding Channels for Housing Capital Flows

This objective might be considered part of expanding total capital flows into housing. It is noted separately here to emphasize its importance. By using innovative instruments and methods, secondary mortgage market institutions have attracted large amounts of money from investors who have not traditionally funded real estate. For example, GNMA has sold over $150 billion in pass-through certificates that are backed by home mortgages. Many of these certificates were purchased by pension funds that otherwise do not invest in real estate. Many pension funds were willing to buy these certificates only because they were covered by federal government guarantees, although the certificates are not quite as liquid as Treasury bills or bonds. FHLMC has also invented several new vehicles for attracting funds into housing markets which would otherwise probably not go there.

In sum, the major institutions in the secondary mortgage markets carry out spatial intermediation (moving funds from capital-surplus to capital-short regions), temporal intermediation (using funds supplied at one set of maturities to invest at another set), and intermediation of market specialties (moving funds collected by specialists in one type of activity, such as bond investing, for use by specialists in another type, such as mortgage lending). These intermediations involve varying degrees of risk that the intermediaries will get caught in unforeseen adversities such as those occurring in 1981–82.

The Rising Importance of Secondary Mortgage Markets

The revolution in real estate finance created two basic reasons that secondary mortgage markets will become more important in the future. One reason is the weakened ability of thrifts to provide long-term mortgage funds, especially for housing. Other institutions capable of buying such mortgages and holding them for long periods must replace much of the thrifts' former portfolio function if housing credit needs are to be met adequately.

The second reason is the need for greater liquidity of real estate mortgages to make them more competitive within the nation's newly integrated capital markets. No longer is any large segment of those markets a legalized "captive" of real estate, as were thrifts before deregulation. Savings and loan associations that maintain 82 percent or more of their assets as home mortgages can hold a larger reserve of bad debt than can those that do not, though this advantage would be changed by some tax reform proposals being considered in mid-1985. This ability reduces their income taxes, thereby making mortgages more attractive to them than other investments. Even so, persons seeking to finance real estate investments must successfully appeal to capital suppliers who can choose among many other investments. Yet direct purchase of real estate mortgages has serious drawbacks compared with those other alternatives. Passing those mortgages through secondary markets removes many of those drawbacks, as explained below.

These two factors are interrelated. Thrifts will no longer hold as many long-term mortgages as in the past, partly because deregulation has reduced their legal requirement to do so. Borrowers must therefore make their instruments more attractive to both thrifts and other investors.

Secondary mortgage markets have already begun to handle a much larger fraction of all residential mortgages than they did before 1979. But these markets will not reach their full potential for channeling funds into real estate until additional changes occur in them (most of these changes are discussed in the rest of the chapter):

—developing more attractive forms for MBSs that permit issuers of those securities to manage cash flows from them;

—encouraging more widespread use of original residential mortgage instruments that are better hedged against potential inflation than long-term, fixed-rate mortgages;

—better defining the specific functions society wants performed by the quasi-governmental agencies that now carry out most secondary mortgage market activities;

—changing the laws and regulations governing these quasi-governmental agencies to enable them to perform those specific functions more effectively (more fully deregulating these agencies, more effectively regulating them, or both);

—encouraging more fully private institutions to package non-FHA-insured residential and other mortgages as bases for issuing MBSs, without using government subsidies;

—exploring the need for, and the possibilities of developing, a more effective secondary market for nonresidential mortgages.

Use of Mortgage-backed Securities

The form in which future mortgage debt is marketed to its holders will probably differ greatly from that prevalent in the past. Until the late 1970s most mortgages had fixed interest rates and were amortized over twenty to thirty years. More recently many variations in terms have been written into mortgages. But all individual mortgages are difficult to transfer from one party to another without extensive documentation of the creditworthiness of the property involved, of the issuer, or of both. Compiling and checking such documentation is costly and time consuming. Equity interests are equally difficult to transfer for the same reason.

Mortgages are therefore relatively illiquid compared with alternative investments competing with them for funds in the nation's newly integrated capital markets. This is true even in secondary markets, as long as the original instruments are the items being resold. Institutions oriented toward real estate still have extensively traded "unsecuritized" mortgages among themselves. Nevertheless, use of these hard-to-handle instruments handicaps real estate in the overall competition for capital, particularly in attracting funds from investors who know little about real estate.

A group of mortgages can be "packaged" together, however, and used as backing for another, more liquid security. Some organization such as GNMA buys many individual mortgages, puts them together into a single group, and issues another security as a liability against that group of mortgages considered as collateral. This other security is an MBS. The buyer of an MBS receives a single periodic payment representing that buyer's share of the interest and principal repayments made on all the mortgages in the package. The issuer of the MBS performs all the required administrative tasks, including evaluating the security of the mortgages to be placed in the package, pricing them, buying them, collecting interest payments from individual borrowers, receiving repayments of principal, handling any loan delinquencies or defaults, and keeping appropriate records.

The MBS is legally a trust that allows the trust manager to collect interest from individual mortgages and pass it through to the trust's owners. The trust manager does not have to pay income taxes on the interest collected in addition to those paid by the trust owners, as long as the management is "passive" and all the income is passed through to the MBS owners. The MBS buyer is thus relieved of all the costly tasks associated with determining whether individual mortgages are worth buying and with servicing them once they have been bought. Moreover, the issuer of an MBS normally provides a guarantee to the buyer to assure the latter that payments will actually be made as scheduled.

The degree of liquidity enjoyed by MBSs depends not only on the relative ease of dealing with them but also on the existence of an active market in which they can be bought or sold at any given moment. In recent years such markets in several different types of MBSs have sprung up. These types include MBSs issued by GNMA, FHLMC, FNMA, and a few private "packagers" of mortgages. Until 1985 almost all secondary markets involved residential mortgages, mainly for single-family homes, rather than industrial or commercial mortgages. These residential markets will probably become even more active in the future.

Indeed, *the future ability of real estate to extract debt funding from fully integrated capital markets depends heavily on greater use of MBSs of various types.* Only their liquidity and ease of handling can hope to appeal to those capital sources that have traditionally focused on corporate and Treasury bonds rather than on real estate mortgages.

The MBSs described above are not the only ones possible. The next section discusses a whole spectrum of possible instruments that may be used in secondary mortgage market transactions.

Costs and Risks of Transactions in Secondary Mortgage Markets

Intermediaries in secondary mortgage markets can use many methods of shifting funds from general capital markets into housing markets. Each method involves a specific type of transaction linking three parties: a capital supplier, a mortgage borrower, and an intermediary. Two important dimensions of these transactions concern the risks and costs borne by the intermediary.[10] The *risks* involve the degree to which the intermediary takes upon itself the possibility of losing from future defaults or adverse interest rate changes. The *costs* involve the amount of resources the intermediary must spend to carry out its role in the transaction.

The nature of *default risk* is self-evident, but that of *interest rate risk* is not. Fixed-rate home mortgages—still the main type in secondary market transactions—are long-term instruments with *uncertain repayment streams* (apart from defaults) because the borrowers may choose to repay faster than the contract requires. If interest rates remain at about the level specified in the mortgage contract, experience shows that home mortgages will be repaid in a certain pattern. Their average life will be about ten years, even though the contract requires full repayment in twenty-five to thirty years. That time pattern for repayment is what most investors expect when they buy mortgages or MBSs.

But if future interest rates fall *below* the contracted rate, borrowers will repay faster than usual in order to refinance at lower rates. This harms the original investors. They must reinvest those funds at

10. The method of analysis in this section was invented by Timothy Howard of FNMA. He also made many other useful suggestions for this and other chapters; I am profoundly grateful to him for his contributions.

the current rates, which are now lower than the original contracted rate. If future rates rise well *above* the contracted rate, borrowers will repay more slowly than usual. Then they can in effect reinvest their loan proceeds at those higher rates. This also harms the original investors, who would then like to get their funds back as quickly as possible to invest them at the now higher rates. But investors who purchase home mortgages cannot know in advance exactly what time pattern of repayment they will actually receive. They usually bear the risk of potential losses caused by deviations from the "normal" repayment pattern that are due to future changes in interest rates.

The two dimensions of cost and risk to the intermediary vary directly with each other. That is, the less risk the intermediary bears, the lower are its costs. Conversely, the more it assumes the risks present in such transactions, the greater are its costs. This relation is not accidental; it is inherent in the nature of such transactions.

This cost-risk correlation can be seen by focusing on the relations between the original borrower and the original capital supplier, as if they were the only two parties in the transaction. The longer the duration of the loan, the greater the possibilities of both default and interest rate changes adverse to the lender, other things being equal. Home mortgages are typically written for twenty-five to thirty years, although they are usually paid off long before that. *Someone* must bear these two types of risk. If the lender charges a fixed interest rate well above the market rate prevailing at the time the loan is made, the lender receives enough "excess compensation" to reduce possible future losses from either default or changes in interest rates. In this case the lender has shifted much of both types of risk onto the borrower. But such excess charges are difficult to obtain from borrowers in a highly competitive market. Usually the fixed interest rate of the contract is close to the prevailing market rate. Then the risk of adverse consequences from default or higher rates falls on the lender. If the interest rate is fully adjustable along with current economic conditions, the borrower bears all future interest rate risk (unless default occurs). If that rate is only partially adjustable in response to current conditions, the risk is split between the lender and borrower.

Under all these circumstances, the transaction can be designed so that an intermediary bears some or all of the risks that would otherwise fall on the lender or borrower. Intermediaries can shift the risks associated with both default and uncertain repayment streams onto themselves by guaranteeing specific repayment streams to the ultimate investors. Then any variations in actual repayments by the mortgage borrowers from the guaranteed pattern must be made up by the intermediary. The intermediaries are "uncoupling" the actual payments on these mortgages from the payments promised to the ultimate investors. There are different degrees of such uncoupling, as described further below.

Prudence indicates that, whichever party bears these risks, the risk bearer should protect itself from possible adverse consequences. Arranging that protection draws down resources; for example, it may require maintaining substantial reserves. The more the financial intermediary bears these risks, the greater are its costs—hence the greater is the compensation it must demand from the other two parties. The intermediary's compensation usually comes from increasing the spread between the rate it receives from the mortgage borrowers and the rate it guarantees to the ultimate investors. That is why investors receive lower interest rates on secondary mortgage market instruments from which repayment risks have been removed than on those which still contain such risks.

The Spectrum of Riskiness and Costs

Because of this fundamental relation, the main types of transactions being carried out in secondary mortgage markets as of early 1985 can be arrayed in the following categories.

GUARANTEED PASS-THROUGH OR PARTICIPATION CERTIFICATES. The intermediary purchases mortgages from originators, places a group of them in a pool, guarantees timely payment of interest and principal by the borrowers as specified in the mortgages, and sells participations in the flow of such guaranteed payments to capital suppliers. The intermediary assumes the full risk of default but does *not* guarantee any specific repayment pattern. Thus the ultimate investor bears all the risk of possible future interest rate changes. The pass-through certificates issued by GNMA, FHLMC, and FNMA fall into this category.

GUARANTEED PARTICIPATION CERTIFICATES (FAST-PAYING AND SLOW-PAYING, WITH DIFFERENT YIELDS). The intermediary purchases a set of mortgages, places them in a pool, guarantees timely payment to the capital suppliers, but then manages the flow of payments and prepayments on those mortgages so that participation certificates can be divided into "fast-paying" and "slow-paying" groups with different yields. These are sold to investors with different preferences for the timing of their repayments. The intermediary bears no greater risks in this case than it does with straight pass-through certificates, since it does not guarantee any particular pattern of repayments. The intermediary has slightly greater operating costs in this case, however, because it must reshuffle the repayment streams and allocate them to different investors. The intermediary also tries to market the two types of investments to different groups, hoping to draw investors into buying MBSs who otherwise would not do so.

"COLLATERALIZED" MORTGAGE OBLIGATIONS.   These instruments are bonds secured by mortgages held by the intermediary, which places all mortgage repayments in a sinking fund from which it makes semiannual payments to the investors. The bonds collateralized by a single pool of mortgages are divided into three groups: those to be repaid fully within a relatively short period, those to be repaid fully within a moderately long period, and those to be repaid only after a long period. Although interest is paid on all three groups semiannually, repayments of principal from the mortgages are all funneled to the first group of bonds until they are fully repaid. Then mortgage principal repayments go to the second group of bonds until they are repaid, and finally to the third group.

The intermediary guarantees that all bonds in each group will be fully repaid by specific dates. If every ultimate mortgage borrower held back repayment as long as contractually possible, all three bond issues might not be fully repaid from mortgage repayments by those guaranteed dates. Then the intermediary would have to advance capital to make the repayments as scheduled. This guarantee thus transfers some (although not much) of the interest rate risk onto the intermediary, which also bears all default risks.[11]

11. For details concerning collateralized mortgage obligations issued by FHLMC, see Federal Home Loan Mortgage Corporation, *Offering Circular: $1,000,000 Collateralized Mortgage Obligations, Series 1983-A* (Washington, D.C.: FHLMC, June 7, 1983), p. 1.

When FHLMC first offered collateralized mortgage obligations, it priced the short-term bonds to provide a slightly higher yield than the other two groups, and the long-term ones to provide the lowest yield. The management of repayment streams required by collateralized mortgage obligations raises operating costs above those for straight pass-through certificates.

Collateralized mortgage obligations are debts on the books of the intermediary that are balanced by the mortgages backing them, which appear as assets. This accounting treatment differs from that of pass-through certificates, which do not appear on the intermediary's books at all. When the intermediary sells a pass-through certificate to an investor, the intermediary is considered to have sold the underlying assets (the mortgages backing the certificate) to that investor; hence nothing remains on the intermediary's books. Collateralized mortgage obligations are not considered "qualifying assets" for savings and loan associations buying them, whereas pass-through certificates are. That is, collateralized mortgage obligations do not count as mortgages in calculating whether each association has maintained enough of its assets in home mortgages to use the special bad-debt reserve.

TRUSTS FOR INVESTMENT IN MORTGAGES. Such trusts are a form of investment that had only been proposed, but not legalized, in early 1985 when this book was written. The form involves establishing a trust that buys mortgages and manages the repayment streams in a manner similar to that described for collateralized mortgage obligations. The trust would not be subject to income tax on the interest collected from the mortgages, since it would pass that interest through to the ultimate investors. But the trust would first actively manage how the interest was distributed among those investors. The trust would presumably provide investors with sufficient guarantees of repayment certainty so that it would have to bear some of the interest rate risk, as well as default risk.

ISSUANCE OF NONCOLLATERALIZED BONDS AND NOTES, THE PROCEEDS OF WHICH ARE USED TO PURCHASE AND HOLD MORTGAGES. This was FNMA's original method of operation, and it is still used. The practice completely uncouples the mortgages purchased from raising the money to purchase them. The bonds and notes issued by the intermediary provide investors with fully specified repayment schedules (although the schedules may allow redemption in advance of the full term). Hence the intermediary bears all the interest rate risk stemming from uncertainty about the repayment streams from the mortgages it buys, plus all mortgage default risk.

In sum, the greater the risks borne by the secondary mortgage market intermediary along this spectrum, the more the intermediary must charge—hence the lower the yield received by the ultimate investor who supplies capital, other things being equal. That investor presumably is willing to accept a lower yield in return for greater certainty of payment, and therefore less interest rate and default risk. Part of the theory of secondary mortgage markets is that lowering those risks inherent in mortgages will broaden the potential market for them more than lowering the yields on the new instruments thus created will narrow that market.

The net result will be a smaller rate differential between instruments used to finance housing and those used to finance other types of activity that the market believes have inherently less risk or more liquidity than "pure" mortgages. That smaller rate differential will lower the ultimate cost of capital to housing occupants, increase the total amount of capital invested in housing, or some combination of both—compared with what would occur without the secondary mortgage market.

But investors can offset risks within their own portfolios by varying the overall mix of different types of assets they hold. Hence some investors would prefer to buy mortgage-oriented instruments with relatively high yields, accepting the risks involved, over those instruments with much lower risks but also lower yields. Experience shows that many investors prefer pass-through certificates to "pure" mortgages because of the greater liquidity of the former, even though both pass interest rate risks fully onto the investor. But it is too early to determine from market reactions whether other instruments that sacrifice more yield to reduce risk further will be well accepted by investors in general.

Because the pass-through type of MBS has clearly demonstrated its market acceptability, much of the analysis in the rest of this chapter and the next chapter focuses on this investment form. Readers should extend the implications of that analysis, however, to other types of mortgage-related securities along the spectrum described above as those securities also demonstrate their market acceptability.

This applies to both existing and yet-to-be-invented forms of such securities.

Mortgage-backed Securities versus Corporate Bonds

MBSs differ from corporate bonds in four important ways. First, the cost of administering the pool of individual mortgages underlying each MBS is greater than the cost of administering one or more corporate bonds of the same denomination. Therefore, if other things are equal, the interest rate spread between what the final recipient of funds pays and what the final supplier of funds receives must be slightly larger for MBSs.

Second, MBSs could in theory be based on ARMs, thereby allowing the investors buying them at least some protection against possible future increases in interest rates, whereas very few adjustable rate corporate bonds exist. As of early 1984 this difference between MBSs and corporate bonds was largely theoretical, since very few MBSs were backed by ARMs. Moreover, there is no theoretical reason prohibiting corporations from issuing variable rate bonds. Nevertheless, in the recent past a much higher proportion of both residential and nonresidential mortgages than of corporate bonds have been issued with some form of variable rates.

A third difference is that each MBS issue is based on many individual debt instruments, from diverse borrowers, that have been pooled, whereas each corporate bond issue is typically from a single borrower. Hence the many mortgages underlying each MBS can be managed so they come from geographically diversified markets. This diversification decreases *default risk* that might arise from acute economic adversity in any one market area. Similar risk reduction is almost impossible for a corporate bond issue originated by a single firm. A firm may have many different products sold in spatially scattered markets, but default risk from adversity to that firm must be considered less diversified than that of the typical MBS pools.

The most important difference between corporate bonds and MBSs is that only the latter suffer from *prepayment risk*, which was described earlier. As a result, when making an initial investment, investors in MBSs cannot accurately determine the ultimate yield they will receive, even though they know the initial interest rate.

Prepayment risk has several aspects. Most mortgages are amortized so that a portion of the principal is repaid as part of each payment. The investor must therefore reinvest portions of the principal periodically over the life of the investment in order to earn income on the full initial amount of the investment. But the yields that will be available at the time such reinvestments must be made cannot be known in advance with much reliability. Hence the investor is not sure what the ultimate total yield will be at the time the initial investment is made. In contrast, most corporate bonds pay interest only until the final payment, when all the principal is repaid at once. Hence the initial amount is fully invested right up to the last day at the contracted rate. Thus the yields on nonamortized corporate securities are more predictable than are those on MBSs.

This problem is aggravated by the ability of individual mortgage borrowers to repay the principal even faster than normal. Prepayment is quite likely in residential mortgages. Most households sell their homes long before the typical amortization period of twenty-five to thirty years and pay their mortgage off at the time of sale. Thus an investor buying an MBS backed by twenty-five-year mortgages can typically count on the mortgages lasting an average of only ten years. Yet the exact duration of the mortgages cannot be forecast reliably.

Moreover, as noted earlier, residential borrowers are likely to repay mortgages much faster than the average if the initial interest rate was quite high and if rates have subsequently fallen. If capital suppliers must then reinvest those funds at lower rates, the total yield on their initial MBS investment will turn out to be lower than they had initially planned. Because of this risk, investors believe that MBSs are biased toward yields lower than initially stated if the general interest rate structure falls. Prepayment risks imply the following conclusions.

—Prepayment is a definite disadvantage of MBSs compared with corporate bonds if all the other basic characteristics are similar. The distinction is analogous to that between callable and noncallable bonds.

—Investors prefer MBSs based on mortgages with interest rates that are relatively low compared with the average prevailing rate and dislike MBSs based on mortgages with relatively high interest rates. Households that made low-interest mortgages will not repay them faster than the normal amortization schedule and may even hold them longer than usual unless those mortgages have due-on-sale clauses. Refinancing those older mortgages at today's higher rates would just raise their monthly payments. Therefore, low-rate mortgages (normally put into MBSs at a discount because of their low rates) have much lower refinancing risk than high-rate mortgages.

—During periods of unusually high interest rates, investors strongly prefer corporate bonds that prohibit or limit prepayment of principal over MBSs that do not, if the other characteristics of both are similar. Hence the interest rate spread between these two types of instruments tends to widen (in favor of corporate bonds) in such periods. During periods of unusually low interest rates, that spread narrows.

—During periods of *unanticipated* inflation, prepayment reduces the overall loss of real purchasing power caused by currency depreciation compared with that suffered by a corporate bondholder. The mortgage holder gets some of the principal back before it has lost as much real purchasing power as it would if not returned until the final maturity date of the loan. But this is an advantage only if the investor plans to spend the principal on consumption as it is returned, rather than to reinvest it. Hence financial markets do not pay much attention to this factor.

Improving the Marketability of Mortgage-backed Securities

These relative disadvantages of MBSs compared with typical corporate bonds require the former to offer higher yields than the latter in order to exert comparable market attraction. Reducing those disadvantages should therefore reduce the yield premium paid by housing for financial capital. How can this be done?

In theory the additional risks inherent in MBSs *borne by the ultimate investor* could be reduced in three ways. One is to prohibit borrowers from repaying principal faster than their original amortization schedule specifies, except when they sell their properties. It would not be practical to ban prepayments altogether because most residential borrowers sell their homes well before the full terms of their loans, but prepayment for reasons other than resale could be eliminated. This prohibition, however, would reduce the choices available to consumers, thereby decreasing their welfare. Moreover, the housing industry is likely to oppose this change if it is made compulsory for all residential borrowers. Therefore this tactic is both undesirable and unlikely to be adopted.

A second approach would require borrowers to pay a higher price for mortgages with prepayment privileges (except for repayment upon sale) than for those without them. This higher price could be an initial fee or a slightly higher interest rate. If the price were made great enough, a large percentage of home purchasers might be encouraged to avoid the cost of prepayment privileges. Then some MBSs could be based solely on mortgages with limited prepayment privileges. Presumably these MBSs would be more attractive to investors than MBSs still carrying a higher prepayment risk. This approach would not, however, eliminate prepayments stemming from either normal amortization or resale.

A third approach would allow a secondary mortgage market intermediary to assume some of the interest rate risk, thereby removing the risk from the ultimate investor. This shifting of risk could be done in several ways set forth in the preceding description of the spectrum of risks and costs among different secondary market transactions. In each case, decreasing this risk would also reduce the yield to the ultimate investor.

The Initial Interest Rate Premium of Mortgage-backed Securities

Despite all the above measures, the disadvantages of MBSs compared with corporate bonds probably cannot be entirely eliminated in the future. Therefore, MBSs may have to offer an initial interest rate premium over these competitive securities to attract sufficient funds into real estate. How large will this rate premium be?

Table 12–1 presents yields for various types of securities with five-year maturities (unless otherwise noted) as published in the *Wall Street Journal* on October 12, 1984. Several conclusions can be drawn from these data.

—MBSs issued by GNMA and industrial corporate bonds had almost identical yields. Both had *lower* yields than securities in Moody's Aaa and Aa Utility Bond Index (although that index showed the same yield as MBSs from GNMA in August 1983). This

Table 12-1. *Comparison of Yields on Bond-like Investments, as of October 12, 1984*
Percent

Issuer or type[a]	Yield	Spread from Treasury bonds	Spread from GNMA
U.S. Treasury bills (90 days)	10.33	−1.83	−2.66
U.S. Treasury bonds	12.16	. . .	−0.83
Federal Home Loan Bank Board	12.44	+0.28	−0.55
Federal National Mortgage Association	12.49	+0.33	−0.50
Adjustable rate mortgages (3-year term)	12.39	+0.23	−0.60
Government National Mortgage Association (12.5% series)	12.99	+0.83	. . .
Recent corporate industrial bonds (unstated maturity)	12.92	+0.76	−0.07
Moody's Aaa and Aa Utility Bond Index	13.60[b]	+1.44	+0.61
Fixed-rate mortgages (30-year term)	13.83	+1.67	+0.84

Source: *Wall Street Journal*, October 12, 1984.
a. Each type of security has a maturity of approximately five years unless otherwise indicated.
b. Estimated from graph of this index.

difference reflects both the widespread acceptance of GNMA and the financial difficulties among public utilities.

—GNMA yields were 83 basis points (100 basis points equal 1 percent) above U.S. Treasury bond yields and were higher than yields on bonds issued by either the Federal Home Loan Bank Board (FHLBB) or FNMA.

—FNMA and FHLBB bonds had higher yields than Treasury bonds but lower yields than corporate bonds.

—Traditional long-term, fixed-rate mortgages had higher yields than any other type of security shown. These were conventional mortgages, not insured by FHA or VA. Mortgage yields were 50 basis points above yields on GNMA pass-through certificates. This reflects the superior acceptability of MBSs compared with mortgages themselves.

Some disagreement arose among the experts I interviewed concerning how large an interest rate spread would separate MBSs from corporate bonds in the future. Some believed there would be no difference, as on the date shown in table 12–1. They thought the lower default risk of MBSs would completely compensate for their higher prepayment risk. Others thought a spread of as much as a percentage point over corporate bonds would be necessary to induce pension fund managers to consider investing in MBSs. Nearly all agreed that the greater is the share of total real estate mortgage funds raised through secondary markets, the greater is the probability that such a spread would rise, and the higher it would be.

The size of any such spread is important because the number of potential homebuyers who can qualify for mortgages depends on the *nominal level* of interest rates. The greater is the spread between mortgage rates and corporate bond rates, the higher is the nominal level of mortgage rates for any given general level of interest rates.

13

Policies Affecting Secondary Mortgage Markets

As of early 1985, when this book was written, secondary mortgage markets suffered from the following deficiencies.

—*The Federal National Mortgage Association (FNMA) was in financially precarious condition in the prevailing climate of volatile interest rates.* Its large existing portfolio of older fixed-rate, low-interest mortgages made its income flows far less flexible than the costs of the bonds and notes underlying that portfolio. Hence, whenever short-term interest rates rose close to or above long-term rates, FNMA began to lose money (as did the entire thrift industry, which it resembles in this respect). If this situation were to continue for long, FNMA could become bankrupt unless it received aid from the federal government.

—*The Federal Home Loan Mortgage Corporation (FHLMC) could not function as effectively as it could as a fully private institution.* If so converted from its quasi-governmental status, FHLMC could carry out all the functions it has performed without any injury to the public interest. Moreover, it would then have greater flexibility and speed of responsiveness, enabling it to innovate and perform even more useful functions.

—*The connections between FNMA and FHLMC and the federal government that have reduced their costs of funds compared with those of fully private institutions without federal deposit insurance were contributing to the imbalance of risk within U.S. financial markets.* That imbalance was analyzed in detail in chapter 10. It extended far beyond secondary mortgage markets, since it involved the use of federal deposit insurance by banks and thrifts as well as the federal connections mentioned above. It was probably inhibiting the entry of more private firms into secondary mortgage market operations, although that cannot be unequivocally proven.

—*These special federal connections within secondary mortgage markets were steering capital flows into housing by reducing the interest costs that housing-oriented borrowers would have had to pay without such connections.* Hence more capital was going into housing than would have if these special connections had not existed. Many people in the home-building and real estate industries consider this condition an advantage rather than a deficiency. Why I view it as a deficiency is discussed later in this chapter.

These conditions reduced the efficiency of capital markets in general and of secondary mortgage markets in particular. They therefore raised the costs for capital users (except for housing-oriented borrowers, whose costs were lowered at the expense of all other capital users). No one knows reliably, however, *by how much* capital costs were changed by these conditions. Nevertheless, I presume that removing these deficiencies would be socially desirable if the costs of doing so are not great. The rest of this chapter, therefore, discusses possible policies for reducing or eliminating these deficiencies.

Setting Goals for Secondary Mortgage Market Institutions

In evaluating possible policies concerning secondary mortgage markets, I will use the principles set forth below. Although they also pertain to the nation's other financial markets, these principles are value judgments that certainly can be debated—the reason that I describe them explicitly here.

—If any function can be performed by either the public or private sector, without any significant difference in social goals served, it should be performed by the private sector. This presumes that private action will be more efficient, other things being equal. It also presumes that as few resources as possible should be routed through the public sector, other things being equal. A corollary is that no function should be performed in the future by either the public or private sector merely because that function has been carried out in the past or is being performed now.

—Arrangements that force financial institutions to compete with each other and to attract resources through markets are superior to those which do not, other things being equal.

—*Additional* government subsidies that reduce the cost of occupying real estate should be made available primarily to low- and moderate-income households and not to middle- and upper-income ones—unless there is high priority for benefiting the latter two groups. This principle covers use of federal credit to reduce mortgage interest rates.[1]

—Small-scale savers and investors should not be required to investigate the security of particular financial institutions in which they place their funds in ways that require costly research. Large-scale savers and investors, however, should be given incentives to conduct such investigations. Detailed research would discourage excessive risk taking by financial institutions trying to attract funds from large-scale savers and investors.

—Private firms should not benefit from special connections with the federal government that give them competitive advantages *unless* those connections serve high-priority social goals that cannot be met in other ways. An example is federal deposit insurance.

—Whenever such special connections cannot be eliminated, other arrangements should be adopted when feasible to reduce the competitive advantages they provide.

—Public agencies that would have to pay the costs if private firms failed should investigate and influence the degree of risk taking of those private firms. Federal agencies that provide deposit insurance thus should—and do—have examination and regulation responsibilities concerning the organizations they insure.

Like most sets of abstract principles, this one contains inevitable

1. Several important *existing* tax benefits and other policies equivalent to housing subsidies primarily benefit middle- and upper-income households. They presumably encourage greater homeownership among all income groups. Whether they should be retained in their present forms is debatable. However, emphasis in this analysis will be upon proposals for *additional* subsidies. For the record, however, my views on this subject are given here. I believe present tax benefits for homeownership should be changed by shifting tax deductibility of mortgage interest and property taxes to a tax credit and by reducing the size of these benefits by an amount sufficient to finance an entitlement program of housing vouchers for all renters with incomes below 50 percent of their area's median incomes. Such a voucher program would leave most homeownership benefits intact. For a discussion of these policy recommendations, see Anthony Downs, *Rental Housing in the 1980s* (Brookings, 1983), pp. 142–47.

conflicts that could lead to inconsistencies in its implementation. Because all human endeavors have multiple objectives, this problem cannot be avoided; it must be overcome through common sense in practice.

Should Federal Connections in Secondary Mortgage Markets Be Used to Aid Housing?

One of the central functions of secondary mortgage markets can only be carried out adequately by agencies with special ties to the federal government. That function is to support federal housing subsidy programs. Sustaining FNMA's large mortgage portfolio may also require an interim tie to the federal government, for reasons discussed later. Several other current uses of these federal connections, however, are not as clearly desirable from society's viewpoint. For one thing, fully private institutions could perform these functions too. Moreover, there are large social costs to using those federal connections, as discussed in chapter 10.

Nevertheless, such connections definitely benefit housing markets compared with what would be the case without them. For example, the Government National Mortgage Association (GNMA) uses Federal Housing Administration (FHA) guarantees and the relatively low cost of federal credit to reduce mortgage interest rates to homeowners. As a result, interest rates on home mortgages financed by GNMA pass-through certificates are lower than they would be if GNMA's and FHA's functions were carried out by fully private agencies. To a lesser extent, the same holds true for home mortgages ultimately financed by activities of FNMA or FHLMC. The "Big Three" agencies plus the Farmers Home Administration act as conduits for large shares of total home mortgage funding. Therefore all home mortgage interest rates are probably lowered by this use of federal connections, although no one knows exactly by how much.

Furthermore, the total flow of capital into housing markets is undoubtedly larger because of these federal connections than it would be without them. The channels funneling capital into housing markets are also more diversified because of them. Finally, homeownership is surely somewhat easier for American households to attain because of the consequent lower interest rates and greater mortgage availability. Thus *housing markets and their many partici-pants clearly benefit* from the pervasive use of federal connections by the major institutions of the secondary mortgage market.

This outcome is certainly regarded as desirable by the home-building industry, the home sales (realty) industry, the thrift indus-try, and many other participants who benefit from it, including millions of home-owning households. Nevertheless, there are three persuasive arguments against these uses of federal connections.

—Extending the umbrella of federal credit ratings to large amounts of essentially private borrowing—as in GNMA participa-tion certificates—raises the average interest rate paid on all federal borrowing. This imposes a cost on federal taxpayers, perhaps a large one (although no reliable measurements have yet been made).

—Giving housing credit a special advantage distorts the overall allocation of capital in the economy, shifting too many resources into housing and leaving too few in other forms of investment that do not have such advantage. This distortion reduces overall economic effi-ciency.

—Use of federal connections in secondary mortgage markets is not necessary to encourage homeownership because homeowners already benefit from other federal connections that reduce their income taxes and mortgage interest rates. The sizable benefits home-owners receive from current income tax laws were discussed earlier. As mortgage borrowers, homeowners also gain from thrifts' ability to attract funds at relatively low interest costs through their feder-ally insured savings accounts.

Whether GNMA sales of pass-through certificates and other fund-ing by quasi-federal agencies in capital markets raise federal interest rates in general is a hotly debated subject. Proponents of allowing GNMA to issue as many mortgage-backed securities (MBSs) as it can argue that its services do not cost taxpayers any money. After all, GNMA covers the expenses of its activities in secondary mortgage markets through user fees. FHLMC and FNMA similarly pay their own operating costs. So why not make the benefits of their low-interest mortgage funding as widely available as possible?

This argument ignores the fact that MBSs issued by GNMA are treated by the market as quasi-governmental securities. Similar issues by FHLMC and FNMA also pay lower interest rates than they would if these agencies had no federal connections. The more issues these agencies sell, therefore, the greater is the total amount of what the market considers federal or federally supported borrowing. This expanded demand for federal credit must raise the average price of such credit; that is, the average federal interest rate. Given the currently huge size of the federal debt, even a tiny marginal increase in federal interest rates is a large sum of money. That added cost falls on federal taxpayers in general.

This upward pressure on average federal interest rates occurs even though the users of GNMA credit pay a *lower* average interest rate than they would if they used fully private funding. GNMA's clients clearly benefit from this federal connection. But the resultant overall expansion in use of its credit causes the *average* interest rate advantage from this connection to decline compared with that in fully private borrowing.

This conclusion would not hold if all federally connected mortgage borrowing were simply substituted for an identical amount of purely private borrowing. Then the total amount of credit demand in the economy would not rise, and the marginal price of credit would be unchanged, other things being equal. Debt offerings in the market would actually have greater average security because a higher percentage of them would have federal connections. Hence average real interest rates might even *fall* compared with what their level would be if secondary mortgage markets were purely private. But simple substitution is not what happens. The lower price of federally connected money to mortgage borrowers *encourages* greater total mortgage borrowing. That follows from the fundamental economic law that the amount of anything demanded rises when its relative price falls. So the total amount of credit demanded must rise, and interest rates at the margin must therefore also rise, other things being equal.

How much higher are interest rates because of this effect? No one knows. For example, the exact size of the burden GNMA places on taxpayers cannot be measured, but it is not a trifling sum. GNMA issued $126 billion in pass-through securities from 1970 through 1981, with a high of $24.6 billion in 1979.[2] During those same twelve years, total federal credit as measured in the Federal Reserve

2. United States League of Savings Associations, *1982 Savings and Loan Source Book* (Chicago: USLSA, 1982), p. 52.

Board's flow of funds accounts was $528.8 billion. Thus, overall, GNMA's securities were equivalent to an additional 24 percent of federal borrowing. In 1979 alone, GNMA's $24.6 billion was equivalent to 65.8 percent of federal credit flows of $37.4 billion. Running these large amounts of essentially private borrowings through the federal funds market surely raises federal interest rates noticeably. GNMA's activities also force private interest rates higher than they would be otherwise because of a rise in the total demand for credit. Thus GNMA's issuance of MBSs is *not* costless to taxpayers. To a lesser degree, the same reasoning applies to credit funneled through FHLMC, FNMA, and the Farmers Home Administration.

Moreover, the imbalance in the rewards and costs of taking risks that is caused by federal connections helps misallocate capital in general. This distortion reduces the efficiency of the economy and loads further potential burdens onto federal taxpayers, as discussed in chapter 10.

How much federal connections in secondary mortgage markets unduly distort the overall allocation of capital, excessively favoring housing over other uses, is even more difficult to determine empirically. One reason is that so many other distorting factors throughout the economy also influence capital allocation. Hence the relevant comparison is not between some "perfect" theoretical allocation and what happens as a result of market imperfections produced by secondary mortgage markets. Rather, it is between an economy already permeated with existing distortions and what happens to overall allocation as a result of adding those distortions in secondary mortgage markets. This subject is discussed further in chapter 14.

How much federal policies should encourage homeownership is not a scientific question but a matter of political and ethical value judgment. Income tax policy and federal deposit insurance, however, already provide great incentives for people to own their own homes. This is one reason that about 65 percent of all American households were homeowners in 1980. Hence I am inclined to agree with the view that it is not necessary to provide further encouragement for homeownership through federal connections in secondary mortgage markets. This view is strongly opposed by homebuilders, mortgage bankers, realtors, and other participants in the housing industry. A more detailed discussion of whether housing should receive a favored position in the allocation of capital was presented in chapter 7.

Taking all these arguments into consideration, I have reached the following conclusions about policies that should be adopted.

—Existing federal connections in secondary mortgage markets that primarily benefit low- and moderate-income households should be maintained. These include supporting mortgages on subsidized housing and raising capital mainly used for mortgages on relatively low-priced housing.

—Existing federal connections in secondary mortgage markets that primarily benefit middle- and high-income households should either be ended or modified so that their benefits go mainly to low- and moderate-income households.

—No additional benefits from federal connections should be created in secondary mortgage markets.

Specific implications of these conclusions are described in the remainder of this chapter.

Dividing Housing-related Functions among Secondary Mortgage Market Institutions

The division of housing-related functions in secondary mortgage markets that I believe should be adopted is based on five key ideas. Each is given below, with a brief rationale for its recommendation. More detailed discussion of these ideas and their justifications are presented in the remainder of the chapter, where nonresidential secondary mortgage markets are also briefly discussed.

First, *GNMA should remain a federal agency and perform those functions that can only be done by such an agency.* Its responsibilities, however, should be restricted to those functions, and its interest-reduction abilities should be focused mainly on low- and moderate-income households. Because GNMA is fully embedded within the federal government, it is better placed than any other agency to carry out those secondary mortgage market activities that require close federal ties. But such ties should not be used to aid middle- and upper-income households. GNMA should therefore be restrained from serving such households, since whatever it does will be affected by its federal ties. This restriction implies, for example, that GNMA should include neither conventional mortgages nor high-valued mortgages (whether conventional or not) within its pools.

Second, *both FHLMC and FNMA should eventually be transformed into fully private, tax-paying firms with no ties to the federal government*. Each should have to operate in credit markets without access to the U.S. Treasury or other special financial advantages over private firms. In return, both agencies should be almost completely free from federal and other regulations about what they can do or how they can do it. Both now serve primarily middle- and upper-income households, even though they are limited by a ceiling of $114,000 on the mortgages they can purchase. But there is no good reason to aid such households through special federal connections that raise federal interest costs in general.

It would be difficult for these two agencies to shift markets so that they served primarily low- and moderate-income households. Moreover, the unsubsidized benefits they would provide to middle- and upper-income households even without federal connections would remain substantial, although smaller than present subsidized benefits. For instance, these agencies would continue to attract far more capital into housing markets than would otherwise go there. Hence it would be socially desirable for them to keep on serving the same clientele they now serve, but without federal connections.

Third, *the special problems posed by FNMA's huge portfolio of low-interest mortgages must be recognized in its transition to fully private status*. Hence FNMA will probably have to retain some ties to the Treasury on an interim basis that could last for quite a few years. These ties are discussed later in this chapter.

Fourth, *more private firms should be encouraged to enter secondary mortgage markets—not through subsidies, but through reducing the competitive advantages now enjoyed by federal or quasi-federal agencies*. Increased "privatization" would stimulate more innovation, a greater volume of activity, and more competitive prices. This conclusion is borne out by what has happened as a result of deregulation in other fields, notably in the airline industry and in financial services themselves.

Finally, *changes should be made in the operation of other portions of real estate financial markets to create a "more level playing field" there too*. The most important of these changes involves federal deposit insurance (analyzed earlier and hence not considered further in this chapter).

Keeping GNMA a Federal Agency but Restricting Its Functions

Some of the functions of secondary mortgage markets cannot be performed by private firms. Financing some federally subsidized housing programs is too risky for such firms. Cutting mortgage interest rates to the lowest possible level requires a tie to the federal Treasury to insure maximum security. Federal Housing Administration (FHA) and Veterans Administration (VA) mortgage insurance shifts the risk to those federal agencies, and GNMA acts as a vehicle for raising the funds attracted by their guarantees.

The only controversial part of my recommendation for GNMA is restricting the agency's provision of low-cost credit to primarily low- and moderate-income households. This limitation would preclude its guaranteeing MBSs based on conventional mortgages. Up to early 1984, GNMA was restricted to insuring securities based only on FHA- or VA-guaranteed mortgages, which had a ceiling of $67,000 (or up to $90,000 in "high-cost" areas). But some experts had proposed that GNMA be able to insure securities based on conventional mortgages, including those of higher value. I believe that GNMA should continue to be restricted to insuring securities based on FHA- and VA-guaranteed mortgages. Moreover, the $67,000 ceiling should be retained even if FHA and VA are allowed to guarantee costlier mortgages (although that ceiling should be adjusted annually to offset inflation).

Why should the deficit-ridden federal government use its credit rating to cut the mortgage costs of middle- and upper-income households? Doing so may be politically expedient, but it seems particularly unwise economically because it would raise federal interest costs to some extent (although no one knows by exactly how much). Subsidizing these nonpoor households at general taxpayer expense would be highly unjust when federal spending on food stamps and other assistance to the poor is being cut back.

Moreover, the leaders of GNMA should be required by legislation to refrain from performing any functions that private firms could perform, even if private firms would do so at a higher cost because they lack GNMA's federal credit rating. The exception would be guaranteeing MBSs based on FHA- and VA-guaranteed mortgages, as discussed above. This recommendation may seem inconsistent with the inherent tendency of bureaucratic officials to expand their activities as widely as they can. Congress has often demarcated such boundaries, however, and can enforce them—if it seeks to do so— vigilantly and persistently.[3]

Transforming FNMA and FHLMC into Fully Private Firms

If GNMA performs the secondary market functions requiring connections to the federal government, FNMA and FHLMC need not be so connected. Rather, their federal ties can be severed, and they can be changed into fully private firms. They should be entirely owned by private stockholders, with no directors appointed by any federal officials or agencies. Nor should they have any access to the Treasury in case of financial difficulties. Each should be free to engage in any type of activity and should be required to pay federal income taxes (FNMA has paid such taxes for years, and FHLMC began to pay them in 1985).

Such privatization would have several advantages. These agencies could no longer use their federal ties to lower mortgage interest rates for middle- and upper-income households. These ties are not restricted to their unique access to possible Treasury "back-stop" financing. FNMA, for example, has several other valuable federal connections. Banks and savings and loan associations can purchase FNMA debt without limits related to their total asset holdings. FNMA is also exempt from Securities Exchange Commission requirements on the securities it sells; its central paying agent is the Federal Reserve Bank. Most important of all, its origin as a former government agency and its congressional charter have created an impression among investors that the federal government would never permit FNMA to go bankrupt.

All these factors convince investors that FNMA is a better credit risk than private firms that do not enjoy these benefits. FHLMC enjoys other special privileges, plus a similar general reputation that the federal government would stand behind its obligations. Hence

---

3. For a discussion of bureaucratic tendencies toward aggrandizement, see Anthony Downs, *Inside Bureaucracy* (Boston: Little, Brown, 1967).

both organizations can raise funds in credit markets at lower interest costs than those incurred by purely private firms. Ending the privileged competitive positions of FNMA and FHLMC would permit other fully private firms to enter secondary mortgage markets without competitive disadvantage.

Such broader competition is strongly in the public interest. As pointed out in chapter 12, about 55 percent of the mortgage funds flowing though secondary markets during 1977–82 were handled by GNMA, FNMA, FHLMC, or the Farmers Home Administration. No market so heavily dominated by a few firms is free from oligopolistic tendencies, regardless of how competently those firms are run. Experience proves that more innovation and dynamism are likely to emerge from markets containing many suppliers.

It is true that a completely "atomized" market, such as that in wheat farming, might not produce much innovation. Each actor would be too small to make the large-scale investments necessary to conduct research and development. Each would be too small to capture enough benefits from new techniques to take the risks involved. That is why agriculture has benefited from centralized research funded by the federal government.

But atomized markets are not the only alternative to markets dominated by three or four large firms. An intermediate possibility is a market in which there are, say, several dozen actors, each a sizable firm but each a much smaller part of the entire market than any one of the Big Three is now. Each such firm would be large enough to make investment in innovations both possible and potentially rewarding.

Moreover, private firms would be free from the regulatory and political constraints that now affect the secondary mortgage market. For example, in early 1983 FNMA proposed using a Netherlands Antilles corporation to attract more European capital into funding U.S. housing. But the Treasury prohibited this scheme because it was then negotiating a new treaty with the Netherlands Antilles. Legislative changes have rendered this particular controversy unimportant, but it illustrates the type of constraint that would not plague a private firm.

In addition, as long as the Big Three remain public or quasi-public agencies, all of them are constrained from undertaking actions that might offend key members of Congress or the administration. Those offended parties might take revenge in various ways involving use of regulatory or legislative powers. Such retaliation could include withholding approval of future changes that these agencies may desire. Fully private firms would be much less sensitive to such influence, and therefore more able to launch new activities potentially beneficial to consumers.

Privatization does not mean that secondary mortgage markets would be totally free from government regulation. Some legal restrictions would undoubtedly be imposed by state governments and federal monetary authorities. But those regulations could be far less restrictive than the constraints now imposed on FNMA and FHLMC.

Rather than making both FNMA and FHLMC two fully private firms, it would be possible to merge them. A merger would be to FNMA's advantage if no satisfactory resolution is found for its portfolio problem (discussed in the next subsection). Without such resolution, FNMA would be at a competitive disadvantage if faced by a fully private FHLMC that had no large portfolio of low-interest mortgages. But more competition is better than less. Therefore I believe that both organizations should be made private separately. At the same time, FNMA's portfolio problem should be resolved in a way that makes FNMA an equal competitor with a private FHLMC. This approach also avoids the difficult problem of trying to merge two highly competent but separate staffs without any loss of ability or enthusiasm detrimental to the market as a whole.

The Special Problem of FNMA's Low-Interest Mortgage Portfolio

An important obstacle to immediately severing the tie between FNMA and the U.S. Treasury is FNMA's huge portfolio of old, long-term, low-interest mortgages.[4] In mid-1983 FNMA owned over $73 billion in mortgages, which could be divided into three categories.

About $6 billion was in forty-year loans with an average yield of about 8 percent and no likelihood of prepayment. These had been made to support various federally subsidized multifamily housing

---

4. Much of the material in this section was developed in conversations with staff members of the Federal National Mortgage Association (FNMA), especially David Maxwell, Tim Howard, and Gary Kopff. I am grateful to them for their help.

programs, and they would probably be held until their full maturities. Another $29 billion was in FHA-guaranteed, fully assumable single-family loans made at very low rates. These loans were also not likely to be retired before their maturity. Homeowners using them could have buyers assume these mortgages at their favorable low rates. Thus about $35 billion in long-term mortgages were both made at rates far below current market levels and unlikely to be paid off before maturity. Financing the holding of these loans with bonds and notes paying interest rates close to current market rates created a net loss of many millions a year. The exact size of the loss depended on how high current interest rates were at any moment.

The remaining $38 billion in FNMA's portfolio consisted of conventional loans with considerably higher interest rates and much greater likelihood of being paid off before their formal maturity dates. Carrying these with bonds and notes at current market interest rates did not create any significant loss. FNMA's net worth in mid-1983 was a mere $1.3 billion. Moreover, its liabilities in the bond market had a much shorter average term than its low-rate mortgage assets. Therefore, whenever short-term rates get close to or above long-term rates, FNMA would begin losing money again—as it did in 1981, 1982, and 1984.

Because FNMA has only a "thin" equity in relation to the huge size of its liabilities, it could not lose money for long without serious danger of default. Hence it might need to use its current relation with the Treasury to remain solvent. Abolishing that relation without making any other changes in FNMA's situation would place it in a highly risky position, which would certainly be perceived by financial markets. FNMA might therefore be unable to continue rolling over its intermediate-term debt without paying prohibitively high interest premiums—if indeed it could roll over this debt at all. Hence immediately eliminating FNMA's call on the Treasury and some of its other unique financial advantages without making any other changes would at least greatly increase its costs, and might jeopardize its financial soundness.

Precisely why this situation has arisen is debatable but not very relevant to determining what to do about it. Some observers believe that FNMA could have built up much more equity, or amassed a much smaller mortgage portfolio, if it had been managed differently. Others argue that FNMA was vigorously pursuing its fundamental function of supplying mortgage funds for housing by borrowing short and lending long. As with the thrift industry, that mission was established by federal policy in a period of low inflation when "inverted" yield curves rarely occurred. Even then FNMA occasionally lost money during periods of high short-term rates, as in 1969–70. But it continued to buy and hold mortgages because part of its mission was to provide funds for housing when other sources were unable to do so.

Recent developments—especially inflation—made this mission unprofitable for such a high fraction of the time as to be considered unworkable. Those adverse developments included federal fiscal and monetary policies that helped create inflation and high short-term interest rates. According to this view, it would be neither wise nor just to penalize FNMA and its stockholders because they vigorously performed the very mission for which they were created—after all, the viability of that mission was undermined by other federal policies beyond their control. Yet it would also be unwise to leave FNMA a heavily regulated quasi-federal agency as it is now. As discussed earlier, that course would perpetuate FNMA's providing credit assistance to middle- and upper-income households because of its federal connection, even though such assistance raised federal interest costs at least slightly.

At least six approaches to coping with this complex problem have been suggested. Their main features are briefly explained below.

LEAVING FNMA'S STATUS UNCHANGED, AND LETTING IT GRADUALLY WORK OUT ITS PORTFOLIO PROBLEM. If no changes were made in FNMA's institutional structure and ties to the federal government as they existed in early 1985, FNMA could only reduce the danger of future bankruptcy through a long-run strategy of gradual improvement. This strategy would involve its lengthening the maturity of its liabilities (notes and bonds), shortening the maturities and raising the average yield of its assets (mortgages), and relying as much as possible on earning fees to add to its profits (especially through issuing MBSs). A primary objective would be to increase its equity capital through retained profits or sale of additional stock. Because of the huge size of that part of FNMA's portfolio bound to lose money, it would take many years for FNMA to work its way out of danger in this way. This tactic has the advantage of not shifting the problem onto the federal government, but it keeps FNMA restricted by federal regulations, leaves it in precarious financial position, and maintains its competitive edge over fully private firms.

That competitive edge does not stem from any eagerness of private secondary market firms to start amassing huge mortgage portfolios such as that of FNMA; few wish to do so. But the connection with the Treasury that would protect FNMA from possible disaster arising from its portfolio is an indivisible asset. By its mere existence, that connection also gives FNMA an advantage over purely private firms in raising funds in capital markets. Hence its effects spill over from the portfolio business into the MBS business, even though the two are really distinct. Moreover, these disadvantages would last for the many years it would take FNMA to work out of danger. Hence entry of other fully private firms into secondary mortgage markets would be inhibited for a long time, as would FNMA's ability to act without restrictive federal regulations.

ENDING FNMA'S FEDERAL CONNECTIONS BUT TAKING NO ACTION TO ASSIST IT IN HANDLING ITS PORTFOLIO. Congress could change FNMA's enabling legislation by eliminating FNMA's back-stop link to the Treasury and its other federal advantages without giving it any aid in handling its existing mortgage portfolio. This would render FNMA a fully private firm but would leave the problem of its large low-interest portfolio unresolved. If short-term interest rates then rose near or above long-term rates, FNMA would start to lose money again. How long it could sustain such losses would depend on how high short-term rates went. But if its losses continued, FNMA would soon become bankrupt. At the end of 1983 FNMA held over 6 percent of all outstanding mortgages on one- to four-unit family homes in the United States—more than the similar holdings of any other single organization.[5] In addition, holders of many FNMA bonds and notes bought them when FNMA had a connection with the Treasury that they thought would protect them in case of possible default. To abandon these investors would be a violation of the federal government's trust. As a result, FNMA's bankruptcy would be a severe blow to maintaining orderly future secondary mortgage markets, or orderly credit markets in general. Hence this policy is unacceptable.

---

5. Board of Governors of the Federal Reserve System, *Federal Reserve Bulletin*, vol. 70 (September 1984), p. A37.

SHIFTING THE PORTFOLIO PROBLEM TO THE U.S. TREASURY. The lowest-rate loans in FNMA's portfolio—say, the $35 billion or so at the bottom rates—could be shifted to the federal Treasury, along with a set of FNMA's bonds of matching size. The Treasury could then either sell these mortgages, at a huge one-time capital loss, or keep holding them at a much smaller annual loss in hopes that current interest rates would fall to the point where that loss disappeared. This tactic would provide great benefits to FNMA. The federal government would receive large potential costs, offset only by the benefit of having a fully private FNMA. That might reduce the average federal borrowing rate slightly. But the resulting gains would appear small from the Treasury's viewpoint compared with the potential losses it might suffer. Moreover, FNMA could create more (at least potential) future liabilities for the Treasury by buying more fixed-rate mortgages (as it did in 1983 and 1984) *after* the initial portfolio was shifted to the Treasury. If short-term rates rose above the rates on these added mortgages, the same problem would exist again—*unless* FNMA's tie to the Treasury were ended when the first portfolio shifted or FNMA were prohibited from buying any more fixed-rate mortgages.

SHIFTING THE LOW-RATE PART OF THE PORTFOLIO TO TAX-EXEMPT SECURITIES. If the two lowest-rate portions of FNMA's mortgage portfolio (as defined earlier above) could be transformed into tax-exempt securities, they could be sold in the market for much lower de facto interest rates than they could without such exemption. Depending on the relation between tax-exempt and taxable rates at that moment, this tactic might allow FNMA to sell these securities at no capital loss or at a very small one. It would, however, impose a cost on federal taxpayers because purchasers of the securities would pay lower federal taxes. This tax loss would probably be much smaller than the capital loss the Treasury would sustain from the preceding tactic. Even so, in a time of huge federal deficits the Treasury might be unwilling to bear that tax loss in return for eliminating the long-run possibility that it may have to bail out FNMA in the future.

SHIFTING SOME OF THE MORTGAGE PORTFOLIO TO GNMA WITH A FNMA FLOATING RATE NOTE. In this arrangement, FNMA would shift all $73 billion of its bonds (which are liabilities) and $35 billion of mortgages (which are assets) to GNMA. It would retain the $38 billion in nonlosing mortgages, and give GNMA a note with floating interest rate for $38 billion in return. FNMA would have no further tie with the Treasury, and its other federal connections could also be ended. Hence FNMA would operate as a fully private firm. GNMA would then be in the same position FNMA is in now, except that $38 billion of its assets would consist of a floating rate note from FNMA. All FNMA bondholders would be protected because their bonds would be the responsibility of a federal rather than a quasi-federal agency (as FNMA is now). If short-term interest rates soared near or above long-term rates again, GNMA would begin to sustain losses, just as FNMA would now. If short-term rates fell, as the Reagan administration has forecast, GNMA would make profits on this portfolio. This is a modified version of shifting the problem to the Treasury. In this version, however, the newly private FNMA would share in some of the costs if short-term interest rates rose because of its floating rate note.

SETTING UP A HOLDING COMPANY OVER TWO FNMAS, ONE PRIVATE AND ONE QUASI-PUBLIC. In this arrangement, the mortgage portfolio would be shifted to the quasi-public FNMA, which would also retain as liabilities all existing bonds that back the portfolio. This shift could be made with the entire portfolio of both bonds and mortgages. Or the private FNMA could retain the $38 billion in relatively high-rate mortgages in return for a note with floating interest rate, as in the preceding tactic. The quasi-public FNMA would maintain the same tie with the Treasury that FNMA has now. Hence FNMA's bondholders would have the same protection they do now, except that the quasi-public FNMA would probably not engage in as many innovative ways of making profits as FNMA is doing now. The quasi-public FNMA could actively manage its mortgage and bond portfolio, gradually shortening the maturities of its assets and lengthening those of its liabilities. But the quasi-public FNMA would be required to wind down its activities gradually as its portfolio was paid off in order to avoid perpetuating the problem caused by that portfolio.

The new, private FNMA would have no ties to the federal government and would therefore be free to operate without restraint. Hence it would probably be more innovative and more profitable than its quasi-public relative. But it could not build up a large portfolio of mortgages by purchasing them during periods of credit tightness. Investors would not believe in the wisdom of such a strategy if no federal connections backed up such purchases, and such a portfolio-acquisition strategy would only put the private FNMA into a potentially even more untenable position than its parent experienced. The need for such back-stop mortgage purchases, however, has been greatly reduced by the deregulation of thrift savings accounts. This last tactic has the advantage of not loading FNMA's problem onto the federal government, either directly or indirectly.

In early 1985 it was not clear which tactic should be adopted. One reason was that many key political players in the financial arena had not yet seriously considered this subject. Until they do, it will be hard to determine which tactics have a chance of gaining enough support to be seriously proposed. At the moment I favor the approach that would create a holding company. But several important questions about that solution remain unanswered. One is whether secondary mortgage markets should operate without any major intermediaries that are willing to build up and hold large mortgage portfolios over time. No fully private organization would take on such a task because it would be too risky without some federal backup. My tentative answer to that question is yes, but it is only tentative. Nevertheless, I hope that spelling out both the central problem and alternative ways to cope with it will help focus more attention on this issue.

Encouraging More Private Firms to Enter the Secondary Mortgage Market

The secondary mortgage market can be divided into several different businesses, as described in the preceding chapter. The mortgage-portfolio business is one of the most important because *someone* ultimately has to hold mortgages if real estate—especially owner-occupied housing—is to be financed. This business is viable only as long as interest rates on the mortgages the organization buys are higher than those it pays to investors who buy its bonds and notes. Most of its profits come from the spread between these two sets of interest rates, although fees also contribute to profits. FNMA has been, and still is, in this business. So are many savings and loan associations that still not only originate mortgages but also hold them as assets.

As long as interest rates remain as volatile as they have been recently, prospects for attracting fully private firms into the mortgage-portfolio business are dim. The problem arises from mismatches between the maturities of the mortgages purchased (the portfolio's assets) and those of the bonds and notes issued (the portfolio's liabilities). If the assets have longer maturities than the liabilities, then sharp increases in interest rates may cause the portfolio holder to lose money. That is precisely what happened to both the thrift industry and FNMA in 1980–82. In the past, mortgages typically have had longer maturities than the liabilities that portfolio holders used to raise money. These fund-raising instruments were savings accounts for thrifts and bonds and notes for FNMA. Interest rate volatility makes it too risky for any fully private firm to undertake mortgage acquisition and holding except as a relatively small part of its total portfolio.

If mortgage maturities could be reduced so that they equaled the maturities of the liabilities used to fund mortgage purchases, then the portfolio business would once again be economically viable. That would be true even in a world of volatile interest rates. One way to accomplish such leveling is through adjustable rate mortgages (ARMs). Their formal maturities might still be longer than those of their corresponding liabilities. But if the rates on those mortgages could be adjusted just as often as rates had to be adjusted on the liabilities, and with equal freedom to raise them, then the mortgage-portfolio business would be far less risky. ARMs were becoming more widely accepted among homebuyers in late 1983 and early 1984 than they had been earlier, but they were still far from dominating the market.

Prospects for fully private firms entering other types of mortgage business within secondary markets, however, were bright in the first quarter of 1985. These include the *mortgage-brokerage, mortgage-dealership,* and *mortgage-conduit* businesses, as described earlier. Several investment banking firms were actively engaged in these businesses or were planning to become so. Eliminating the competitive advantages then held by the Big Three would make those prospects even brighter. Leveling the field would require making FNMA and FHLMC fully private, as described above. It would also require keeping GNMA's operations limited to FHA- and VA-guaranteed mortgages having values not exceeding the 1984 ceiling of $67,000.

If FNMA and FHLMC are not made private, their operations in

MBSs could also be limited to the lower-priced end of the market. Such a limitation would reserve the higher-priced end to fully private firms. That division is already occurring to some degree because of the ceiling on mortgages that FNMA and FHLMC can use for MBSs. But private firms are uncertain whether this ceiling will be changed; hence many hesitate to enter this market without knowing whether they would soon have to compete with FNMA and FHLMC or perhaps GNMA. Until FNMA and FHLMC are made fully private, or until uncertainty about future mortgage ceilings is greatly reduced in some way unknown now, private intermediaries are probably not going to enlarge greatly their present participation in secondary mortgage markets.

It is true that some packaging of mortgages has already been done by private firms other than the Big Three. One Minnesota-based firm has successfully bought conventional home mortgages—many with values larger than the limits in effect for FNMA and FHLMC—and has sold MBSs based on those mortgages. Some home-building firms have similarly packaged mortgages issued against homes they have built. Some banks have bought mortgages and issued MBSs based on them, using private mortgage insurance rather than FHA insurance to improve market acceptability. Yet all these fully private efforts combined have been small compared with the activities of the Big Three.

Certain other policy developments would increase fully private activity in secondary mortgage markets. One would be to legalize the management of cash flows received by mortgage trusts without requiring the managers to pay income taxes, as discussed in chapter 12. Legislation enabling trusts for investment in mortgages was supposed to come before Congress in 1984.

Another is to reduce regulations that prohibit certain types of firms from engaging in mortgage-related activities, or from operating across state lines, or from operating in multiple locations. Such deregulation would increase the potential number of participants in packaging mortgages, thereby enhancing competition. It is especially important to allow large-scale operators such as Sears, Roebuck and Prudential to enter this field, as well as smaller firms. Only sizable firms are big enough to compete relatively evenly with FNMA and FHLMC, once the two agencies are fully private and no longer enjoy special advantages.

It would also be desirable to prevent state or local governments from adopting certain regulations that restrict mortgage terms. These regulations make it impossible for market forces to balance rationally the costs and rewards of accepting certain risks connected with lending.

For example, some states prohibit mortgage lenders from charging prepayment penalties while also prohibiting them from "calling" their loans before the basic term expires. This combination of rules distributes interest rate risk asymmetrically and unfairly. People who borrow at high interest rates can pay off their mortgages and refinance at lower rates, without paying any penalty, whenever interest rates fall. But lenders cannot require borrowers who make low-interest loans to refinance at higher rates when rates rise. As a result, high-rate loans are often refinanced before they mature, whereas low-rate loans are often held for periods longer than average. The actual average interest rate over the lifetimes of all home mortgage loans is therefore lower than the average rate at which those loans are initially made. In effect, these are variable rate mortgages with rates that can vary only downward. Hence lenders are compelled to bear a disproportionate share of interest rate risk. It is only fair for them to be able to obtain compensation by charging borrowers a fee for exercising prepayment privileges. Alternatively, lenders could charge two different initial fees (or even two different interest rates) for loans with and without prepayment penalties, giving borrowers a choice. These arrangements should be left to market forces rather than be restricted by regulations.

Other regulations limit the amount or percentage by which a lender can raise mortgage interest rates or payment sizes each year, or the number of raises allowed in a year. For years many states had usury laws limiting interest rates on mortgages and other loans. Usury laws had the unintended effect of drastically reducing the volume of lending in those states whenever prevailing market interest rates exceeded the legal ceilings. Lenders who could exercise choice switched their activities elsewhere.

All such restrictions are economically undesirable because they prevent both lenders and borrowers from rationally distinguishing among different combinations of loan terms by means of different prices (that is, by interest rates and fees). Yet such price distinctions are necessary for a reasonable balance of risks and rewards in these markets. Most state regulations favor borrowers over lenders. If they make the balance of risks unreasonably favorable to borrowers and prohibitively difficult for lenders, mortgage finance will be less able to attract funds from capital suppliers. Then borrowers will either suffer shortages of funds or have to pay the higher interest rates necessary to overcome this imbalance of risks.

How can states be prevented from restricting mortgage markets in these ways? Federally regulated financial institutions could be allowed complete freedom concerning such terms, thereby pressuring state regulators to follow suit. Such freedom occurred for variable rate mortgages when the Federal Home Loan Bank Board removed virtually all restraints on specific terms for federal savings and loan associations while some states still had restraints on state associations. Or Congress could preempt state laws on these subjects, as it did for usury rates on home mortgages.

A Secondary Market for Nonresidential Mortgages

Development of a secondary market for nonresidential mortgages has lagged far behind that for residential mortgages for several reasons. First, there has been far less political pressure for the federal government to help provide financing for nonresidential properties. After all, housing is a basic necessity of life. People unable to afford housing of good quality by themselves must either live in substandard housing or receive assistance from someone else. Their plight and the adverse neighborhood effects of poor housing create strong pressures for the federal government to do something to help them.

In contrast, most nonresidential properties are used by profit-making businesses or nonprofit organizations as part of their means of production. Most of these entities are expected to provide for their own quarters. Their failing to do so harms mainly themselves, with few external effects injurious to the rest of society. Consequently there has been no major governmental effort to develop secondary market institutions for nonhousing properties comparable to the creation of FNMA, GNMA, and FHLMC. Nor is any such effort likely in the foreseeable future. There is simply no pressing social need for such development.

Another obstacle to secondary mortgage markets for nonresidential properties is the relative lack of standardization both among such properties and among mortgages made using them as collateral. There are over 88 million housing units in the United States, including over 58 million single-family homes.[6] Many of these homes are quite alike, and the mortgage instruments used to finance them are even more similar. Indeed, considerable effort has been made over the past fifteen years to standardize those instruments so they can be easily sold in secondary markets. Moreover, there have been decades of experience with repayment patterns for residential mortgages and the relation of such patterns to particular characteristics of borrowers and properties, and these correlations have been analyzed exhaustively by federal and academic experts.

In contrast, there were "only" about 4.2 million nonresidential buildings in the United States in 1980, and no more than 600,000 of the dominant type (office buildings).[7] There was far less standardization of structural characteristics among these buildings than among single-family homes. Moreover, there is much less homogeneity of either space requirements or income-stream reliability among the potential users of nonresidential buildings than there is among the nation's 80 million households. As a result, the marketability of a "typical" nonresidential building cannot be assumed to be nearly as well established as that of a "typical" single-family home. Therefore, in the absence of specific investigation by an investor, the security of nonresidential buildings as collateral for loans must be considered much less reliable than that of single-family homes.

More important, the mortgage arrangements used to finance nonresidential buildings have not been standardized either. Nor has there been any extensive compilation and analysis of the payment history of nonresidential mortgages that would relate their security to specific traits of either property or borrower. Consequently there is nothing in nonresidential markets comparable to the "plain vanilla home mortgage" with some payment seasoning that is found in housing markets. Nor are any large institutions devoted to creating such a standard investment vehicle. This absence of standardization is a serious obstacle to establishing effective secondary mortgage markets for nonresidential properties.

A third reason that such markets have not come into being is the

6. U.S. Bureau of the Census, *Statistical Abstract of the United States, 1982–1983* (Government Printing Office, 1982), p. 751.

7. Ibid., p. 764.

adequacy of existing arrangements for nonresidential financing. Many observers believe that substandard housing is an important social and economic problem in the United States, but few feel the same way about substandard nonresidential structures. The nonresidential building cycle described in chapter 6 has produced enough space, in the absence of a secondary mortgage market, to create large-scale space surpluses during each general business recession. The building cycle has also quickly remedied whatever nonresidential space shortages arose during the boom phase of each business cycle.

Thus *there is little social need for public policies to encourage the development of a secondary mortgage market for nonresidential properties.* If some inadequacy of existing markets creates a need for such a market in the future, private firms will probably appear capable of meeting that need. Despite the lack of any pressing social need for such a market, however, *one is likely to be developed by some private organizations in the near future.* Potential arbitrage offers attractive profit possibilities to large and imaginative investment banking firms from such development. These possibilities arise from the difference in *quality of credit* between the usual tenants in some properties—especially high-class office buildings—and the buildings themselves.

Large firms that occupy office buildings typically can borrow money from banks or through commercial paper at relatively low interest rates on the basis of their general creditworthiness. These rates are notably lower than the rates that developers of office buildings must pay for mortgages, using those buildings as collateral. That difference arises because ownership of a specific building involves risks of vacancy as well as risks of default by tenants. Hence the creditworthiness of the tenants is not the only factor influencing mortgage lenders; they also must worry about filling the building if they get it back through default.

If a large number of mortgages for specific occupied properties can be pooled together, however, the diversity of those properties reduces the joint risk from vacancy. This is especially effective if the mortgages are seasoned (that is, the properties have been operating long enough so that it is clear they will not default in the initial years—the highest-risk period). Then the overall risk from the mortgage pool can be pushed closer to equality with the risk stemming from the creditworthiness of the tenants. Because the latter risk commands a smaller premium than the former, it should be possible to buy mortgages on individual properties originally financed at one rate and to resell them through the pool at a lower rate closer to the tenants' creditworthiness rate. Mortgages would be bought at lower prices than they are resold. Even though the difference between these two rates may be quite small—less than a percentage point—it can result in huge profits when applied over a large enough number of properties.

In early 1985 when this book was being finished, at least one major Wall Street investment banking firm (Salomon Brothers, Inc.) was working on creation of a secondary mortgage market for nonresidential properties to capitalize on this arbitrage potential. Moreover, both FNMA and FHLMC might start developing nonresidential secondary markets if they were fully deregulated. Then they would no longer be politically pressured to focus all their efforts on improving housing finance. They might actually prefer to go into nonresidential finance to diversify their activities and to reduce their dependence on housing markets.

Moreover, both FHLMC and FNMA are large and experienced enough, and command enough attention in the marketplace because of their size, to overcome the lack of standardization that has inhibited a secondary mortgage market for such properties. But neither has the political freedom to do so as long as each is heavily regulated and compelled by political pressure to devote all its efforts to housing finance. If these two giants ever become fully private, both would have incentives at least to explore development of nonresidential secondary mortgage markets.

14

National Economic Strategy and Financial Deregulation

W HET HER real estate markets will obtain the financing they need for high levels of activity in the late 1980s will depend in large measure on two sets of national policies. One is the *national economic strategy* carried out by the federal government. The other is the amount of *additional financial deregulation* that occurs. This chapter explores these two issues and their possible effects on real estate finance.

Elements of Overall National Economic Strategy

The nation's economic strategy consists of the monetary policy adopted by the Federal Reserve Board, plus the fiscal policy adopted by Congress and the federal administration. Three principal causal factors and five important results of such strategy will be especially crucial for real estate. The causal factors are:

—the level of total federal spending, measured as a percentage of current total real output (gross national product [GNP]), and the total real output that would prevail under conditions of full employment;

—the mixture of taxation and borrowing used to finance federal spending;

—the tightness of monetary policy, as measured by the rate of growth of the money supply.

The results of such strategy are:

—the level of nominal interest rates;

—the rate of inflation;

—the level of GNP, measured both absolutely and as a percentage of real output under full employment;

—the growth path of GNP over time;

—the composition of GNP; that is, its division into investment and consumption.

The relations among these variables are extremely complex; indeed, they constitute nearly the whole of macroeconomic theory. Therefore it is impossible to describe them fully in this analysis. The following discussion focuses only on those aspects most relevant to real estate markets.

Effects of High Federal Spending

Whenever federal spending accounts for a relatively high percentage of the total real output that would prevail under full employment, a conflict can arise between federal and private demands for resources. That conflict will not become intense as long as total output is well below the full employment level. Then private demands can expand by drawing on idle resources, so that their expansion will not drive up prices or interest rates.

But when GNP approaches the full employment level, as in the prosperity phases of most business cycles, further growth of private demands can no longer be supplied from idle resources. Moreover, federal resource requirements normally take precedence over private ones. The federal government can expropriate private resources directly through taxation. It also can outbid private buyers in product and factor markets or can outbid private borrowers in credit markets, where it pays whatever interest rates are necessary to obtain the funds it needs.

This conflict between federal and private resource demands arises at full-employment GNP no matter what the level of federal spending is. But the higher that level, the fewer resources are available for private activities at full employment.

Effects of Different Means of Financing Federal Spending

How the conflict between federal and private resource demands will affect financial markets depends both on how federal spending is financed and on federal monetary policy. Federal spending can be financed through current taxation, borrowing, or both. When federal spending is financed almost entirely through taxation, its economic burden falls directly on the current income streams of households and businesses. This burden reduces both consumption and savings. Curtailment of consumption is much greater absolutely because a much higher share of current income is consumed than saved. Hence the effects on private capital markets come mainly from a reduced inflow of savings, and partly from smaller demands for investment because of lower overall private demand.

When a large share of federal spending is financed through borrowing in the form of deficits, the economic burden falls more directly on capital markets. The federal government competes there with private borrowers for funds, pushing interest rates higher than they would otherwise be. By how much this federal borrowing will raise interest rates depends on several other factors. One is the magnitude of such borrowing: large deficits will clearly have greater effects than small ones, other things being equal.

But even large deficits may not raise interest rates much when private borrowing is relatively weak, as in a recession or in the early phases of an economic recovery. Deficits then generate faster real economic growth, thereby increasing savings too. So the level of actual real GNP compared with full-employment real GNP is also important. The closer the economy is to full employment, the more government borrowing to finance big deficits will crowd out private borrowing.

Equally vital is monetary policy. If the Federal Reserve Board tightly restricts growth of the money supply, perhaps to combat inflation, a relatively small increase in credit demands may raise nominal interest rates sharply. If the Federal Reserve allows the money supply to expand extensively when credit demands rise, interest rates may not increase much initially, even when federal borrowing is large.

Two important differences between financing high federal spending mainly through taxation or heavily through deficits are the different effects each strategy has on interest rates and the general price level. The greater the use of deficit financing, the more interest rates will rise, other things being equal. Deficit financing does not reduce private spending by directly expropriating private funds, as does taxation. Hence the federal government must obtain the funds with which to buy resources by outbidding private borrowers in credit markets. It does so by raising the interest rates it will pay.

Deficits also place greater upward pressure on the general price level. Private market demands are not directly reduced, as through taxation, so public demands are added to them. Hence total demand pressures in product and factor markets increase. If the economy is near full employment, and monetary policy is not restrictive, these pressures push prices upward. Those private demanders who cannot afford such higher prices are forced out of the market as the federal government bids for the resources it needs. Hence deficit financing often involves price rationing of resources, rather than the direct rationing effected through taxation. The extent to which deficits thus increase inflation depends greatly on how close the economy is to full-employment output (the closer it is, the greater the inflationary effect) and on how accommodating monetary policy is (the more accommodating, the greater the inflationary effect).

The inflationary effects of deficits also tend to reinforce their effects on interest rates. Greater inflation raises long-term nominal interest rates as lenders seek to protect themselves from future currency depreciation. The Federal Reserve can postpone this effect for a while by rapidly expanding the money supply. But once the economy is near full employment, it is difficult to do so without causing rapid inflation, either immediately or soon thereafter.

Higher interest rates from large deficits tend to reduce those activities that are quite interest sensitive. These include all housing transactions, plus investments in other types of real estate and in industrial equipment. In contrast, greater use of direct taxation to finance federal spending tends to reduce consumption more and investment less. Hence *the choice of how to finance federal spending greatly influences the composition of total real output.*

The effect of federal deficits on private activities also depends on how large the deficits are in comparison with net private savings flows (after subtracting depreciation allowances). Deficits can be relatively large compared with GNP without greatly curtailing private investment if the society involved has high savings rates, as in Japan. But when large deficits absorb a large fraction of net private savings, they do not leave much for private investment. Thus the level of private savings indirectly influences the effect of national economic strategy on the availability of real estate capital.

Within each society the savings level tends to remain relatively constant over time. It is therefore difficult to change through public policies. The United States has one of the lowest levels of net private saving among all developed nations. Hence we have a relatively restricted ability to accommodate federal deficits without adversely affecting private investment.

If relying heavily on deficits to finance high levels of federal spending reduces private investment, it will thereby reduce future improvements in productivity. That reduction will in turn decrease the economy's long-run real growth rate, compared with what that rate would be *either* if federal spending were a lower share of GNP or if a smaller portion of federal spending were to be financed by borrowing.

Effects of National Economic Strategy on Real Estate Finance

Assume that the economy starts from recessionary conditions—high unemployment, low inflation, and total real output far below capacity levels—as in 1982. An economic strategy of high-level federal spending and large deficits, with an accommodating monetary policy, would initially encourage rapid real growth of private consumption and investment, as occurred in 1983. Repeated stimulation from large federal deficits, accompanied by low interest rates, would cause rapid general economic expansion as long as total output stayed below the economy's capacity level.

When output approached capacity, competition in credit markets between federal deficit borrowing and rising private borrowing would become intense. Moreover, the rapid money growth necessary to accommodate large deficits without high interest rates might be causing faster general price increases. Both these developments would raise nominal interest rates.

How much rates would increase would depend in part on whether the Federal Reserve continued its accommodating posture or tightened considerably. Eventually, rising inflation and general economic "overheating" would almost certainly cause monetary policy to tighten. Thus *financing high levels of federal spending through repeated large deficits eventually produces relatively tight monetary policy and high interest rates*, even if the deficits are initially accommodated by a "looser" monetary policy.

Under an initially accommodating monetary policy, however,

elected officials gain the political benefits of one or more years of rapid real growth in both consumption and investment. This growth is presumably faster than it would have been if the Federal Reserve had adopted a more restrictive monetary policy from the start. In addition, interest rates are initially lower under this accommodating scenario. Variations in the timing of these policy effects are often vital to elected officials. They must run for office at specific times and at relatively frequent intervals. As a result they usually have short-run horizons, and rarely do they take account of consequences likely to occur over entire decades or even over business cycles.

Thus monetary policy greatly influences whether adoption of a national economic strategy featuring large deficits will cause relatively high interest rates immediately or only after several years. In either case prolongation of large federal deficits will almost certainly generate high interest rates eventually. Moreover, if high rates have been deferred by initially accommodating monetary policy, interest rates will probably reach higher levels than if monetary policy had been relatively stringent from the start. In the latter case increases in real output will have been more restrained, so general economic pressures and inflation will be lower.

National Economic Strategy and the Relative Social Priority of Housing

Real estate transactions—especially those involving single-family housing—are among the most sensitive to interest rates of all activities. Hence they are especially likely to be curtailed under a fiscal strategy involving high-level federal spending, large deficits, and relatively stringent monetary policy. Yet, when this book was being written in early 1985, that fiscal strategy seemed extremely likely to prevail throughout the mid- and late 1980s. Moreover, because of the Federal Reserve's relatively restrictive monetary policy, high nominal and real interest rates lasted much longer than usual during 1979–83. This development drastically reduced housing market activities in 1980–82 and restricted the market's recovery after that.

In essence, the nation's political leaders were awarding *much higher social priority to continuing high-level federal spending without raising federal taxes than to interest-rate-sensitive activities, including housing market transactions.* The increases in federal spending that were keeping it a relatively high fraction of GNP consisted mainly of greater outlays for defense, interest, social security, and medical aid. Political leaders were deciding that to expand these activities, without raising taxes, was more important than to stimulate housing production or greater investment in improved industrial plant and equipment. With these priorities in force, the prevailing federal fiscal strategy—high federal spending, big deficits, and relatively high interest rates—was not likely to be changed.[1]

Is there any reason to believe that the relative social priority of housing might rise later in the decade? On the basis of events in 1979–83, U.S. political and financial leaders consider housing to have low priority. Moreover, American households were better housed in 1980 than ever before, judging from the levels of crowding, substandard physical conditions, unit size, and amenities revealed by the 1980 Census. The nation's main housing problem was the high cost of good-quality units in comparison with the low incomes of millions of poor households. This problem could be conceived as mainly an income or poverty problem, rather than a lack of decent housing.

During 1980–82 production of new housing units was indeed low for an abnormally long period. Nevertheless, few if any critical shortages of housing existed in early 1985. The only exception might be a scarcity of housing for low-income households in a few markets that were experiencing rapid in-migration (such as East Los Angeles). Even the problem of affordability plaguing first-time buyers did not yet deserve high social priority in the nation as a whole, as shown in chapter 9. Affordability was a serious problem in some regions, but restrictive policies concerning new building enacted in these same regions were among the primary causes. Hence nationwide pressures for federal remedies to problems of affordability were not likely to become strong.

If new housing production remains at very low levels for pro-

---

1. This conclusion is confirmed by the National Association of Homebuilders' launching a national campaign in 1983 to reduce the federal deficit. The generality of this campaign probably doomed it to having little direct influence on Congress or the administration. But it shows that homebuilders were well aware of the effects of federal fiscal strategy on their activity levels.

longed periods, serious shortages might eventually appear. But housing starts (excluding mobile homes) rose to about 1.7 million in both 1983 and 1984 despite continuing high real interest rates. That was only 5 percent below the annual average of 1.786 million for the 1970s, the highest decade for housing construction in U.S. history. Thus housing starts averaged 1.375 million for the first half of the 1980s, down 19 percent from 1.703 million in the last half of the 1970s and only 3 percent below the 1.415 million during the last half of the 1960s.[2] This is not an enormous drop, given the accompanying slowdown that has occurred in net household formation. Hence, as of 1984, the case for greatly increasing the relative social priority of housing did not seem likely to become very persuasive.

Other arguments against the prevailing U.S. fiscal strategy, however, were more persuasive. These focused on the long-run importance of stimulating more productivity-raising private investment in industrial equipment, training, research and development, and plant modernization. Whether these arguments would prove effective could not be clearly foreseen when this book was written in early 1985. Yet it did not appear that anything short of a very clear and pressing economic emergency would persuade the elected officials benefiting from the prevailing fiscal strategy that it should be significantly changed before the 1990s.

For the rest of the decade, then, the nation's dominant economic strategy is likely to remain a combination of high federal spending (as a fraction of GNP), large deficits (as a fraction of net private saving), and high average nominal and real interest rates (compared with average levels since 1945). That is not a very favorable climate for real estate, especially housing. Consequently, housing markets will probably continue to experience lower average levels of activity in the remainder of the 1980s than they did in the 1970s.

Some Key Issues of Future Financial Deregulation

As discussed earlier, financial deregulation since about 1978 has already had profound effects on the nation's capital markets, especially on real estate finance. But such deregulation could go much

2. U.S. Bureau of the Census, *Statistical Abstract of the United States, 1984* (Government Printing Office, 1983), p. 743.

further than it had when this book was written. Exactly how much further it goes, and what forms it will take, are issues crucial to the future of real estate finance.

Important regulatory questions remaining to be answered include the following.

—Should savings and loan associations and other thrift institutions be permitted to diversify into nonhousing and non-real-estate-related activities as much as they wish? Or should they be encouraged, even required, to remain focused mainly on housing-related investments? If they do remain so focused, what specific restraints on them should be adopted? What limits, if any, should be placed on the activities that commercial banks and bank holding companies can undertake? What should their relations be to:
  —real estate development;
  —real estate brokerage;
  —stockbrokerage;
  —underwriting of corporate and municipal bonds;
  —insurance underwriting;
  —operation of equity mutual funds?
If limits are placed on their ability to engage in any of these activities, what forms should those limits take?

—How should the operation of federal deposit insurance be changed to encourage more prudent risk taking by institutions using it? Should access to such insurance be made more or less restrictive?

—Should interstate operations of banks and thrift institutions be allowed? If such operations are to be permitted, should they be phased in gradually over time or allowed immediately? What limits, if any, should be placed on them?

—Should the various specialized regulatory and insurance agencies now serving commercial banks and savings and loans remain separate, or should they be merged into a single superagency, or into one regulatory agency and one insurance agency?

—What should be the respective functions of state and federal regulatory agencies concerning the operations of financial institutions?

—Should tied sales between financial and nonfinancial activities be permitted or restricted? An example would be Sears, Roebuck's offering discounts on furniture to homebuyers who have financed their homes with mortgages provided by Allstate Insurance, one of its subsidiaries, or who have used brokerage services provided by Coldwell Banker, another of its subsidiaries.

—What limits, if any, should be placed on the activities of the "Big Three" secondary mortgage market agencies: the Government National Mortgage Association (GNMA), the Federal National Mortgage Association (FNMA), and the Federal Home Loan Mortgage Association (FHLMC)? What ties should the Big Three have to the U.S. Treasury as backing for their financial obligations? Should FNMA and FHLMC be encouraged to become fully private organizations?

—Should real estate investment continue to benefit from the relatively short depreciation periods, adopted in recent tax laws, that have made syndication one of the lowest-cost ways to raise funds? Or should tax benefits be modified to reduce this advantage accorded to real estate?

Two Illustrative Strategies for Future Financial Deregulation

It is not possible within the scope of this book to formulate possible answers to all these questions and to analyze their implications.[3] But it is possible to define two different directions that future deregulation might take and to discuss their implications for future real estate finance. These two strategies form the extremes on a broad spectrum of possible approaches to future financial deregulation. Although neither extreme is likely to be adopted, examining them both will illuminate the more likely possibilities that lie between them.

MAXIMUM FURTHER DEREGULATION. One extreme would be to extend deregulation of all financial markets to the greatest extent possible. The goal would be to make those markets as free as feasible from all encumbrances—and benefits—caused by government regulations or ties to federal or state government. Only the minimum of regulations and ties required for effective operation of the overall financial system would be retained.

This strategy would permit both savings and loans and banks to diversify their activities as much as they wished. It would allow

3. Another study is being undertaken by the Brookings Institution to explore many of these aspects of financial deregulation.

unrestricted interstate operations by all types of financial institutions. But it would require institutions offering federal deposit insurance to pay premiums based on the riskiness of their investments. Tied sales of financial and nonfinancial services or goods would be permitted. Both FHMA and FHLMC would be made fully private. Present ties linking them and other financial institutions to the Treasury would be abolished.[4] Existing regulatory and insurance agencies for banks and thrifts would be merged into a single set, or even a single superagency, to eliminate differences in the ways those institutions are treated. Regulations required by both federal and state agencies would be pared as much as feasible. Real estate tax benefits would be made no more advantageous than tax benefits from other types of investment.

This strategy would seek to reduce financial specialization based on legal distinctions between different types of institutions. Specialization would still exist, but it would originate entirely in voluntary concentration on specific functions by different organizations. The approach assumes that maximum freedom from regulation is desirable because it would promote intensive competition, greater innovation, and the lowest possible costs of services to consumers.

MINIMUM FURTHER DEREGULATION. At the opposite extreme would be a strategy to hold further financial deregulation to a minimum.[5] This approach would aim to retain compulsory specialization of financial institutions. Hence it would halt further homogenization of banks, thrifts, insurance companies, investment bankers, and other financial actors. Banks would be prohibited from entering the brokerage, mutual fund, insurance, and real estate development businesses. Firms now in those businesses would remain limited to specialized functions and would not be allowed to acquire banks or thrifts or to perform any more of the functions of banks or thrifts. FNMA and FHLMC would remain quasi-governmental agencies partly linked to the Treasury, but with no greater powers of asset acquisition or operation than they have now.

---

4. This would require adopting some arrangement relieving FNMA from the burden of its existing portfolio of long-term, low-rate mortgages, as discussed in chapter 13.

5. Reinstating regulations already removed would be even more extreme. I am not considering that strategy because I believe it is neither practical nor politically possible.

Existing separate regulatory institutions would continue, although federal rules would take precedence over state rules, thus preventing additional diversification from sneaking in. Interstate financial operations would be prohibited, and the partial movement already made toward such operations would be reversed. Federal deposit insurance would be retained in its present form, thereby continuing the benefits it confers on banks and savings and loans. Existing tax benefits enjoyed by real estate would also be continued.

Clearly these two strategies as defined are contrasting extremes. Many intermediate strategies could also be defined that might have a greater probability of actually occurring. But these intermediate possibilities are so numerous that it would be impossible to consider all of them in this analysis. Hence I will arbitrarily focus on the two extremes to illustrate what differences, if any, adoption of each would make for real estate finance during the rest of the 1980s.

Likely Effects of Maximum Financial Deregulation

Maximum financial deregulation would eventually cause real estate capital users to compete against all other capital users in a virtually homogeneous capital market. This outcome would emerge only gradually over the long run. Eventually all capital seekers would obtain their funds from the same basic sources because any source could interact with any user. Hence the interest rates paid by each capital user would reflect the general level of rates, plus the specific advantages or handicaps of that type of investment.

During the past decade the general level of interest rates has become extremely volatile, varying by as much as 100 percent within short periods. For example, the bank prime rate rose from 9.06 percent in 1978 to 18.87 percent in 1981, then fell to 10.73 percent in mid-1983.[6] Longer-term interest rates did not move quite so dramatically, but they varied far more than in most past periods.

Borrowers of capital to finance housing purchases—by far the largest single real estate capital use—would suffer from two important disadvantages in a largely unregulated general competition for funds. One is inherent in the present structure of home mortgage loans, although it could be partially altered by changes in that structure. It is the prepayment possibility that makes mortgages or mort-

6. Bureau of the Census, *Statistical Abstract, 1984*, p. 521.

gage-backed securities less attractive to capital suppliers than other investment instruments. It means that seekers of capital for home mortgages will probably have to pay interest rates at least as high as those paid by any other capital users, and perhaps slightly higher. This handicap could be reduced, albeit not fully eliminated, through the changes in mortgage structure and pricing discussed in chapter 9.

The second handicap is inherent in housing markets; hence it cannot be removed. It is that the interest rate sensitivity of home mortgage borrowing is greater than that of most other capital uses. American households are compelled by local laws to occupy homes that are quite expensive in relation to the costs of achieving the minimum standards required for health and safety. Moreover, most Americans strongly desire such costly homes because of widespread cultural pressures and their own personal expectations. Hence the typical household wants to own a home costing much more than its total annual income. To buy such a home it must borrow most of the purchase cost, to be repaid over a long period.

Monthly payments of long-term, amortized loans contain a very high fraction of interest. A relatively small increase in interest rates therefore greatly raises the size of the monthly payment required. But lenders will not permit borrowers to use more than certain limited fractions of their income to repay loans. So a relatively small increase in interest rates can cause a large percentage decline in the number of households that can afford to purchase homes. Other demands for capital are far less adversely affected by similar increases in interest rates. These include borrowing to finance purchases of nondurable consumer goods, durable consumer goods, industrial equipment, stocks, bonds, commercial real estate, and industrial real estate.

This extreme interest rate sensitivity makes housing market activity vulnerable to wide cyclical swings. Both new starts and sales of existing units will fluctuate sharply as long as interest rates in general move cyclically and are periodically high enough to cut down housing demand. For new construction, wide fluctuations in activity levels have undoubtedly raised average building costs over time.[7]

7. See Thomas Cooley and Carol Corrado, *The Cost of Cyclical Instability in the Construction Industry* (Cambridge, Mass.: MIT-Harvard Joint Center for Urban Studies, September 1977).

Decreasing this undesirable effect has been one of the justifications for most of the housing-related policies adopted by the federal government over the past forty years. Examples include the creation of FNMA, GNMA, and FHLMC. Yet all attempts of public policy to eliminate or even reduce greatly housing's cyclical swings have failed to do so. This failure is proven by the tremendous volatility in housing starts during the past decade. They plunged from 2.40 million in 1972 to 1.17 million in 1975, then soared to 2.00 million in 1977 and 1978, but dropped to 1.10 million in 1981 and 1982.[8] These huge swings were actually much greater in percentage terms than those during 1950–70, before many "anti-instability" policies had been adopted. Thus the inherent interest rate sensitivity of housing markets cannot be eliminated by feasible public policies.[9]

Because of these two competitive disadvantages, whenever the general level of nominal interest rates rises relatively high, persons seeking capital to finance home purchases will be forced out of the market before those seeking capital for other purposes. As a result, the number of new and existing homes sold will vary more widely than other activities financed with similarly long-term capital. Nearly complete deregulation of financial markets thus would not eliminate, or even greatly lessen, the cyclical nature of activity in housing markets, if interest rates in general continued to experience cycles containing periods of relatively high rates.

This arrangement would not be socially harmful if the general level of interest rates remained relatively low, on the average. Then periods when high interest rates sharply reduced housing market transactions would be offset by those in which low rates stimulated such transactions. So no large, cumulative shortages of housing units would build up over time.

But the average levels of nominal and real interest rates will be quite high for the remainder of the 1980s if the nation persists in its current economic strategy of high federal spending, large deficits,

8. Bureau of the Census, *Statistical Abstract, 1984*, p. 743. These data exclude mobile home shipments.

9. Such cyclical swings in housing transactions might have been even greater without these policies, adopted in part to reduce the average amplitude of the fluctuations. In addition, other policies were simultaneously adopted that tended to decrease stability. Hence it is difficult to isolate the effects of these particular policies on cyclical instability in housing markets. Yet it remains indisputable that volatility in those markets has not significantly declined.

and tight monetary policy. The particular strategy the nation adopts will be determined mainly by Congress, the federal administration, and the Federal Reserve Board, rather than by more housing-oriented agencies and financial institutions. Continued interest rate volatility will frequently raise interest rates from this high average to levels high enough to cause substantial erosion of housing demand.

As a result, housing transactions will remain well below their average levels in the 1970s, when interest rates were much more favorable to real estate borrowers. Over time, cumulative shortages of adequate housing units might build up in some markets. Combining maximum financial deregulation with this overall fiscal strategy would thus cause lower levels of new housing production and lower sales of existing units than might be socially desirable. These outcomes are not certain, but they are likely enough to be worrisome.

Likely Effects of Minimum Financial Deregulation

A central purpose of financial deregulation was to allow thrift institutions to escape from having to borrow short and lend long in an era of volatile interest rates. That arrangement had caused thrifts to lose money whenever the short-term rates they paid savers exceeded the long-term rates they collected from mortgage borrowers. In the 1950s and 1960s such an "inverted yield curve" almost never happened, partly because federal regulations limited the short-term rates that thrifts could pay savers. Then vulnerability to such losses was not important. But when monetary policies and other factors caused short-term rates to exceed long-term rates for long periods, thrifts faced a financial dilemma: if they did not pay those higher rates to savers, the latter shifted their money into other institutions that did. This large-scale shift of funds would have caused a liquidity crisis among thrifts if allowed to continue. Hence regulatory authorities allowed thrifts to offer accounts with variable rates.

But if thrifts did pay higher rates to savers, they sustained operating losses because their income from long-term, fixed-rate mortgages did not rise commensurately. The resultant losses reduced the net worth of thrift institutions, thereby threatening their survival. Thus, in 1982, the entire industry was drifting toward bankruptcy. Many individual institutions had to be rescued from collapse through mergers or infusions from the Federal Savings and Loan Insurance Corporation (FSLIC). In late 1982 a change in the Federal Reserve's monetary policy moved the industry out of danger—at least temporarily. But in mid-1984 another rise in short-term interest rates again pushed many thrifts back to the brink of bankruptcy.

Financial deregulation was supposed to remove this danger permanently in two ways. First, thrifts could shift into activities other than making long-term loans based on short-term deposits. Deregulation made this possible by reducing restrictions both on the percentage of assets that thrifts had to maintain in home mortgages and on the other types of activity they could perform. Second, thrifts could adopt adjustable rate mortgages (ARMs) that would more closely match their income flows from assets (mortgage interest collections) with their outflows to current liabilities (interest payments on savings accounts). It would take many years, however, for most thrifts to use these new powers enough to end their vulnerability to prolonged high short-term interest rates.

As of early 1985 few thrifts had changed their behavior enough to protect them from serious losses if short-term rates again rose above long-term rates. Most savings and loans still had large portfolios of older mortgages with interest rates below their current costs of funds. Moreover, they had not significantly shifted their activities out of making and holding home mortgages. Although most were making slight operating profits, the industry as a whole was still likely to lose money if short-term rates rose sharply, as they had from 1980 through 1982.

It is true that the Federal Home Loan Bank Board (FHLBB) had adopted accounting rules that allowed thrifts to write off losses from selling their old loans over long periods of time rather than at the time of sale. The FHLBB had also created "certificates of net worth" that it could lend to individual institutions in trouble to enable them to appear solvent even when their liabilities exceeded their other assets. But these moves did not fully eliminate the vulnerability of the industry to dangerous losses during another period of very high short-term interest rates.

The strategy of minimum further financial deregulation makes several important implicit assumptions about this situation. First, it assumes that thrifts do not need greater legal abilities to undertake activities other than home mortgage lending. This strategy seeks to keep thrifts focused primarily on such lending. But how can this position be reconciled with the continuing vulnerability of thrifts to the type of economic disaster that stimulated deregulation in the first place?

The answer lies in the third and fourth assumptions implicit in this strategy. One is that thrifts can shift from fixed-rate mortgage loans into ARMs fast enough so that future increases in short-term rates will not cause them serious economic losses. The other is that short-term rates will not rise very high before thrifts are ready to endure such rates without danger. If the United States follows a national economic strategy of large deficits and high interest rates throughout the second half of the 1980s, these two assumptions are likely to prove wrong. Thrifts had certainly not moved out of potential danger as of early 1985, and they do not seem likely to do so very quickly. Yet higher short-term interest rates seem quite possible in late 1985 or 1986, when thrifts would still be threatened by such rates.

Thus the strategy of minimum further financial deregulation risks further weakening of the thrift industry if short-term interest rates rise sharply during the late 1980s. The first defense against that risk is declaring that short-term rates will not rise. A second defense is declaring that such rates will not rise until after the thrift industry has protected itself by shifting into new activities or adopting new mortgage forms. The third defense is that, in case rates do rise before that, the thrift industry can be saved by the same tactics the FHLBB and the FSLIC used in 1982. The weakness of those defenses is a major drawback of this deregulation strategy.

The Instability and Undesirability of Maintaining the Status Quo

The strategy of minimum further deregulation also implies that the existing division of functions in financial markets is both stable and desirable. Hence there will be no major "market invasions" by some types of institutions of the functional territories of others. Or, if such invasions occur, they will not threaten the viability of any institutions whose survival is in the public interest. In addition, the existing division of functions, and whatever changes are likely to arise from it without further deregulation, will provide services to consumers at the lowest possible costs consistent with the continued viability of the nation's financial system.

The desirability of the status quo in financial markets, however, has been strongly questioned by many observers. Paul A. Volcker, chairman of the Federal Reserve Board, presented a contrary view before a U.S. Senate committee on September 13, 1983:

> New combinations of firms in the financial services area, new services, and new combinations of older services are proceeding. No doubt, much of this change reflects a natural, and potentially constructive, effort to respond to market incentives, customer needs, and new technology. What is so disturbing is that much of this activity is forced into "unnatural" organizational form by the provisions of existing law and regulation. The consequences are obvious and serious. In some cases, the services are less readily available, at higher cost, than would otherwise be the case. Important competitive inequalities exist, as some institutions are able to take advantage of loopholes or ambiguities in the existing legal fabric and others are not. And in some cases, important objectives of public policy embodied in existing law are threatened or undermined. The pervading atmosphere of unfairness, of constant stretching and testing of the limits of law and regulation and of circumvention of their intent, and of regulatory disarray is inherently troublesome and basically unhealthy. . . .
>
> We are at a crucial point. We can turn the system toward creative innovation consistent with certain broad and continuing concerns of public policy. Or, left unattended, we can continue to see the financial system evolve in haphazard and potentially dangerous ways—ways dictated not just by natural responses to market needs but by the often capricious effects of existing and now outmoded provisions of law. . . .
>
> The present situation is untenable. . . . We must either move forward, or we must define more precisely, carefully, and equitably the boundaries of existing law dealing with the separation of banking and commerce and of activities within the financial sector.[10]

Thus, at the very least, the strategy of minimum further deregulation requires much clearer definition of the powers of different types of institutions than existed in early 1984. Only such greater clarity

10. *Moratorium Legislation and Financial Institutions Deregulation*, Hearings before the Senate Committee on Banking, Housing, and Urban Affairs, 98 Cong. 1 sess. (GPO, 1984), pp. 146–47, 147, 148–49.

could halt certain major changes then under way in the division of functions among existing institutions. These changes included the following:

—Several large banks and savings and loans were already conducting interstate operations and planned on expanding these operations. They had gotten started through regulatory mergers with failing institutions in other states. Yet many other banks and thrifts desiring to start similar operations were blocked from doing so by existing laws.

—Some states were authorizing banks to sell insurance, and others were authorizing insurance companies to own banks. Yet many states prohibited both these joint activities, as did some federal regulators.

—Some banks, insurance companies, and thrifts were starting real estate syndications or subsidiaries carrying out such syndications. Stockbrokerage and investment banking firms were already conducting large-scale syndications.

—One stockbrokerage and investment banking firm had initiated credit-card operations that involved cashing checks at remote teller locations. Other such firms had for several years been operating money market funds that permitted some check writing and cashing. Yet these firms were not regulated by the same agencies regulating banks.

These and other developments suggest that the status quo in early 1985 was certainly not in equilibrium. Instability made it unwise to freeze further deregulation without major additional changes. The changes required would probably have to extend the legal powers of several types of institutions to place them in a more equally competitive position with certain others.

Thus, as of early 1985, *the strategy of minimum further financial deregulation was untenable.* It would not sufficiently protect the thrift industry from continued vulnerability to injury from high short-term interest rates. Equally important, halting all further deregulation would leave financial markets in disequilibrium marked by inequitable and unstable divisions of functions among different types of institutions. Therefore, at least some further changes in regulations and clarifications of functions were required. Many such changes and clarifications have been described in earlier chapters of this book.

REVOLUTION IN REAL ESTATE FINANCE

Conclusions for Future Financial Deregulation Strategy

Each of the two extreme deregulation strategies described above suffers from serious drawbacks. Maximum further deregulation would work well if the general interest rate structure remains relatively low, on the average. But, moving into the second half of the 1980s, the United States appears likely to continue an overall economic strategy based on high deficits, tight monetary policy, and high interest rates. On the one hand, maximum further deregulation under such conditions would lead to relatively low average levels of both new housing construction and existing home sales. If these low levels persisted for long, shortages of adequate housing might appear in some markets, although few shortages existed in early 1985. Hence this strategy runs the risk of generating future housing problems.

On the other hand, minimum further financial deregulation would essentially stop further changes in the complex, confusing, inequitable, and seriously obsolete rules and regulations that governed financial markets as of early 1985. But the situation then existing was not a stable one that could be "frozen" without adverse consequences. On the contrary, it already involved dynamic forces of change likely to cause instability and even rather chaotic developments in financial markets if existing rules and regulations were not both clarified and altered. Moreover, one of the fundamental purposes of financial deregulation—rescuing thrift institutions from performing a basically untenable primary mission—had not yet been achieved. So a return of short-term rates higher than long-term rates would once again threaten the survival of the thrift industry. Hence this "minimalist" strategy is almost certain to perpetuate existing problems throughout financial markets.

If society had to choose between these two strategies, maximum further financial deregulation would be far superior. It would be wiser to risk encountering the *possible but uncertain future problems* that might arise from selective housing shortages than to endure the *certain present and future difficulties* of maintaining wholly inadequate rules and regulations. But society need not confine its choices to these two extremes. Rather, it can move toward greater financial deregulation by adopting clearer and less restrictive rules and regulations without eliminating all restraints on the behavior of financial institutions.

Because the national economic strategy adopted by the federal government has such great effects on financial markets, it might seem desirable to adapt the specific rules and regulations governing those markets to whatever strategy is most likely to prevail in the near future. But national economic strategies can be changed quickly—they have sometimes been radically altered by presidential elections, such as those of 1932 and 1980. And they are much more often significantly modified over time. In contrast, the rules and regulations governing financial institutions are much more difficult to change. Moreover, their implications tend to become embedded in myriad and complex institutional and legal structures. Hence the rules and regulations governing financial institutions should be designed to work relatively well under any likely national economic strategy.

It has been beyond the scope of this book to analyze how existing rules and regulations governing all financial markets should be changed and to present a full set of such recommended policies. Preceding chapters have discussed many alternative changes relevant to real estate markets—and have made specific recommendations concerning them. Taken together, they constitute a partial strategy much closer to maximum financial deregulation than to minimum further deregulation, but identical to neither. This intermediate position seems the most prudent, in view of both the present turmoil among financial institutions and the high probability of continued interest rate volatility. Hence that partial strategy should be incorporated into whatever more comprehensive approach is ultimately taken toward developing a consistent financial deregulation strategy over the long run.

Appendix A

Detailed Analysis of the Fundamental Structure of Real Estate Financial Markets

THIS APPENDIX examines certain elements of real estate financial markets in greater detail than set forth in chapter 4. Information on the structure of secondary mortgage markets was given in greater depth in chapter 12.

Past Sources of Mortgage Origination

Although real estate capital consists of both equity and debt, far better information exists on the sources of real estate debt (mortgages) than on the sources of real estate equity. The U.S. Department of Housing and Urban Development has compiled data for three different kinds of mortgages originated in 1970–81 by eleven types of financial institutions.[1] These data do not include mortgages originated by individuals or households, such as the "purchase-money mortgages" involved in real estate "creative finance."

As shown in figure A-1, savings and loan associations supplied 37.7 percent of total mortgage originations in the United States in 1970–81—48.2 percent of all mortgages for one- to four-unit family

---

1. U.S. Department of Housing and Urban Development (HUD), Office of Financial Management, *The Supply of Mortgage Credit, 1970–1979* (Government Printing Office, 1980); and HUD, Office of Public Affairs, "Survey of Mortgage Lending Activity, August 1982," HUD News Release no. 82-227, October 29, 1982.

Figure A-1. *Major Institutional Mortgage Originators, 1970–81*

A. Percentage of total dollars of mortgage originations, all types

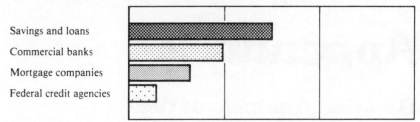

Savings and loans
Commercial banks
Mortgage companies
Federal credit agencies

B. Percentage of total dollars of originations, one- to four-unit family housing

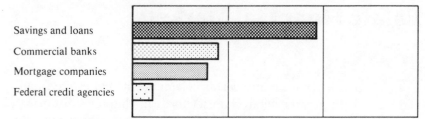

Savings and loans
Commercial banks
Mortgage companies
Federal credit agencies

C. Percentage of total dollars of originations, multifamily housing

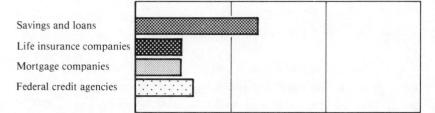

Savings and loans
Life insurance companies
Mortgage companies
Federal credit agencies

D. Percentage of total dollars of originations, nonresidential properties

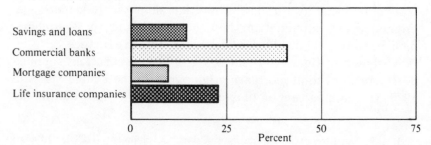

Savings and loans
Commercial banks
Mortgage companies
Life insurance companies

```
0          25          50          75
              Percent
```

Source: U.S. Department of Housing and Urban Development, Office of Financial Management, *The Supply of Mortgage Credit, 1970–79* (Government Printing Office, 1980), and supplements.

homes, 32.0 percent of all mortgages for multifamily dwellings, and 14.3 percent of all mortgages for nonresidential properties. Commercial banks were the second-largest source of mortgages, putting up 24.7 percent of total funds, the largest supplier of nonresidential mortgage funding (40.9 percent), the second-largest supplier of mortgage funds for one- to four-unit family housing (22.3 percent), and the sixth-largest supplier of multifamily mortgage funds (10.0 percent). Mortgage companies were the third-largest overall source of funds (15.9 percent); their contribution included 19.6 percent of funding for one- to four-unit family housing, 11.7 percent of multifamily funding, and 9.6 percent of nonresidential funding.

These three major sources combined accounted for 78.3 percent of all mortgage originations during 1970–81. Only three other sources contributed more than 2 percent each to total funding. Federal credit agencies—including the Federal National Mortgage Association (FNMA), the Federal Home Loan Mortgage Association (FHLMC), and the Government National Mortgage Association (GNMA)—put up 7.2 percent of all mortgages, mostly for multifamily housing (14.8 percent of the total for that category). Life insurance companies supplied 6.8 percent of mortgage funding, mainly for nonresidential properties (22.8 percent of total nonresidential funding). Mutual savings banks put up 5.4 percent of total mortgage originations, mainly for multifamily housing (10.2 percent of the total for that category).

The relative importance of these different sources of mortgage funding changed only slightly over this twelve-year period. Savings and loan associations contributed their largest share (about 43 percent) in 1975–77, when they were flooded with new savings. Their market share dropped sharply during 1980–81, when high interest rates caused them to lose deposits to money market funds and to suffer sharp declines in net worth. The market share of commercial banks held relatively steady during 1970–81. The activity of mortgage companies moved in inverse proportion to that of savings and loan associations. The market share of mutual savings banks declined steadily throughout the period.

Despite these shifts in relative importance among funding sources, savings and loans, commercial banks, and mortgage companies clearly remained the key institutional originators of mortgages throughout this period.

Mortgage-holding Savings Depository Institutions

Institutions or households willing to provide cash for mortgages that they will hold for periods similar to the duration of the underlying real estate transactions are essential to most such transactions. Without such "ultimate lenders," most purchasing or refinancing of real properties could not occur because the buyers or owners could not provide the required funds themselves. Therefore, *getting enough institutions and other actors to hold mortgages as investments over long periods is far more important than getting enough parties to originate mortgages.*

At the end of 1983, outstanding mortgages of all kinds in the United States totaled $1,826.4 billion.[2] The eight most important holders of these mortgages, in descending order of importance, were:

—savings and loan associations (27.0 percent);

—commercial banks (18.0 percent);

—individuals and minor institutions (15.6 percent);

—GNMA mortgage pool investors (8.8 percent); this category overlaps with the others because many of the others hold GNMA securities—hence their totals are slightly too low;

—life insurance companies (8.3 percent);

—mutual savings banks (7.5 percent);

—FNMA (4.3 percent);

—federal land banks (2.8 percent).

The relative importance of each of these institutions as a mortgage holder has changed somewhat during the past two decades. Savings and loans have remained the largest holders throughout. Their share rose from 29 percent in 1960 to about 35 percent in the mid-1970s, then declined to 27 percent at the end of 1983. The share of commercial banks has gradually risen, from about 14 percent in 1960 to 18 percent in 1983. Life insurance companies experienced a sharp drop in their share, from 21 percent in 1960 to less than half that in 1983. The share of mutual savings banks also fell by about half during that period. In contrast, FNMA's share doubled to 4.3

2. Board of Governors of the Federal Reserve System, *Federal Reserve Bulletin*, vol. 70 (September 1984), p. A37.

percent, and that of GNMA pools went from almost nothing to 8.75 percent.[3]

Annual net changes in mortgages outstanding and annual mortgage originations are both much smaller than the total inventory, so that relative shares in that inventory shift only gradually over time. In 1977–83, the average total amount of mortgages outstanding was $1,424.9 billion, whereas the average annual net gain in such mortgages was $133.8 billion, or 9.4 percent. Average total mortgage originations during 1977–81 equaled $219.8 billion, or 16.9 percent of average mortgages outstanding in that period. Hence massive shifts in annual shares of activity among different types of institutions would be required to have much effect on their shares of the total outstanding inventory.

Longer-run variations in mortgage holdings among different institutions are the result not only of differing total asset size but also of tremendously varying institutional orientation toward real estate. Some financial institutions have invested heavily in real estate because they were legally required to do so until recent deregulation. These include savings and loan associations and mutual savings banks. Others with broader investment powers have nevertheless amassed large real estate investments. These include life insurance companies and commercial banks. Still others have shown little preference for real estate. Their managers either were confronted by legal obstacles to such investment or were overwhelmingly oriented toward stocks and bonds by past experience. Pension funds are in this category.

The major financial institutions supplying capital for real estate, their total assets, the assets they have invested in real estate, and their real estate investments as a fraction of their total assets are set forth in table A-1 (data used are for December 1983).

The particular estimate of the real estate holdings of pension funds shown in this table almost certainly understates the true size of those holdings. It does not include pension fund investments in

---

3. The Government National Mortgage Association (GNMA) does not really hold all the mortgages in its pools; rather, the mortgages are in effect held by the owners of its mortgage-backed securities. But most other "ultimate" holders of mortgages are also intermediaries who finance their possession of those mortgages by offering deposits or selling notes and bonds to others, especially to households.

Table A-1. *Share of Institutional Assets Invested in Real Estate,*
December 31, 1983
Billions of 1983 dollars unless otherwise specified

Type of institution	Total assets	Real estate assets	
		Amount	As percentage of total
Commercial banks	1,969.5	334.6	17.0
Savings and loans	771.7	493.4	63.9
Mutual savings banks	193.5	97.4	50.3
Life insurance companies	659.0	174.3	26.4
Pension funds[a]	1,089.7	39.3	3.6
Total	4,683.4	1,139.0	24.3

Sources: Board of Governors of the Federal Reserve System, *Federal Reserve Bulletin*, vol. 70 (August 1984), p. A26, for data on savings and loans, mutual savings banks, and life insurance companies; pp. A15 and A17, for data on commercial banks. Pension fund data are from Federal Reserve Board, *Flow of Funds Accounts, Assets and Liabilities Outstanding, 1957–1980* (The Board, 1981), p. 27, and *Flow of Funds Accounts, Second Quarter 1984* (The Board, 1984), p. 28. Basic estimate of 1982 and 1983 pension fund assets is from American Council of Life Insurance, *1982 Pension Facts—1983 Update* (Washington, D.C.: ACLI, 1984), p. 5. Total assets for 1982 were increased by adjusted amounts indicated as net asset acquisitions by pension funds in 1983. The estimates of real estate assets were taken from these sources and supplemented by the author's estimates; it was assumed that 10 percent of the pension fund assets added in 1983 consisted of real estate assets.
a. Pension fund investments in real estate are probably greatly underestimated, as discussed in the text.

GNMA mortgage-backed securities, or all the real estate investments in those portions of pension funds held by life insurance companies. Yet, even if pension funds hold three times as much real estate as indicated in table A-1, less than 11 percent of their total assets would be in real estate. That small fraction is one reason that so many people concerned with real estate finance regard pension funds as an important potential source of additional real estate capital.

Household Savings and Increases in Savings in Depository Institutions

The importance of household savings to real estate finance can be confirmed by the close relation of household savings to savings held in those depository institutions that hold most mortgages. Table A-2 shows annual increases (in current dollars) in categories of deposits held by major financial institutions in 1971–82.[4] At the bottom of

4. Federal Reserve Board, *Federal Reserve Bulletin*, vol. 70 (September 1984), p. A37.

the table the annual totals for these increases in deposits are compared with annual increases in net acquisition of financial assets by households, also taken from Federal Reserve Board flow of funds data. Although year-to-year totals for these two variables differ considerably, their sums for the entire twelve-year period are less than 1 percent apart. This correlation indicates that household savings form the basis for increased deposits in these institutions over any moderately long period.[5]

The eight types of savings institutions shown in table A-2 held about two-thirds of the mortgages outstanding in late 1982; households and minor financial institutions held another 20 percent.[6] FNMA held another 4.3 percent, but most of the FNMA bonds backing those mortgages were in turn held by the eight types of institutions or by households. These major institutions, plus households and minor institutions, thus accounted for over 90 percent of all outstanding mortgages at the end of 1982.[7]

The next-to-last column of the table shows the percentage of total savings-type deposits made in each of these eight kinds of institutions over the entire 1971–82 period. Commercial banks received the largest share, slightly over one-third of all household savings deposits when all checkable deposits (deposits on which checks can be written) are included. Because checkable deposits may include many nonhousehold funds, this figure may somewhat exaggerate the share of commercial banks in purely household savings. Pension fund reserves were second in size, capturing just over one-fourth of all household savings. Increases in pension fund reserves include earnings on existing assets as well as additional contributions from household incomes, but both represent increases in household assets. Savings and loan associations were the third-largest recipient of household savings, gaining somewhat more than one-sixth in 1971–

5. To show that the close matching of these totals is not just a coincidence, I also added up totals for the first five years and last six years of this period separately. In 1971–75 the totals were $694.6 billion for the savings deposits in the table and $634 billion for net acquisition of financial assets, or a difference of 8.7 percent. In 1976–81 the totals were $1,452.0 billion and $1,528.3 billion respectively, a difference of 4.9 percent.

6. This conclusion assumes that the 7.0 percent of outstanding mortgages in GNMA pools were held by these institutions.

7. Federal Reserve Board, *Federal Reserve Bulletin*, vol. 70 (September 1984), p. A37, and vol. 66 (August 1980), p. A41.

Table A-2. *Annual Increases in Savings Deposits at Major Financial Institutions, 1971–82*
Billions of current dollars unless otherwise specified

Depository institution	1971	1972	1973	1974	1975
All commercial banks (checkable, large time, small time, and savings deposits)	54.6	62.1	63.4	56.5	37.6
Savings and loan associations (deposits)	27.8	32.6	20.2	16.0	42.8
Mutual savings banks (deposits)	9.8	10.2	4.7	3.1	11.2
Life insurance companies (reserves)	6.3	6.7	7.4	6.6	8.5
Pension funds (net increase in liabilities, including federal pension funds)	36.4	46.5	25.4	29.6	34.9
Money market mutual funds (net share issues)	0.0	0.0	0.0	2.4	1.3
Credit unions (shares)	2.9	3.2	2.9	3.0	5.5
Mutual funds (net share issues)	8.6	3.5	−0.2	0.9	−0.3
Total increase in savings deposits at these institutions	146.4	164.8	123.8	118.1	141.5
Net household acquisition of financial assets	103.0	114.8	132.5	127.0	156.7
Ratio (net to total)	0.704	0.697	1.070	1.075	1.107

Sources: Board of Governors of the Federal Reserve System, *Flow of Funds Accounts, First Quarter 1983* (The Board, May 1983), pp. 6–7, 16–17, 22–29; Federal Reserve Board, *Flow of Funds Accounts, Assets and Liabilities Outstanding, 1957–1980* (The Board, 1981).

82. Although the share of savings and loans dropped off sharply in 1980, and especially in 1981, it rose again in 1982 and was over 25 percent in 1983 (thanks to new accounts without interest ceilings). Commercial banks, pension funds, and savings and loans together accounted for 79.0 percent of the increase in household savings in major financial institutions over this period.

Behind these three were money market mutual funds, life insurance companies, and mutual savings banks, in that order, which accounted for another 16.6 percent. Thus, during 1971–82, these six types of financial institutions captured 95.6 percent of all current household savings flowing into credit markets. Unless household saving habits change markedly in the future, these institutions— especially banks, pension funds, and savings and loans—will continue to be the main recipients of current household income streams

Table A-2 *(continued)*

1976	1977	1978	1979	1980	1981	1982	Total (1971–82)	Percentage of total (1971–82)
52.7	78.7	87.2	69.7	97.1	100.5	108.1	868.2	35.12
50.2	50.9	44.2	39.1	41.8	19.3	45.5	430.4	17.41
13.0	11.1	8.6	3.4	7.5	3.0	5.4	91.0	3.68
8.2	11.3	11.7	12.3	11.4	9.9	11.3	111.6	4.51
44.0	55.9	61.8	55.6	78.2	88.4	97.9	654.6	26.48
0.0	0.2	6.9	34.4	29.2	107.5	24.7	206.6	8.36
6.0	7.7	6.4	4.4	8.3	3.1	13.0	66.4	2.69
−2.4	0.9	−0.1	0.1	5.0	7.7	19.6	43.3	1.75
171.7	216.7	226.7	219.0	278.5	339.4	325.5	2,472.1	100.00
183.9	205.5	251.8	265.0	297.6	324.5	333.0	2,495.3	. . .
1.071	0.948	1.111	1.210	1.069	0.956	1.023	1.009	. . .

available for investment. Therefore, they will also be the major potential sources of capital for real estate finance.

Availability of Mortgage Capital from Portfolio Income and Turnover

Current household income flows are not the only sources of funds for financing real estate investments. Also important are current earnings from assets already held in the portfolios of financial institutions, plus funds repaid to those institutions as their portfolio assets mature or turn over. Each type of financial institution provides more investable resources each year (1) the bigger is its aggregate portfolio, (2) the higher is its portfolio yield, and (3) the more rapidly debts in its portfolio are paid off.

What are the sizes and characteristics of these major outstanding asset portfolios? Some data on asset portfolios containing large amounts of mortgages have already been presented, but they need to be placed in a broader perspective. At the end of 1983 nonfinancial domestic and foreign sectors of the U.S. economy owed a total of $5,500.6 billion in debts to each other, to financial institutions, to households, and to foreign lenders. Of this amount, $1,177.9 billion (21.4 percent) was owed by the federal government and its agencies, and $245.2 billion (4.5 percent) was foreign credit held in the United States. The remaining $4,077.4 billion (74.1 percent) was owed by private domestic nonfinancial sectors. The major types of *domestic* debt, their outstanding amounts at the end of 1983, and their percentages of total debt at that time, are shown in table A-3.

How much of this capital will be repaid each year and will therefore be available for reinvestment? Undoubtedly this fraction varies greatly with prevailing economic conditions. Nevertheless, on the average both nonresidential (commercial and industrial) and resi-

Table A-3. *Outstanding Domestic Credit Market Debt Owed by Nonfinancial Sectors, 1983*

		Percentage of total	
Type of debt	Amount (billions of dollars)	Of all domestic debt	Of private sector domestic debt
Federal	1,177.9	22.4	. . .
State and local bonds	371.0	7.1	9.1
Other tax-exempt securities	113.6	2.2	2.8
Corporate bonds	421.3	8.0	10.3
Mortgages	1,820.0	34.6	44.6
Home	1,214.4	23.1	29.8
Multifamily	147.9	2.8	3.6
Commercial-Industrial	348.0	6.6	8.5
Farm	109.6	2.1	2.7
Consumer credit	493.0	9.4	12.1
Other bank loans	507.2	9.6	12.4
Other domestic credit	351.3	6.7	8.7
Total	5,255.3[a]	100.0	100.0

Sources: Board of Governors of the Federal Reserve System, *Flow of Funds Accounts, Second Quarter 1982: Annual Revisions* (The Board, 1982), p. 56; *Flow of Funds Accounts, First Quarter 1983* (The Board, 1983), pp. 56–59; and *Flow of Funds Accounts, Second Quarter 1984* (The Board, 1984), p. 61. Figures are rounded.

a. Total private-sector domestic debt equaled $4,077.4 billion, or 77.6 percent of total debt. Total credit held by foreigners equaled $245.2 billion, and is not included in the above table. Hence the total of *all* debt was $5,500.6 billion.

dential borrowers either refinance or sell mortgages ten years after obtaining their loans, regardless of the formal loan maturities involved.[8] Total mortgage debt outstanding at the end of 1983 was $1,826 billion. If 10 percent of that amount is repaid each year, then about $183 billion yearly becomes available for reinvestment from all mortgages held by institutions and households.

I have no confirmed basis for estimating repayment of other types of debt held by major institutions. I presume, however, that repayment of nonmortgage debt would occur faster than repayment of real estate debt because many types of nonmortgage debt (such as consumer and business loans) have shorter maturities. At the end of 1983 the institutions listed in table A-1 held about 62 percent of all mortgages, or an estimated $1,139 billion. Because their total assets equaled about $4,560 billion, they held about $3,430 billion in other assets. It is reasonable to guess that the total annual repayment of debt associated with these assets is at least 10 percent of amounts outstanding. If so, about $468 billion would be available for reinvestment in 1983 from the existing portfolios of these institutions, counting all repayments from mortgages they held but not counting any net additions to those portfolios.

All these calculations up to now have ignored the annual net earnings from these massive asset portfolios. Yet such earnings are also available for investment to the extent that they are not distributed to the asset owners. If all assets earned annual yields of 5 percent net of operating expenses, that would add another $234 billion in 1983 dollars available for investment, including income from existing real estate assets.

How much of these repayments and earnings are available for investment in real estate? Consider first those from assets not in real estate. It would be unrealistic to expect any significant fraction of such repayments and earnings to shift into real estate unless there were specific reasons for a substantial increase in the relative attractiveness of real estate. Yet this large flow of repayments and earnings from nonmortgage assets is a potential source of funds that could be tapped by making real estate relatively more attractive.

It is much more realistic to expect that most of the funds repaid

---

8. This conclusion is based on my conversations with members of the Real Estate Investment Department of Aetna Life and Casualty Company in Hartford, Connecticut, and with other real estate lending practitioners across the nation.

from outstanding mortgages will be reinvested in real estate. In many cases mortgages will be repaid when properties are sold, and the new owners will refinance them—often with even larger mortgages than before. That likelihood would seem to increase total mortgage financing requirements rather than to reduce them. But the proceeds of the original sales eventually are deposited in some financial institution, expanding its ability to make offsetting loans. (Even if the sellers turn around and buy other properties, the sellers of *those* properties must put their sales proceeds somewhere, and so on.) Moreover, the owners or new buyers of the properties originally sold often refinance with funds from different institutions than those which made the original loans. Hence, from the viewpoint of each individual capital supplier, final loan repayments represent funds available for reinvestment in different properties.

Furthermore, during most of the lifetime of many mortgages, the borrowers are making periodic payments without selling or refinancing their properties. These payments also become available to lenders for reinvestment. Yet most of these funds will eventually be reinvested in the same properties, although often by different lenders. Therefore, from the viewpoint of the economy as a whole, it would be unrealistic to consider these repayments as *net additions* to the household savings made available for added mortgage financing each year. This is true even though repaid mortgage funds that are reinvested are counted as mortgage originations, even if used to finance the same properties again. Mortgage originations are thus much larger than total increases in mortgage debt during each year.

The potential resources represented by repayments and earnings from existing asset portfolios are shown in table A-4. The current dollar amounts from 1983 data have also been translated into 1972 dollars.

Recent Changes in Net Homeowner Equity in Relation to Personal Savings

Homeowners benefited from a huge net gain in equity in their homes during the 1970s, and that equity buildup indirectly helped finance many home sales in the early 1980s. Table A-5 shows how this increase in equity took place. The number of one- to four-family

Table A-4. *Annual Investable Funds of Institutions Providing Real Estate Finance, 1983*
Billions of dollars

Item[a]	From mortgage debt	From all other debt
	1983 dollars	
Annual repayments	114.0	354.4
Annual earnings	57.0	177.2
Total	171.0	531.6
	1972 dollars[b]	
Annual repayments	52.9	164.6
Annual earnings	26.5	82.3
Total	79.4	246.9

Sources: Tables A-1 and A-3. Assets, from repayments and earnings, are those held by the institutions listed in table A-1.

a. Annual repayments are assumed to be 10 percent of total amount outstanding. Annual earnings assume a yield of 5 percent net of operating expenses.

b. Based on an inverted deflator for 1983 GNP of .4644.

housing units rose 27.9 percent in 1970–82, but the median price of these units rose 194.7 percent.[9] Home prices rose especially fast during 1975–81. Then the *average* price of existing single-family homes sold increased at a compound rate of 12.3 percent a year, and the *median* price increased at 11.1 percent. In contrast, the consumer price index rose 9.1 percent a year.[10] The hypothetical gross market

9. I have used all one- to four-unit family housing because total mortgage debt is calculated for that category and because most of such units are operated as small investments by individual households. Hence the equity in such units constitutes an asset on the balance sheets of individual households comparable to their equity in the homes they both own and occupy. The average price of units in two- to four-family structures, however, is undoubtedly lower than that of single-family units. Therefore, I used the *median* price for existing single-family homes sold to estimate gross market value rather than the *average* price, which would be the statistically correct variable. The median price of existing single-family units sold runs between 80 percent and 90 percent of the average price; for the calculation here, I assume that it is 90 percent. Also, units in two- to four-family structures make up about 15 percent of all one- to four-family units. Hence using the median price instead of the average price amounts to an implicit assumption that units in two- to four-family structures have market values equal to only one-third of those of single-family units. This assumed value is surely too low, but it produces estimates of total homeowners equity that are almost certain to be conservative by a significant degree. Therefore I have retained this approach, even though it underestimates actual homeowner equity.

10. National Association of Realtors, *Monthly Report: Existing Home Sales*, January 1982, p. 10, and President's Council of Economic Advisers, *Economic Indicators, September 1983*, p. 23.

Table A-5. Growth of Net Homeowner's Equity in Nominal and Real Terms, 1970–82

Million dollars unless otherwise specified

	Inventory (millions of units)			Median sales price (thous.)	Total 1–4 family gross value	Outstanding 1–4 family mortgage debt	Homeowner's equity gain in current dollars					Homeowner's equity gain in 1972 dollars					
							Total net home-owners equity (1)	Annual gain in homeowner's equity		Total personal savings (2)	Ratio (1)/(2)	Inverted GNP deflator (72=100)	Homeowner's equity	Annual gain in homeowner's equity		Personal savings (4)	Ratio (3)/(4)
Year	Single family	2–4 family	Total					Nominal value	Percent					Real value (3)	Percent		
1970	46.79	9.00	55.80	23.0	1,283,353	361,459	981,895	...	...	56,200	...	1.094	1,074,193	...	...	61,483	...
1971	48.29	9.22	57.51	24.8	1,426,191	339,710	1,086,481	104,586	10.65	60,500	1.73	1.042	1,132,113	57,920	5.40	63,041	0.92
1972	49.79	9.43	59.22	26.7	1,581,075	377,960	1,203,115	116,634	10.74	52,600	2.22	1.000	1,203,115	71,001	6.27	52,600	1.35
1973	51.29	9.64	60.93	28.9	1,760,761	416,211	1,344,550	141,436	11.76	79,000	1.79	0.946	1,271,407	68,292	5.68	74,702	0.91
1974	51.28	9.45	60.73	32.0	1,943,360	449,371	1,493,989	149,439	11.11	85,100	1.76	0.869	1,298,276	26,870	2.11	73,952	0.36
1975	52.62	11.94	64.59	35.3	2,278,897	490,761	1,788,136	294,147	19.69	94,300	3.12	0.795	1,421,568	123,292	9.50	74,968	1.64
1976	53.61	12.33	65.94	38.1	2,512,428	556,456	1,955,972	167,836	9.39	82,500	2.03	0.756	1,477,933	56,364	3.97	62,337	0.90
1977	54.33	12.56	66.89	42.9	2,869,538	656,566	2,212,972	257,000	13.14	78,000	3.29	0.714	1,580,062	102,129	6.91	55,692	1.83
1978	55.52	10.75	66.28	48.7	3,227,690	765,000	2,462,696	249,718	11.28	89,400	2.79	0.665	1,637,196	57,134	3.62	59,433	0.96
1979	57.04	9.73	66.76	55.7	3,718,699	880,000	2,838,699	376,009	15.27	96,700	3.89	0.612	1,737,000	99,804	6.10	59,171	1.69
1980	58.30	10.82	69.12	62.2	4,299,015	986,979	3,312,036	473,337	16.67	110,200	4.30	0.560	1,854,078	117,078	6.74	61,690	1.90
1981	59.20	10.82	70.02	66.4	4,649,062	1,065,294	3,583,768	271,732	8.20	135,300	2.01	0.512	1,833,098	-20,980	-1.13	69,206	-0.30
1982	59.85	10.82	70.67	67.8	4,791,155	1,112,352	3,678,803	95,034	2.65	125,400	0.76	0.483	1,776,126	-56,971	-3.11	60,543	-0.94
Annual average	...	...	...	...	...	...	2,149,470	224,742	11.71	...	2.69	...	1,426,086	58,494	4.33	63,552	0.92
Comparable growth rate, 1970–82 (percent)	2.07	1.54	1.99	9.43	11.60	11.49	11.64	...	...	6.92	...	-6.59	4.28	...	...	-0.13	...

Sources: Data on housing inventories are from U.S. Bureau of the Census, *Annual Housing Surveys*, various years; data on housing prices are from National Association of Realtors, *Monthly Report: Existing Home Sales*, December 1982, p. 10; data on personal savings and GNP deflator are from Council of Economic Advisers, *Economic Indicators*, various years; and data on mortgage debt are from Board of Governors of the Federal Reserve System, *Federal Reserve Bulletin*, and U.S. Bureau of the Census, *Statistical Abstract of the United States*, various years.

value of all existing units in one- to four-family structures soared 273 percent, from $1,283.4 billion in 1970 to $4,798.2 billion in 1982.[11] At the same time the mortgage debt held against those units increased 268 percent, from $301.5 billion in 1970 to $1,112.4 billion in 1982. *Net homeowner equity* consequently soared to $3,700 billion in 1982, or by 279 percent—a compound rate of increase of 11.7 percent a year.[12]

Annual increases in net homeowner equity were much larger than annual personal savings out of current incomes in every year during 1970–81, although they were smaller in 1982. In eight of these twelve years, gains in net homeowner equity were more than twice the size of personal savings, and in four of these years more than three times the size.

Individual households can reasonably consider net increases in homeowner equity as savings comparable to deposits in financial institutions from their current incomes. Both cause the assets on household balance sheets to rise in the same way. Yet net increases in homeowner equity generated solely by rising home prices are actually gains in *financial capital* only, since equity increases do not involve any changes in society's real resources. In contrast, savings out of current incomes are *real capital* flows because they make real resources generated by human effort available for current investment. Hence such savings are included in the flow of funds accounts and in gross national product accounts, whereas net gains in homeowners' equity are not included in either.

Thus two forms of asset gain that appear identical from each

11. This is a hypothetical value because it assumes that *all* existing units of this type have a market value equal to the median sale price of those relatively few units actually sold each year. The percentage of existing single-family units sold each year varied from about 3.4 in 1970 to 7.0 in 1978. See National Association of Realtors, *Monthly Report: Existing Home Sales*, October 1982, p. 4. During 1970–81, however, 32.3 million sales of such units occurred, counting multiple sales of individual units separately but not counting the initial sales of newly constructed units. Because there were about 59 million single-family units in 1981, a large fraction of them had been sold at some time during the preceding eleven years. Hence it is not unrealistic to use recent sales prices to evaluate the entire inventory.

12. Net homeowner equity rose faster than gross equity because outstanding mortgage debt did not rise as fast as gross equity. This lag occurred because the presumed prices of *all* existing homes in the minds of their owners went up whenever the prices of *those few actually sold* increased, but the mortgage debt on most of those homes not actually sold did not increase. The realism of this method of evaluating homeowner equity is discussed in note 11.

individual household's perspective are quite different from society's overall perspective. Yet because many households perceive both in the same way, net increases in homeowner equity can affect the allocation of real resources. During the late 1970s, net increases in homeowner equity were three to four times larger than total personal savings out of current income. Some households may have been encouraged by the large increases in their balance-sheet assets to use more of their current incomes for consumption and to save less than they otherwise would have. That tendency may be one reason that the rate of savings out of personal income was lower in the last half of the 1970s than in the first half. It is difficult to prove this conclusion unequivocally, however, because there are so few observations, and so many other factors may also have influenced household savings rates.

Gains in net homeowner equity *adjusted for inflation* were much smaller both absolutely and relative to personal savings than those in current dollars, as shown by the last few columns in table A-5.[13] Homeowners actually sustained net losses in their real equity in housing units in one- to four-family structures in both 1981 and 1982. Nevertheless, real net homeowner equity rose 4.3 percent a year compounded in 1970–82, equaled at least 90 percent of real personal savings in nine of these twelve years, and exceeded real personal savings in five years of the period. Hence, even in real terms, increases in homeowner equity had major effects on household balance sheets.

During much of the time homeowners were benefiting from large increases in real home equities, however, they also were suffering large losses in the real value of their financial assets because of inflation. During 1971–79, total financial assets held by households,

---

13. Real annual equity gains were made smaller *in relation to personal income* by the process of changing nominal values to real values. The figure for personal income that I deflated was a single nominal value for each year. But the figure for annual equity gains was the difference between two year-end nominal totals, each of which was deflated separately before the earlier was subtracted from the later. The later annual total was deflated by a larger amount to allow for higher inflation. Therefore the difference between them shrank more than the single annual total for personal income shrank when it was deflated. This relation makes the ratio of the annual gain in net homeowner equity to personal income smaller when stated in real terms than when stated in nominal terms (even though it might seem that ratios should not be changed by deflating both of their elements).

personal trusts, and nonprofit organizations rose from $2,151 billion to $3,861 billion. Their total financial liabilities also went up, from $551 billion to $1,394 billion, so their net worth in financial instruments increased from $1,600 billion to $2,467 billion. If all these figures are translated into 1972 dollars, however, that would be a *drop* of $158 billion, or a 9.5 percent decrease. During those same years, total net homeowner equity in 1972 dollars rose by $606 billion (table A-5). Thus, declines in the real value of financial assets (including corporate equities) offset about 26 percent of the net gain in homeowner equity in 1971–79.

But the situation changed dramatically during 1979–82. Partly because of a 43 percent rise in the current value of corporate equities, the net financial worth of this household sector (as measured in the Federal Reserve's flow of funds accounts) increased from $2,467 billion in 1979 to $3,654 billion in 1982. Translating those values into 1972 dollars shows a rise of $255 billion in three years, or 16.9 percent (5.3 percent a year compounded in real terms). During these three years, total net homeowner equity went up $39.1 billion in 1972 dollars, even though real homeowner equity fell in two of these three years. That amount is only 15 percent of the gain in net value of financial assets. Thus gains in real homeowner equity not only more than offset declines in the real value of household financial assets during 1971–79, but also added to increases in that real value during 1979–82.

But how can increases in net homeowner equity caused mainly by rising home prices—an almost *purely financial* development—thus affect the *real wealth* of society, when such increases do not directly involve any change in society's real resources? Most of the immediate effect is not real but redistributional. It is part of the fundamentally redistributive effect of inflation itself.

Inflation causes money prices to rise in general, but the prices of some assets—both real and financial—rise faster than the prices of others. The owners of assets with prices that rise faster than the general price level gain wealth in real terms. Increases in the *relative prices* of their assets provide them with greater real purchasing power than at the outset of the inflation. Conversely, owners of those assets with prices that rise more slowly than the general price level lose wealth in real terms. Thus inflation in any period typically redistributes the real purchasing power of the total stock of assets that existed when that period began, without directly affecting the total amount of that purchasing power.

During the 1970s owner-occupied homes were among the assets with prices that increased faster than the general price level. Yet monthly payments on the debt owed by owner-occupiers were usually set in fixed-dollar terms, even though the owners' incomes rose along with inflation. Thus the net equity in those homes rose even faster than their market prices. This "leverage" provided by fixed-payment mortgage debt during a period of inflation was an important reason that home prices rose faster than the general price level. Investors were attracted to homeownership by the possibility of capturing such net equity gains. Their demands bid up home prices faster than prices in general. Hence homeowners experienced a large net gain in their real wealth in the form of the current and potential future purchasing power of the equity in their homes.

Their gain was presumably offset by losses in the real wealth of persons who owned either real or financial assets that did not rise in price as fast as the general price level. Among these losers were owners of the mortgages financing most homes. Thus homeowners gained in real wealth from a purely financial change that redistributed claims to society's total real wealth without producing any net change in that real wealth.

Past Use of Seller Financing Based on Homeowner Equity

During the period of high interest rates in 1980–82, the number of existing homes sold fell sharply. Rising interest rates reduced the size of the loan that any household with a given income could afford to carry. Many potential buyers therefore could not qualify for traditional mortgage loans large enough to pay the high prices being asked by sellers, given the downpayments those buyers were able to provide.

Nevertheless, many sellers needed to sell their homes but were reluctant to accept lower prices. Some had paid high prices to buy their homes within the past few years, and they did not want to get less when selling. In addition, most sellers thought that the high interest rates in 1980–81 were temporary, so they did not want to sell their homes at lower prices than they might be able to get a few years later.

To help consummate sales under these conditions, thousands of sellers accepted unsecured "purchase-money mortgages" from buyers in lieu of cash. This practice of seller "take back" differed from the norm, in which sellers received all cash, including the proceeds of mortgages obtained from financial institutions. Seller financing was especially common for homes that already had mortgages at relatively low interest rates, which the new buyers could assume without any changes in terms. These older mortgages typically covered a relatively small fraction of the sale prices desired by the sellers, as did the downpayments that the buyers could muster. Hence there remained sizable gaps that the sellers filled by accepting IOUs from buyers.

This debt was usually for short terms of three to ten years and usually carried interest rates well below market rates then prevailing. A survey made by the National Association of Realtors in early 1982 revealed that about 70 percent of the recent transactions made by 900 realtors involved seller take-back financing.[14] On the basis of data from that survey, I estimate that 26 percent to 30 percent of the combined sale prices of all the homes sold by these realtors was being supplied through seller financing. A similar survey of 420 realtors by the California Association of Realtors, covering their transactions in the first half of 1982, showed that seller financing was involved in about 52.5 percent of all such home sales.[15] This survey implied that 19.7 percent of the combined sales prices of all the homes sold by these realtors was being supplied by sellers.

When below-market interest rates were involved, the sellers were implicitly discounting the prices of their units if the transactions were viewed in purely economic terms. The market values of these loans were below their face values because their interest rates were below market rates.[16] Hence the true market value received by

14. National Association of Realtors, *Monthly Report: Existing Home Sales*, October 1982, p. 10; and Council of Economic Advisers, *Economic Indicators*, *November 1982*, p. 23.

15. California Association of Realtors, *1982 Housing Finance Study* (Los Angeles: CAR, September 1982), p. 16.

16. For example, if a seller took back an interest-only mortgage for $10,000 at 12.5 percent, the annual payment on that mortgage would have been $1,250, assuming only one payment per year. If the market rate of interest for such loans was then 17.0 percent, that payment would have supported a market value for the loan principal of only $7,353, since $1,250 is 17.0 percent of that amount. Thus, the seller's loan was worth 26.5 percent less than its face value of $10,000. If the seller's loan represented 25.0 percent of the entire sales price, then that price would have in

sellers was actually less than the nominal sum of the downpayment and seller financing, plus the assumed mortgage. The sellers anticipated, however, that market interest rates would soon fall to eliminate such discounts. Although mortgage rates remained high much longer than most people anticipated, they *did* fall in late 1982 and in early 1983. That decline eliminated the discounts on most such notes held until that time.

Realtors called such seller lending "creative financing" to encourage it. They recognized that the level of sales from which they obtained their commissions would have fallen even more drastically than it did without such financing. There had always been some second-mortgage financing with funds supplied by third-party investors, but the surge of such financing with funds supplied by sellers which took place in 1980–82 was unprecedented. In reality, sellers were protecting the unrealized equity buildups they had previously received from significant erosion owing to higher interest rates. They did so by helping buyers finance purchases at higher prices than would otherwise have prevailed. But most sellers viewed this tactic as temporary. Many planned to liquidate the loans they made as soon as interest rates fell back to "normal" levels, which they did within two years.

Can Homeowner Net Equity Help Finance Future Real Estate Transactions?

The "creative" behavior of seller take-back financing raises the possibility of financing future real estate transactions through loans made against existing equities, rather than through loans based on

---

effect been discounted by 6.6 percent (26.5 percent of 25.0 percent). These calculations assume, however, that the seller could have received 17.0 percent by using the same money that he or she advanced to the buyer to invest somewhere else. In many cases, sellers could not realistically have gotten as high yields on their funds as current market mortgage interest rates; hence the "target" rate to use in calculating their discounts should be lower. Moreover, sellers were looking at these transactions as multiyear events and anticipating lower interest rates later, which did happen. Hence they may have actually suffered no discount over a period of several years. This discussion illustrates the difficulty of determining the "true price" of a home sold with seller financing. That difficulty is compounded when corrections for inflation are also taken into account.

current savings out of personal income. Under some economic conditions, future savings flows out of current income might prove too small to finance "needed" home sales and other real estate transactions plus all other claims against those savings, such as federal deficits and industrial investment. In contrast, there is still an enormous buildup of largely unrealized homeowner net equity remaining from the inflationary surge in home prices during the 1970s. In current dollars, this buildup exceeded $3,600 billion in 1982. Even in 1972 dollars, such equity was 65 percent larger in 1982 than it had been in 1970 (see table A-5). Could future home sales be even more significantly financed by claims against the past buildup of homeowner equity?

Use of homeowner equity can increase the total dollar volume of home sales beyond the volume that could be financed from current savings flows only if society is willing to hold larger amounts of its total assets as financial assets, without converting them into real resources. Homesellers themselves normally accomplish this by accepting IOUs from borrowers instead of cash. Because those unsecured obligations are hard to sell to other parties, the sellers are forced to hold them until maturity. If a seller can subsequently trade such debt for cash, then he or she can either continue to hold the proceeds as financial assets (such as cash, a savings deposit, a purchase-money mortgage, a bond, or the like) or convert those proceeds into real resources by consuming or investing (as in taking a vacation, buying a new car, or building a new home).

But seller financing that taps homeowner equity does not make more real resources available to society through any act of genuine production. Hence any conversion of sales proceeds into real resources during the accounting period in which the sales occurred (for example, the same year) must still be financed by genuine savings flows from current real income in that same period. If the stream of real savings in that period does not rise, neither can the volume of home sales financed by such savings if the same share as before is ultimately converted into real resources.

From the viewpoint of the real estate sales and home-building industries, it would be extremely desirable to expand the volume of home sales capable of being financed from a given volume of real personal savings during periods when high interest rates would otherwise greatly reduce that volume. Such an expansion would require society as a whole to hold a higher-than-normal proportion of home sales proceeds as financial assets, without converting them to real resources. How might society be induced to do so?

The most effective method has been to convince sellers who desperately want to sell their homes, but also want to maintain high prices, that they must take back and hold purchase-money mortgages, as explained above. However, the amount of seller-financed lending that households are willing to hold might be increased by development of an effective, large-scale secondary market for such loans. Sellers who accepted notes from buyers could then easily resell those notes for cash provided by the secondary market buyers. Although the receivers of such cash would be tapping into society's current real income stream as soon as they bought current goods and services with this money, an efficient secondary market in seller-financed notes might increase households' confidence that they could liquidate such notes if necessary. That knowledge might increase their willingness both to make such loans in the first place and to hold them longer. Hence such a market might make possible greater use of homeowner equity buildup as a basis for financing current transactions both absolutely and in relation to any given amount of current real savings.

During the credit stringency of 1980–82, FNMA tried to help develop such a secondary market by publicizing its willingness to purchase sellers' mortgages brought to it through authorized mortgage bankers. These mortgages had to conform to certain underwriting and informational requirements to be acceptable. Some executives of savings and loans criticized this policy because it encouraged buyers to assume existing low-rate first mortgages, thereby perpetuating these mortgages within institutional portfolios. More complete enforcement of the due-on-sale clause in first mortgages, authorized by a recent Supreme Court decision, will probably curtail such assumptions quite drastically. That clause requires homeowners who have such mortgages to pay them off fully whenever they sell their homes and not allow the buyers to assume the obligation of making the monthly payments at the original interest rate.

In 1982 most real estate practitioners believed that seller financing would virtually disappear once nominal interest rates declined, as they did in late 1982. During 1983 there indeed was a sharp drop in the share of all home sales involving seller financing. But for such financing to remain at the very low levels typical before 1979 presumes that enough added mortgage funds will be available from current savings to help finance purchases by all those households wanting to buy homes. If that is not true, households trying to sell their homes may again be forced to choose between accepting much lower prices than they desire or accepting illiquid debts from buyers.

Two conclusions about seller financing seem clear. First, it will diminish to a relatively small share of total financing whenever adequate current savings flows are available to borrowers on acceptable terms. Hence it will be an important factor only when very high nominal interest rates sharply curtail the number of potential buyers who can qualify for loans large enough to consummate the sales they desire. Second, whenever such latter conditions arise, seller financing will be extensively used. Knowledge of how seller financing works has become widespread because of its popularity in the early 1980s. Given that knowledge, sellers and buyers will not hesitate to use its power again when traditional sources of financing become prohibitively expensive.

Appendix B

Estimating the Effectiveness of Specific Subsidies for Low-Income First-Time Homebuyers

THIS APPENDIX presents a detailed analysis of the specific subsidies for the first-time homebuyer that were discussed in chapter 9. It focuses on the effectiveness of each subsidy in making housing more affordable for the prototypical low-income household (household A) described in that chapter (the effectiveness of these subsidies in aiding the other two prototypical households is also described in chapter 9). Effectiveness is measured by how much each subsidy reduces the amount of time that the prototypical household needs to save the downpayment required to buy the home with which it was "matched" in chapter 9.

A Tax-Free Savings Account for Accumulating Housing Downpayments

One subsidy often suggested by thrift institutions is a tax-free downpayment savings account for households that are accumulating funds for their first homes. For the household with a low income ($11,400 annually in 1983), elimination of income taxes on interest would raise the after-tax interest rate from 8 percent to 10 percent. That would reduce the time required to amass the necessary downpayment (assuming 5 percent annual increases in home prices,

334

household incomes, and rents) from 20.68 years to 17.75 years if the family rented its own quarters, or from 6.52 years to 6.23 years if it "doubled up" with relatives at no expense while saving to buy a home. This tactic is not very effective, partly because first-time buyers who need help are in relatively low marginal tax brackets.

A 100 Percent Tax Credit for Deposits in a Downpayment Savings Account

Such a subsidy for first-time buyers would reduce the household's federal income tax that year by a certain percentage of each dollar saved. This credit would be more equitable than permitting savers to deduct each dollar saved from their taxable incomes. Unlike a deduction, a tax credit would not benefit high-bracket households more per dollar saved than low-bracket households.

Nonrefundable tax credits provide little benefit to households that pay low income taxes, as most low-income households do. If a household's tax credit exceeds its total tax liability, it cannot get the full benefit of that credit unless the difference is refunded in cash by the government. I have assumed that this tax credit would not be refundable, because Congress is reluctant to adopt that type of credit. A household with a 1983 income of $11,400 would typically pay about 5 percent of its income ($570) in federal income taxes after allowing for all deductions.[1]

The effectiveness of a tax credit also depends partly on how much taxes are reduced for each dollar saved. If the credit were 100 percent (but not refundable in case of negative amounts), the typical household earning $11,400 could deposit an amount equal to its $570 taxes without any net additional cost because its taxes would fall by the same amount that it saved. This would increase its total contributions to savings by $47.50 a month. That contribution would cut the time to save the necessary downpayment (with taxable interest) from 20.68 years to 14.59 years (down 29 percent) if

1. Data are from U.S. Bureau of the Census, *Statistical Abstract of the United States, 1982–1983* (Government Printing Office, 1982), pp. 256–59. The income tax liabilities of all three households shown in table 9-1 were estimated from this source. These liabilities are assumed to be computed after taking into account all the deductions connected with homeownership.

the household lived in rented quarters, or from 6.52 years to 5.72 years if it lived with relatives rent-free. In the latter case, the household would be putting $4,560 a year, or 40 percent of its income, into savings until it actually purchased a home. Tax credits of less than 100 percent would result in the same or smaller improvements in this household's position.[2] Such a tax credit would cost the federal government more in revenue lost than would eliminating taxes on the interest paid by the savings account.

A Direct Downpayment Assistance Grant

The net budgetary effect per beneficiary of this subsidy to first-time buyers would depend on the size of the grant provided for each household. However, its costs to taxpayers for aiding any particular household would be concentrated entirely within the year when the household received the grant, whereas the costs of aiding a household with a tax credit on savings would probably be spread over several years. Congress is usually reluctant to adopt any subsidy with such a concentrated budgetary effect. A downpayment grant could provide benefits larger than total tax liabilities to households with low federal taxes, but the process of applying for the grant would be more complex than the process of taking a tax credit and would create a larger and more ponderous bureaucracy.

If a one-time, tax-free grant of $2,000 were made to help the low-income household with its downpayment after it had saved the remainder, the total it would have to save would be reduced by that same amount. The time required would be decreased only from 20.68 years to 20.44 years if the household were renting, or from 6.52 to 6.28 years if it were living rent-free. Hence this subsidy would be extremely ineffective per dollar of cost.[3]

2. A 50 percent tax credit provides the same benefits to this household as a 100 percent tax credit because of the small size of its total tax liability. The amount saved eligible for a 100 percent tax credit cannot exceed the total tax payment of $570, whereas the amount saved eligible for a 50 percent tax credit could be up to twice as large as that tax payment. But the amount of taxes saved cannot exceed the household's total tax liability, because I have assumed that the credit is not refundable. In both these cases, the household has all its taxes wiped out by the amount it planned to save anyway, if it lived rent-free with relatives.

3. The consequent reduction in required savings time is so small partly because annual increments in the total savings account balance are rather large after over

State or Local Mortgage Revenue Bonds Free from Federal Income Taxes

This approach is already widely used and was recently renewed by Congress.[4] Bond purchasers do not pay federal taxes on their interest, so they are willing to accept lower rates than they would otherwise. States and localities can offer funds from such bonds as mortgage loans at lower interest rates than those offered by normal market sources.

If state revenue bonds dropped the interest rate on the mortgage used as an example in chapter 9 from 13 percent to 10 percent, the household could afford to carry a mortgage of $27,649 rather than $22,322. This would reduce the required downpayment for a $50,000 home from $27,668 to $22,351. The time required to save the downpayment would fall from 20.68 years to 17.63 years (down 15 percent) if it were renting a home, or from 6.52 years to 5.39 years if it were living rent-free (assuming that the 10 percent interest on its savings was taxed at a 20 percent rate).

This subsidy would thus assist potential eligible homebuyers in saving for downpayments *before* they actually purchased homes, even though they could not collect the subsidy until *after* such purchases. It would do so by enabling each household to carry a larger mortgage from a given income, thereby reducing the downpayment needed to buy a home of any given price.

The subsidy involved in such bonds is the U.S. Treasury's loss of taxes that it otherwise would collect on the bond interest. The revenue lost is much greater than the interest saved by the households that purchase homes with such funds; hence this subsidy is inefficient. Moreover, floating many such bonds drives up interest rates

---

twenty years of compounding at 8 percent net interest. Hence the $2,000 payment equals only about one-fourth of the last annual increment.

4. Congressional authorization for use of tax-exempt mortgage revenue bonds expired at the end of 1983 but was renewed in 1984. About $5 billion in such bonds for housing were issued in the first nine months of 1983, compared with $10 billion in the two years 1981–82. The median income among persons aided by such mortgage funding in 1982 equaled about 96 percent of the median income for all households, according to a study by the General Accounting Office quoted in the *Washington Post*, November 27, 1983. This proportion shows that a significant share of such aid was going to households with incomes above the median.

on all state and municipal securities, increasing the cost of all such public borrowing. Hence this subsidy is not economically desirable.

Yet mortgage revenue bonds are extremely efficient politically. State and local governments adopting them receive important political benefits without paying any measurable costs because the costs are spread over all federal taxpayers. Hence this subsidy is highly popular among state and local governments, even more so among municipal bond traders.

In the early 1980s Congress tried to restrict housing revenue bonds to low- and moderate-income households and in other ways. But state and local politicians resisted such restrictions, partly because high market interest rates made providing lower-rate mortgage funds especially appealing politically. Hence every issuer of such bonds adopted some income limits on eligibility, but those limits were usually far above each area's median income. With mortgage revenue bonds thus available to a large percentage of all households, rather than only to first-time buyers, the revenue losses sustained by the Treasury vastly outweighed the benefits derived by first-time homebuyers. Hence this subsidy is undesirable unless stringently restricted to low-income first-time buyers—and perhaps it is undesirable even then.

A Tax Credit Substituted for Part of Mortgage Interest Deductibility

Another subsidy passed by Congress in 1984 substitutes a tax credit for part of mortgage interest deductibility. This was suggested as an alternative to tax-exempt mortgage revenue bonds that would involve less Treasury revenue loss per dollar of homebuyer aid received. Each state agency able to issue tax-exempt mortgage revenue bonds would also be able to issue mortgage credit certificates, up to 14.35 percent of the amount of such bonds that it could issue each year. Any household eligible for aid from mortgage revenue bonds under each state's rules would also be eligible for such certificates.

Individual households could receive certificates ranging from 10 percent to 50 percent of their total mortgage deductions, depending on prevailing interest rates and state rules. Recipients would have to reduce their mortgage interest deductions from taxable income by an amount equal to the credits used. These credits would presumably not be refundable and would be of value only after a household actually purchased a home, rather than while it was saving to buy one. By reducing a buyer's after-purchase taxes, however, such credits would increase the percentage of income usable for mortgage payments, thereby raising the mortgage supportable from a given income. That would reduce the required downpayment, thus cutting the time required to save it.

How effective would such aid be to the household analyzed above? A tax credit equaling 50 percent of its mortgage interest deduction would wipe out its initial income tax liability of $570. The amount of this tax credit, however, would have to be subtracted from its deduction, thus adding $114 back to its income tax. Because it did not use all the tax credit it was eligible for in reducing its taxes by $570, the household could apply more credit to this $114 tax liability. After several repetitions of this process, the household would eliminate its entire federal income tax. If it used its former tax funds for making a larger mortgage payment, it could afford to carry a mortgage of $26,589 rather than $22,332. This would cut its required downpayment enough to reduce the time required to amass that amount from 20.68 years to 18.41 years (down 11 percent) if it rented its own housing, or from 6.52 years to 5.58 years if it lived rent-free with others. Hence this subsidy would not be very helpful to households with low incomes.

Index

341